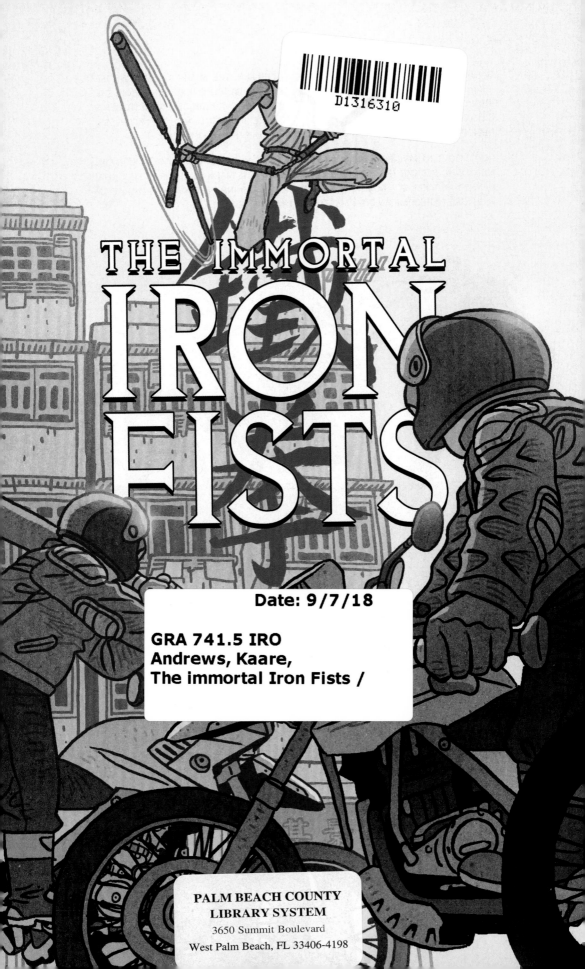

THE IMMORTAL
IRON
FISTS

DANIEL RAND IS A MAN OF TWO WORLDS: K'UN-LUN, THE MYSTICAL LAND WHOSE PEOPLE TOOK HIM IN AS AN ORPHAN AND TRAINED HIM TO BE THEIR CHAMPION, THE IRON FIST; AND NEW YORK CITY, WHERE HE PRESIDES OVER HIS DECEASED FATHER'S BILLION-DOLLAR COMPANY AND FIGHTS FOR THE INNOCENT AND THE HELPLESS. RECENTLY THOSE TWO WORLDS CLASHED, NEARLY DESTROYING K'UN-LUN.

IN THE FIGHT TO SAVE BOTH HIS HOMES, DANNY WAS JOINED BY PEI, A TWEEN K'UN-LUN MONK WHO BECAME THE YOUNGEST TO EVER BEAR THE MARK OF THE IRON FIST. NOW DANNY HAS TAKEN THE POSITION OF THUNDERER, TRAINING PEI FROM HIS MANHATTAN HIGH-RISE TO BECOME AN IRON FIST IN HER OWN RIGHT.

COLLECTION EDITOR MARK D. BEAZLEY ✦ ASSISTANT EDITOR CAITLIN O'CONNELL
ASSOCIATE MANAGING EDITOR KATERI WOODY ✦ SENIOR EDITOR, SPECIAL PROJECTS JENNIFER GRÜNWALD
VP PRODUCTION & SPECIAL PROJECTS JEFF YOUNGQUIST ✦ SVP PRINT, SALES & MARKETING DAVID GABRIEL
BOOK DESIGNERS JAY BOWEN WITH ANTHONY GAMBINO

EDITOR IN CHIEF C.B. CEBULSKI ✦ CHIEF CREATIVE OFFICER JOE QUESADA
PRESIDENT DAN BUCKLEY ✦ EXECUTIVE PRODUCER ALAN FINE

IMMORTAL IRON FISTS. Contains material originally published in magazine form as IMMORTAL IRON FISTS #1-6. First printing 2017. ISBN 978-1-302-90536-1. Published by MARVEL WORLDWIDE, INC., a subsidiary of MARVEL ENTERTAINMENT, LLC. OFFICE OF PUBLICATION: 135 West 50th Street, New York, NY 10020. Copyright © 2017 MARVEL No similarity between any of the names, characters, persons, and/or institutions in this magazine with those of any living or dead person or institution is intended, and any such similarity which may exist is purely coincidental. Printed in Canada. DAN BUCKLEY, President, Marvel Entertainment; JOE QUESADA, Chief Creative Officer; TOM BREVOORT, SVP of Publishing; DAVID BOGART, SVP of Business Affairs & Operations, Publishing & Partnership; DAVID GABRIEL, SVP of Sales & Marketing, Publishing; JEFF YOUNGQUIST, VP of Production & Special Projects; DAN CARR, Executive Director of Publishing Technology; ALEX MORALES, Director of Publishing Operations; SUSAN CRESPI, Production Manager; STAN LEE, Chairman Emeritus. For information regarding advertising in Marvel Comics or on Marvel.com, please contact Jonathan Parkhideh, VP of Digital Media & Marketing Solutions, at jparkhideh@marvel.com. For Marvel subscription inquiries, please call 888-511-5480. Manufactured between 11/24/2017 and 12/26/2017 by SOLISCO PRINTERS, SCOTT QC, CANADA.

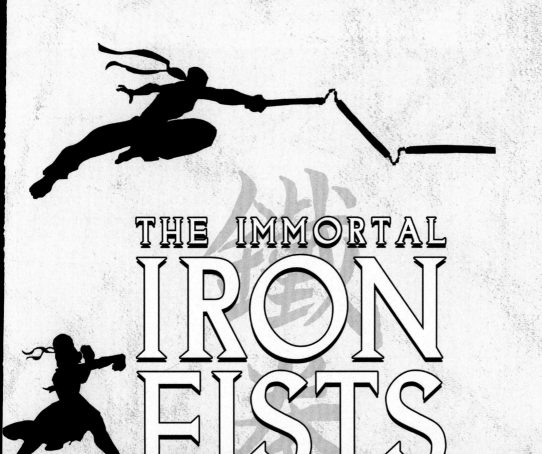

THE IMMORTAL IRON FISTS

WRITER
KAARE ANDREWS

ARTIST
AFU CHAN

COLOR ARTIST
SHELLY CHEN

IN THE DOJO
KAARE ANDREWS

SO WHY IRON FISTS? WHY NOW?

I DID MY THING ON IRON FIST — I SAID WHAT I WANTED TO SAY. I HAPPILY HANDED OFF THE BATON AND FOCUSED ON NEW PROJECTS, NEW WORKS AND NEW IDEAS. THAT'S THE DEAL YOU MAKE WITH SUPER HERO COMICS, YOU TAKE YOUR TURN AT BAT AND SWING FOR THE FENCES… HOPEFULLY YOU ROUND THE BASES AND FIND YOUR WAY HOME, THEN THE NEXT PLAYER TAKES THEIR TURN. YOU CHEER THEM ON AND WATCH THEM SWING…

BUT THEN I GOT THE CALL. MARVEL WAS INTERESTED IN THIS LITTLE ASIAN MONK GIRL I CREATED, THE NEXT IN THE LINE OF IRON FISTS. AND THEY WANTED TO KNOW IF I HAD ANY INTEREST IN CONTINUING HER ADVENTURES. AND IN THAT VERY INSTANT, I KNEW I COULDN'T STAND BY AND WATCH THIS LITTLE LADY BE RAISED BY OTHER "PARENTS." WHAT BROUGHT ME BACK WAS PEI. I JUST NEEDED TO MAKE SURE SHE HAD A GOOD START, THE RIGHT PUSH, THE RIGHT SWING…BEFORE LETTING HER GO.

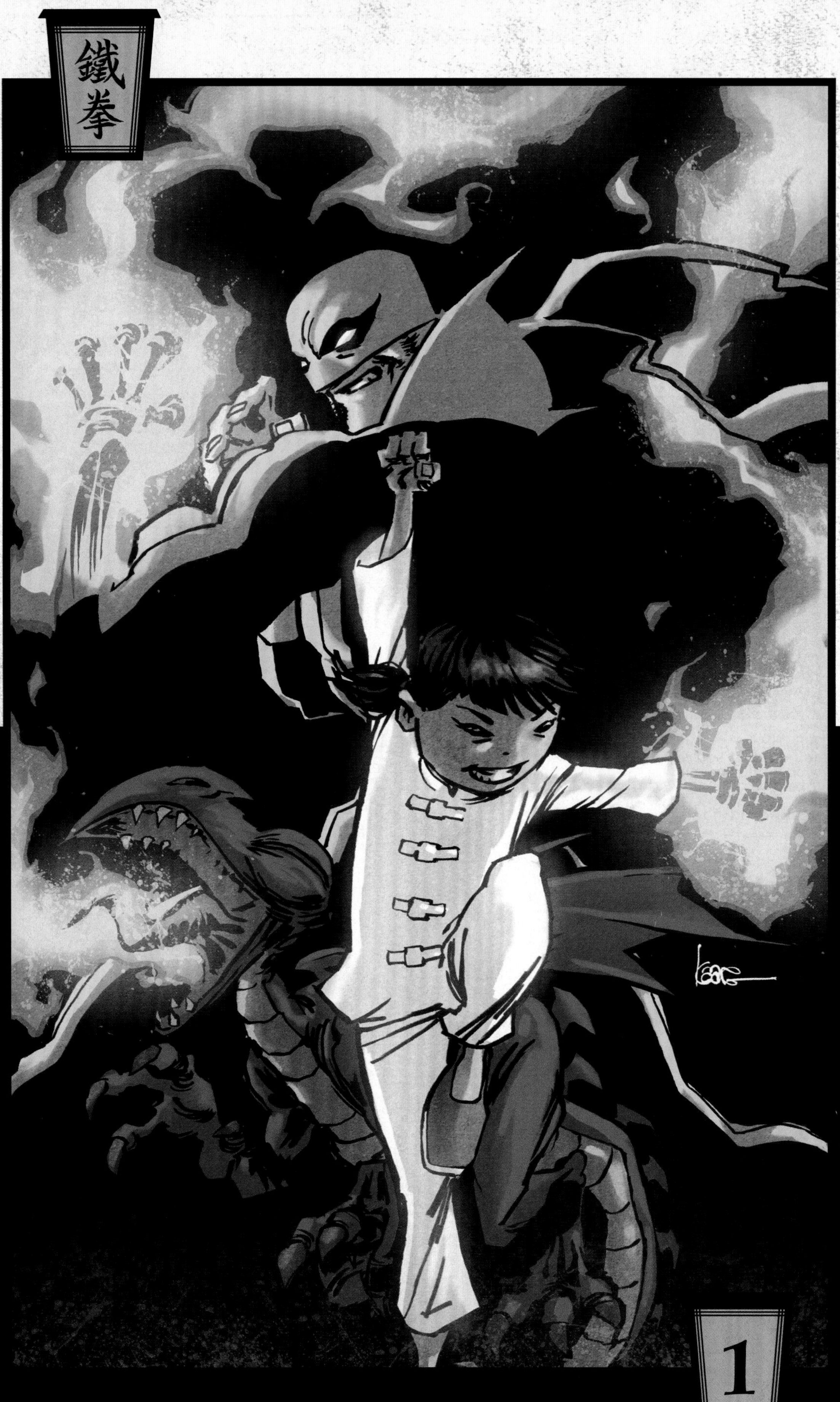
鐵
拳
1

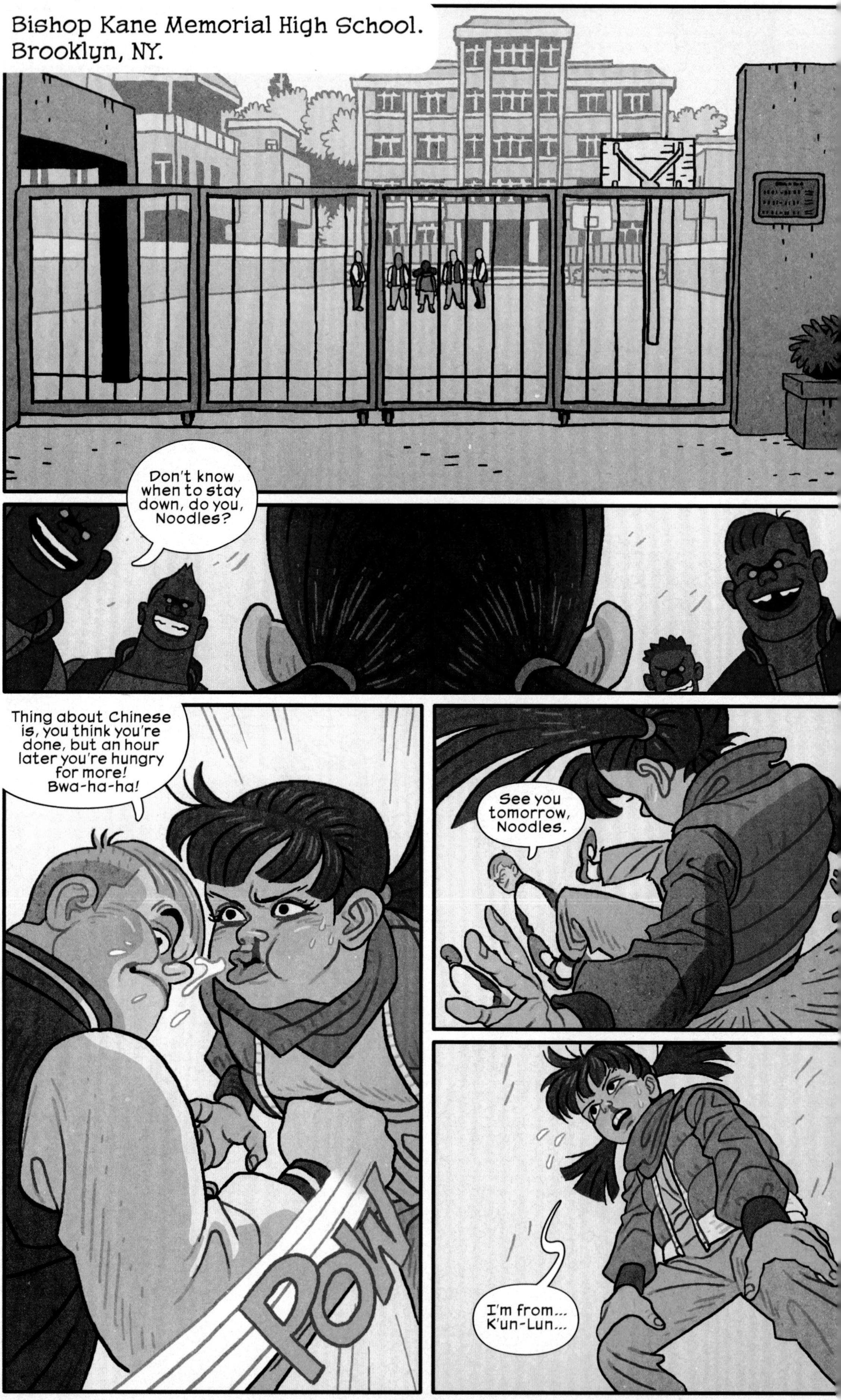
Bishop Kane Memorial High School.
Brooklyn, NY.
Don't know when to stay down, do you, Noodles?
Thing about Chinese is, you think you're done, but an hour later you're hungry for more! Bwa-ha-ha!
POW
See you tomorrow, Noodles.
I'm from... K'un-Lun...

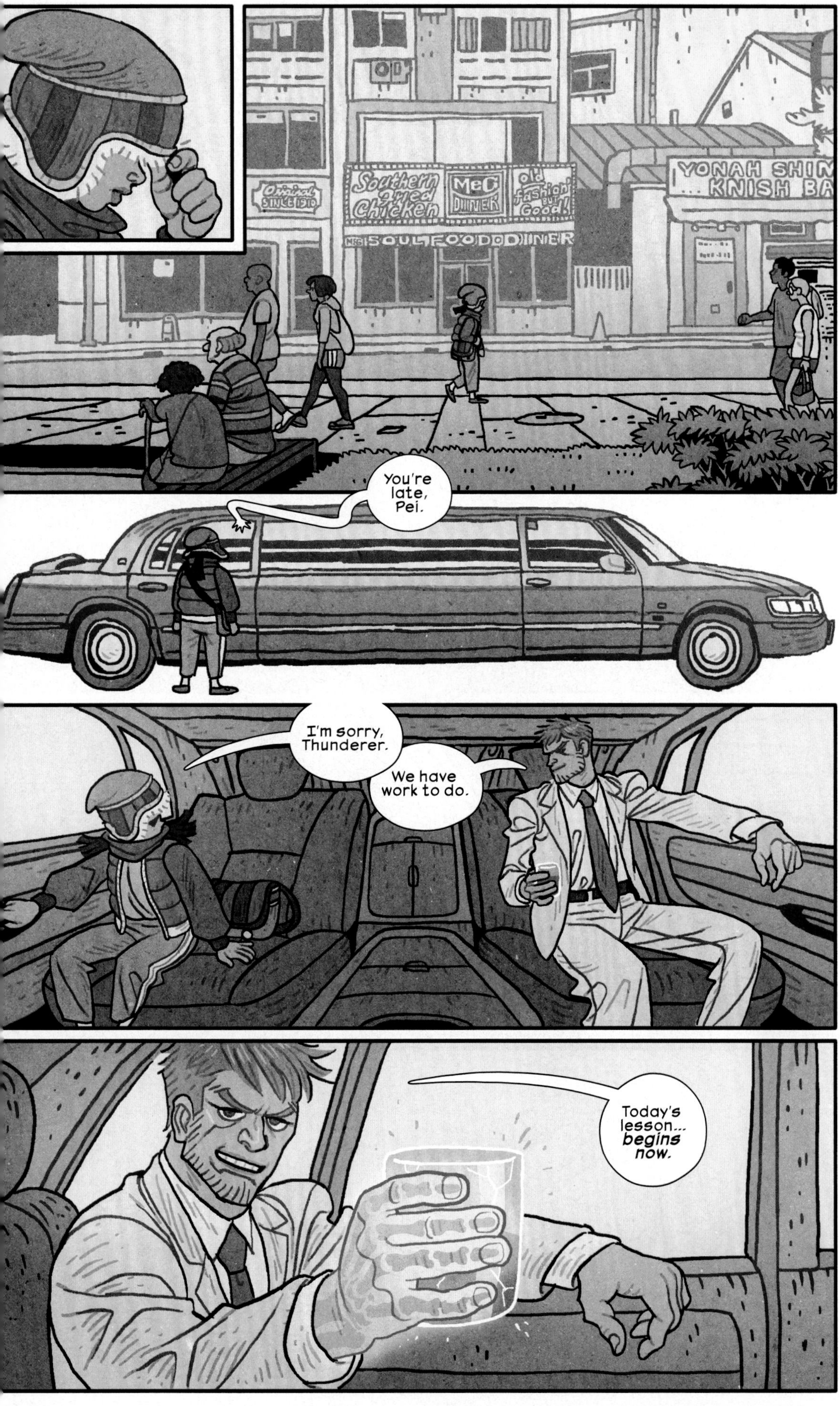
Original SINCE 1910
Southern Fried Chicken
McG DINER
Old fashion BUT Good!
McG SOUL FOOD DINER
YONAH SHIM
KNISH BA
You're late, Pei.
I'm sorry, Thunderer.
We have work to do.
Today's lesson... *begins now.*

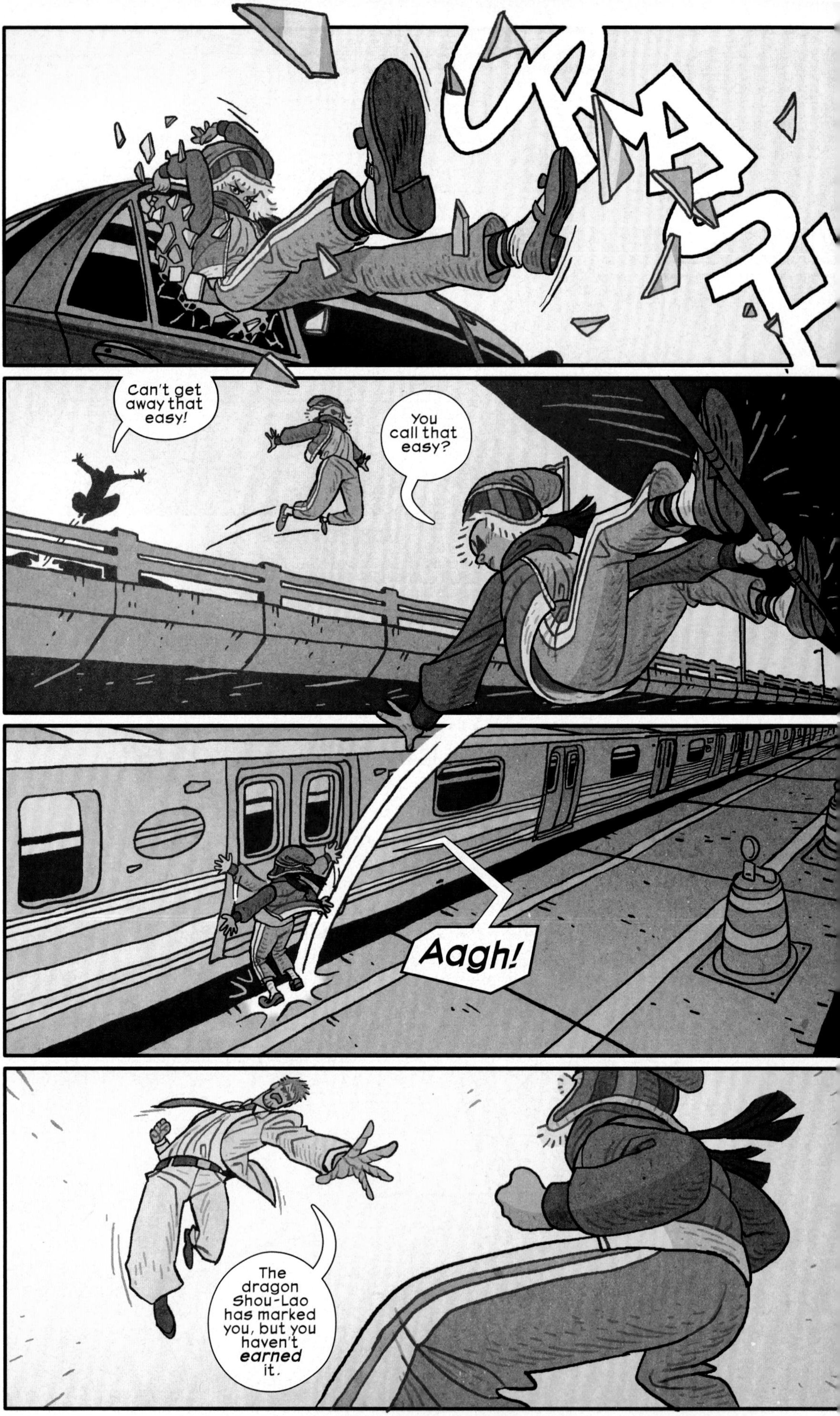
CRASH
Can't get away that easy!
You call that easy?
Aagh!
The dragon Shou-Lao has marked you, but you haven't *earned* it.

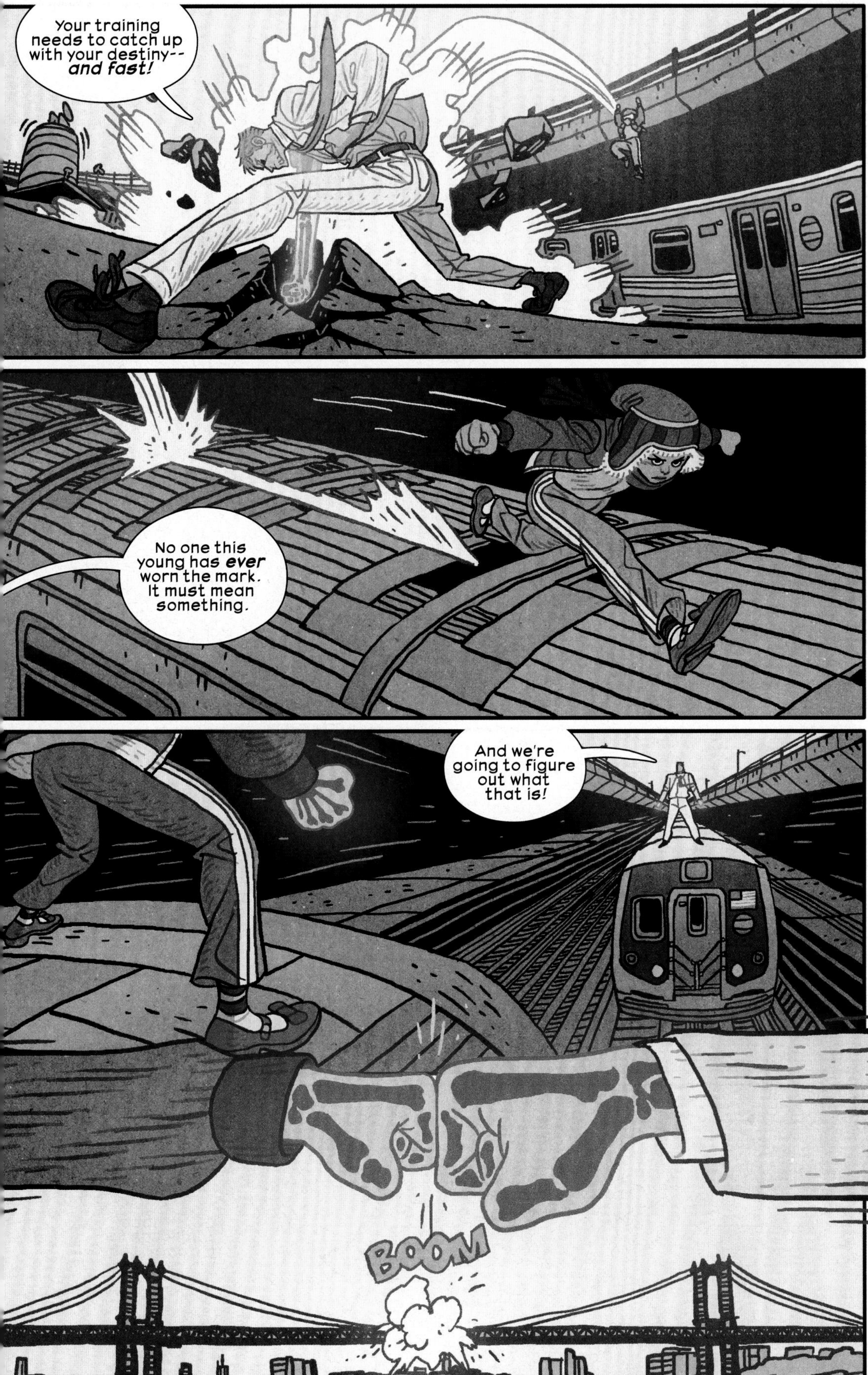
Your training needs to catch up with your destiny-- *and fast!*
No one this young has *ever* worn the mark. It must mean something.
And we're going to figure out what that is!
BOOM

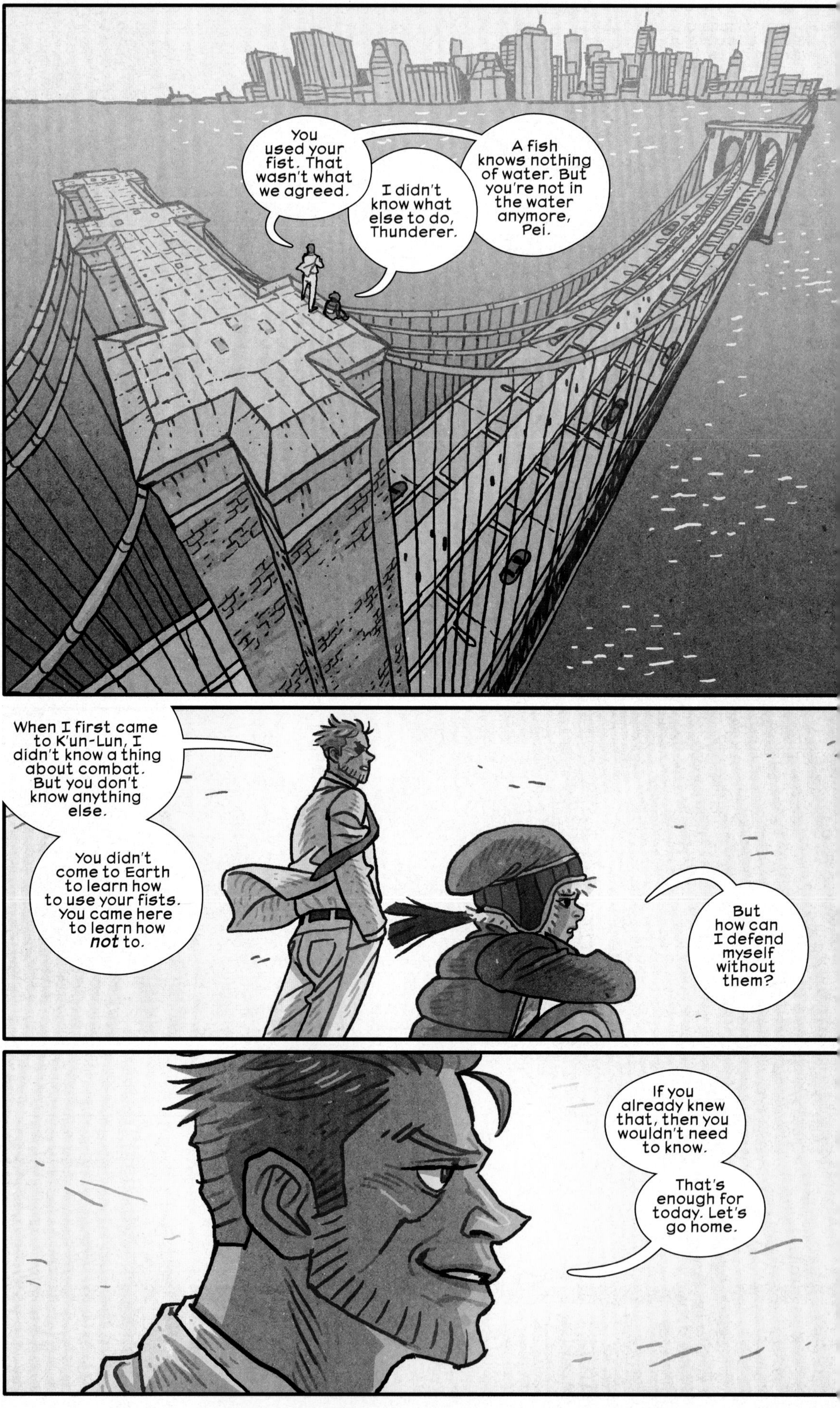
You used your fist. That wasn't what we agreed.
I didn't know what else to do, Thunderer.
A fish knows nothing of water. But you're not in the water anymore, Pei.
When I first came to K'un-Lun, I didn't know a thing about combat. But you don't know anything else.
You didn't come to Earth to learn how to use your fists. You came here to learn how *not* to.
But how can I defend myself without them?
If you already knew that, then you wouldn't need to know.
That's enough for today. Let's go home.

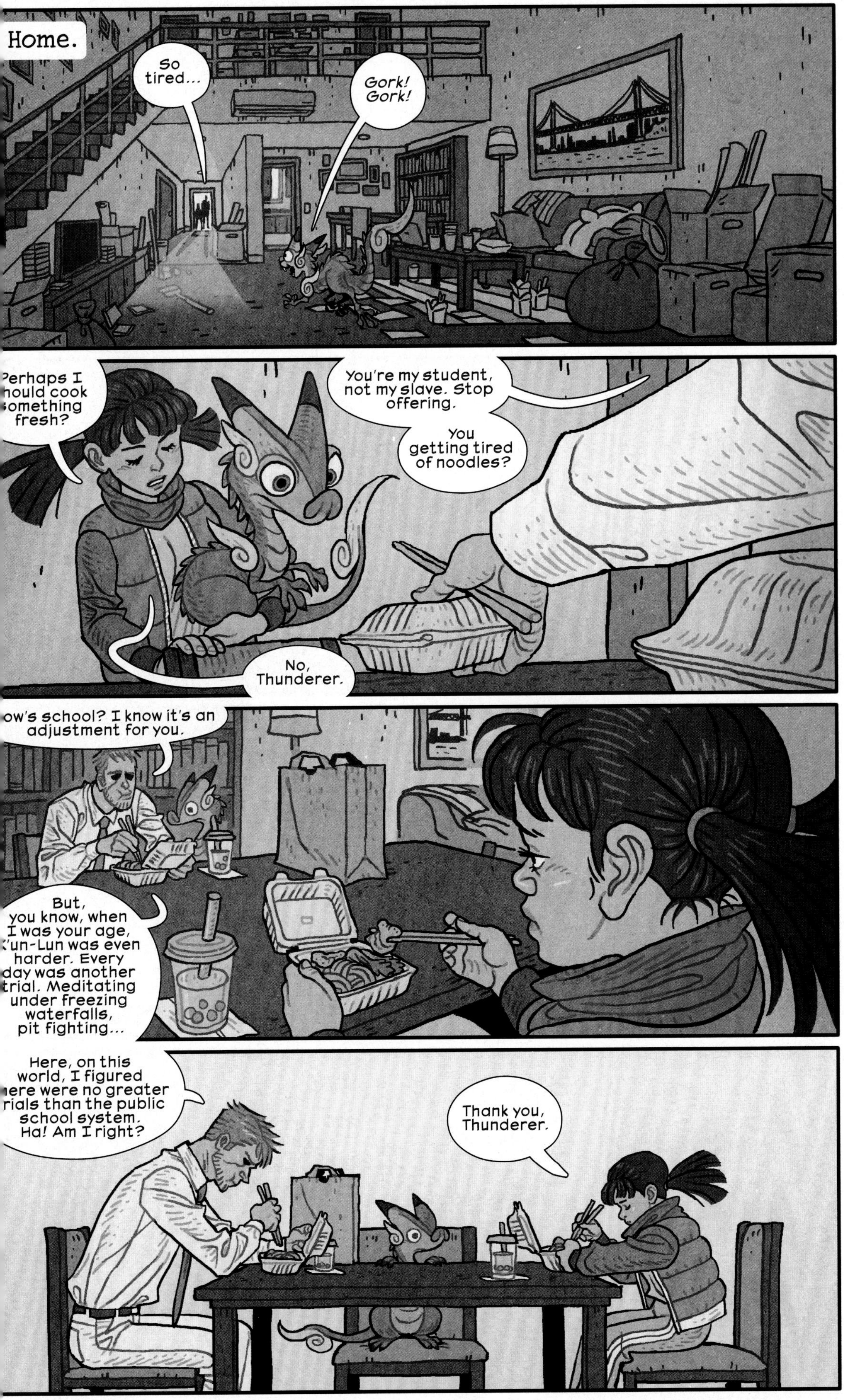
Home.
So tired...
Gork! Gork!
Perhaps I hould cook omething fresh?
You're my student, not my slave. Stop offering.
You getting tired of noodles?
No, Thunderer.
ow's school? I know it's an adjustment for you.
But, you know, when I was your age, 'un-Lun was even harder. Every day was another trial. Meditating under freezing waterfalls, pit fighting...
Here, on this world, I figured ere were no greater rials than the public school system. Ha! Am I right?
Thank you, Thunderer.

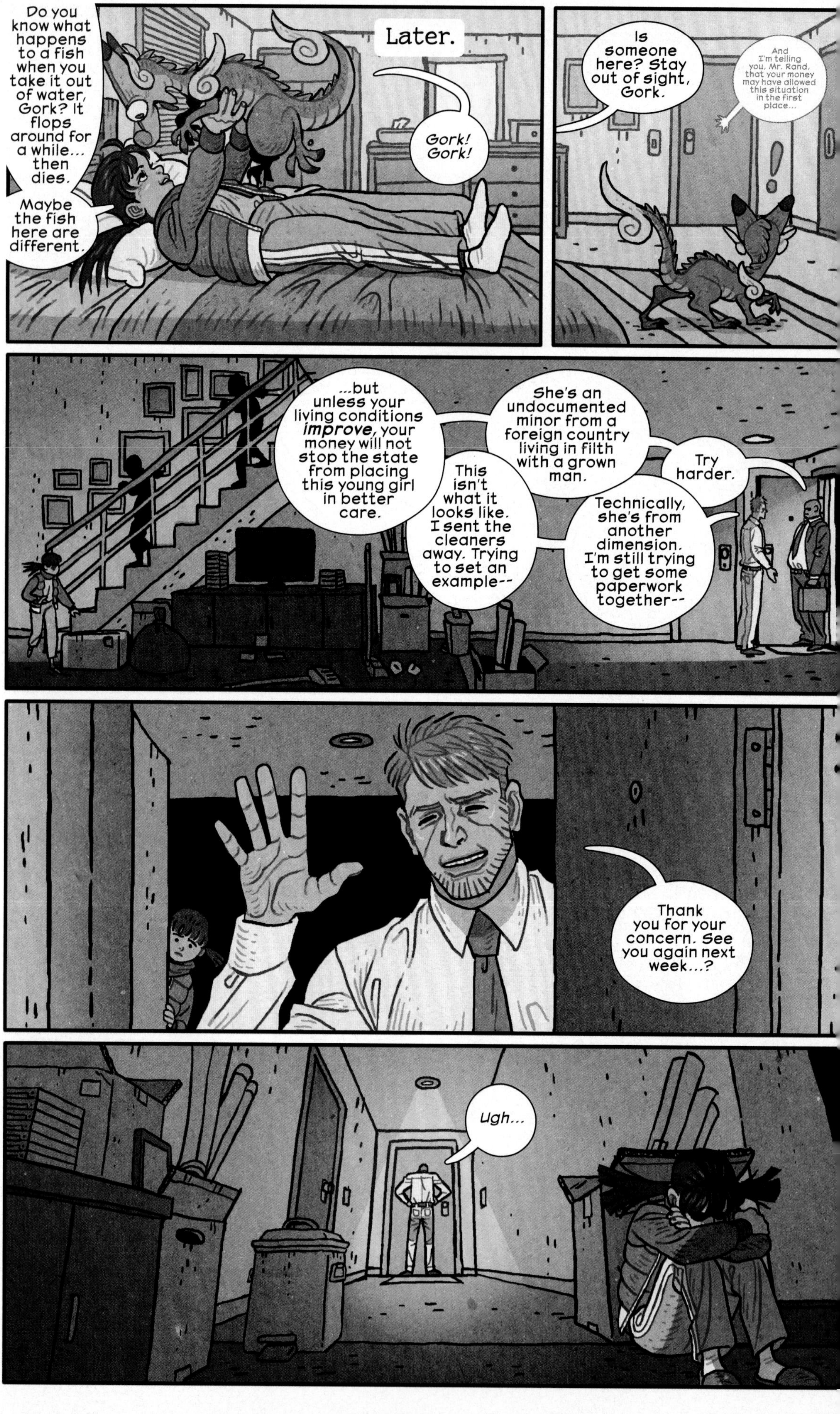
Later.
Do you know what happens to a fish when you take it out of water, Gork? It flops around for a while... then dies.
Maybe the fish here are different.
Gork! Gork!
Is someone here? Stay out of sight, Gork.
And I'm telling you, Mr. Rand, that your money may have allowed this situation in the first place...
...but unless your living conditions improve, your money will not stop the state from placing this young girl in better care.
This isn't what it looks like. I sent the cleaners away. Trying to set an example--
She's an undocumented minor from a foreign country living in filth with a grown man.
Technically, she's from another dimension. I'm still trying to get some paperwork together--
Try harder.
Thank you for your concern. See you again next week...?
Ugh...

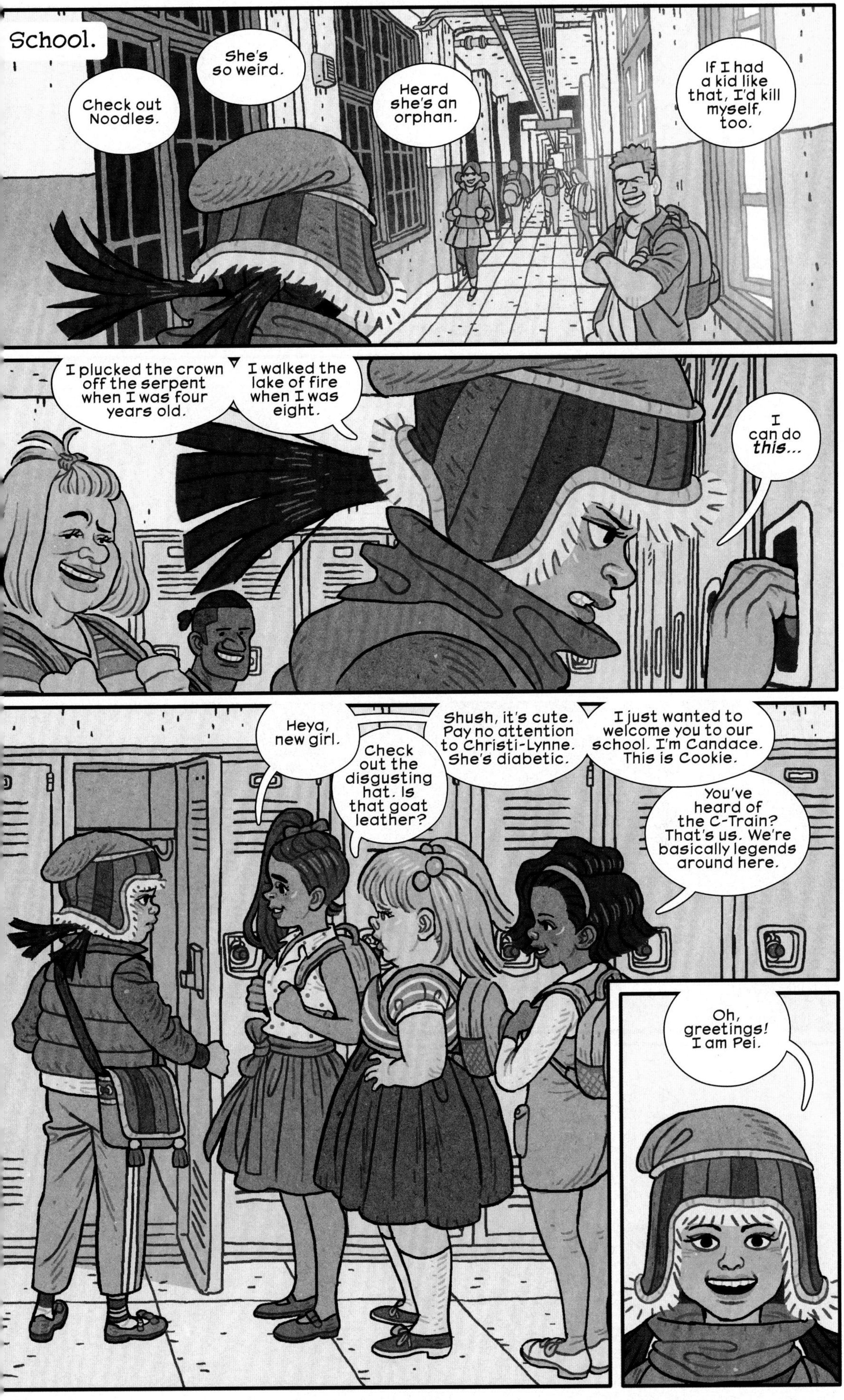
School.
Check out Noodles.
She's so weird.
Heard she's an orphan.
If I had a kid like that, I'd kill myself, too.
I plucked the crown off the serpent when I was four years old.
I walked the lake of fire when I was eight.
I can do *this*...
Heya, new girl.
Check out the disgusting hat. Is that goat leather?
Shush, it's cute. Pay no attention to Christi-Lynne. She's diabetic.
I just wanted to welcome you to our school. I'm Candace. This is Cookie.
You've heard of the C-Train? That's us. We're basically legends around here.
Oh, greetings! I am Pei.

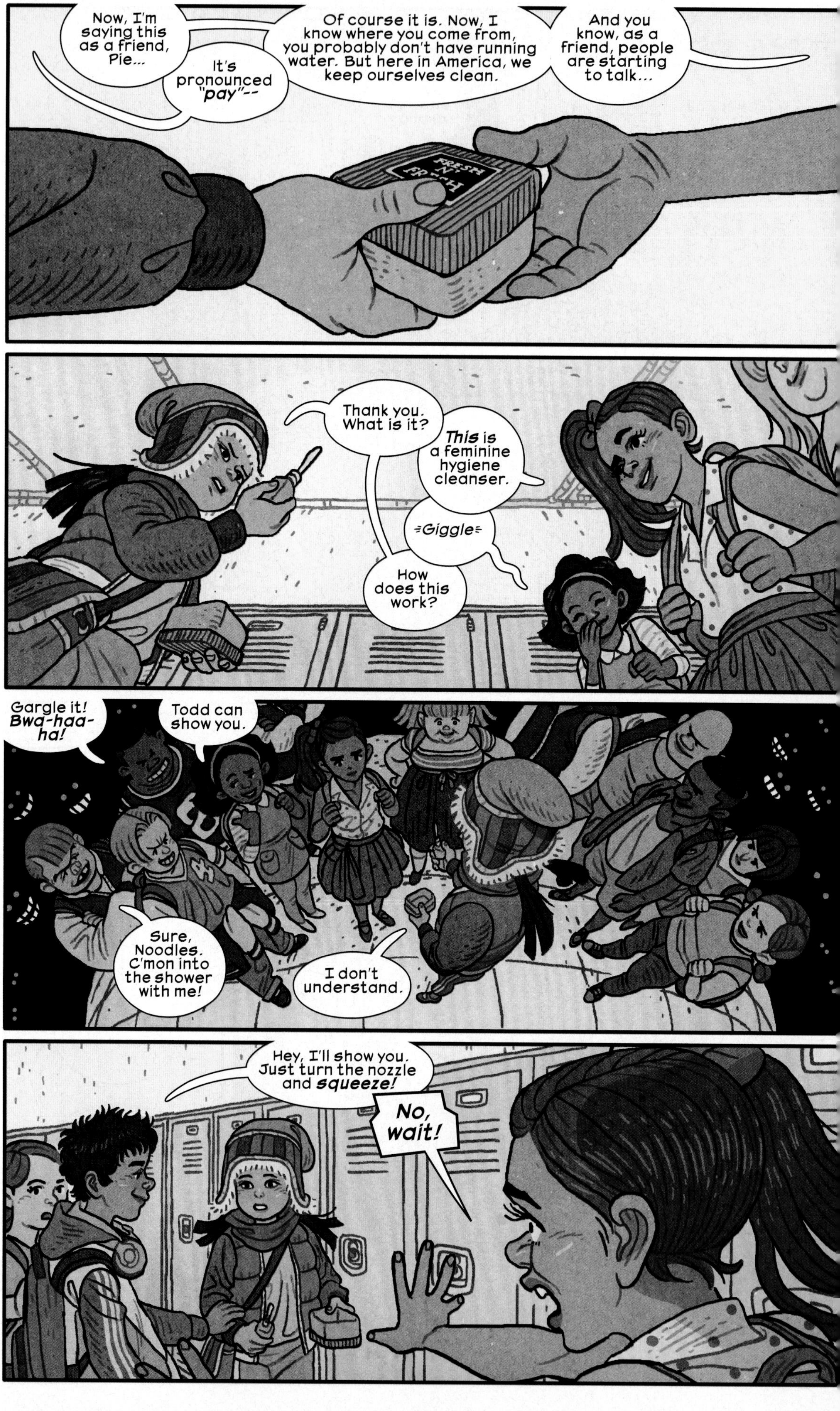
Now, I'm saying this as a friend, Pie...
It's pronounced "pay"--
Of course it is. Now, I know where you come from, you probably don't have running water. But here in America, we keep ourselves clean.
And you know, as a friend, people are starting to talk...
FRESH 'N' FRESH
Thank you. What is it?
This is a feminine hygiene cleanser.
Giggle
How does this work?
Gargle it! Bwa-haa-ha!
Todd can show you.
Sure, Noodles. C'mon into the shower with me!
I don't understand.
Hey, I'll show you. Just turn the nozzle and squeeze!
No, wait!

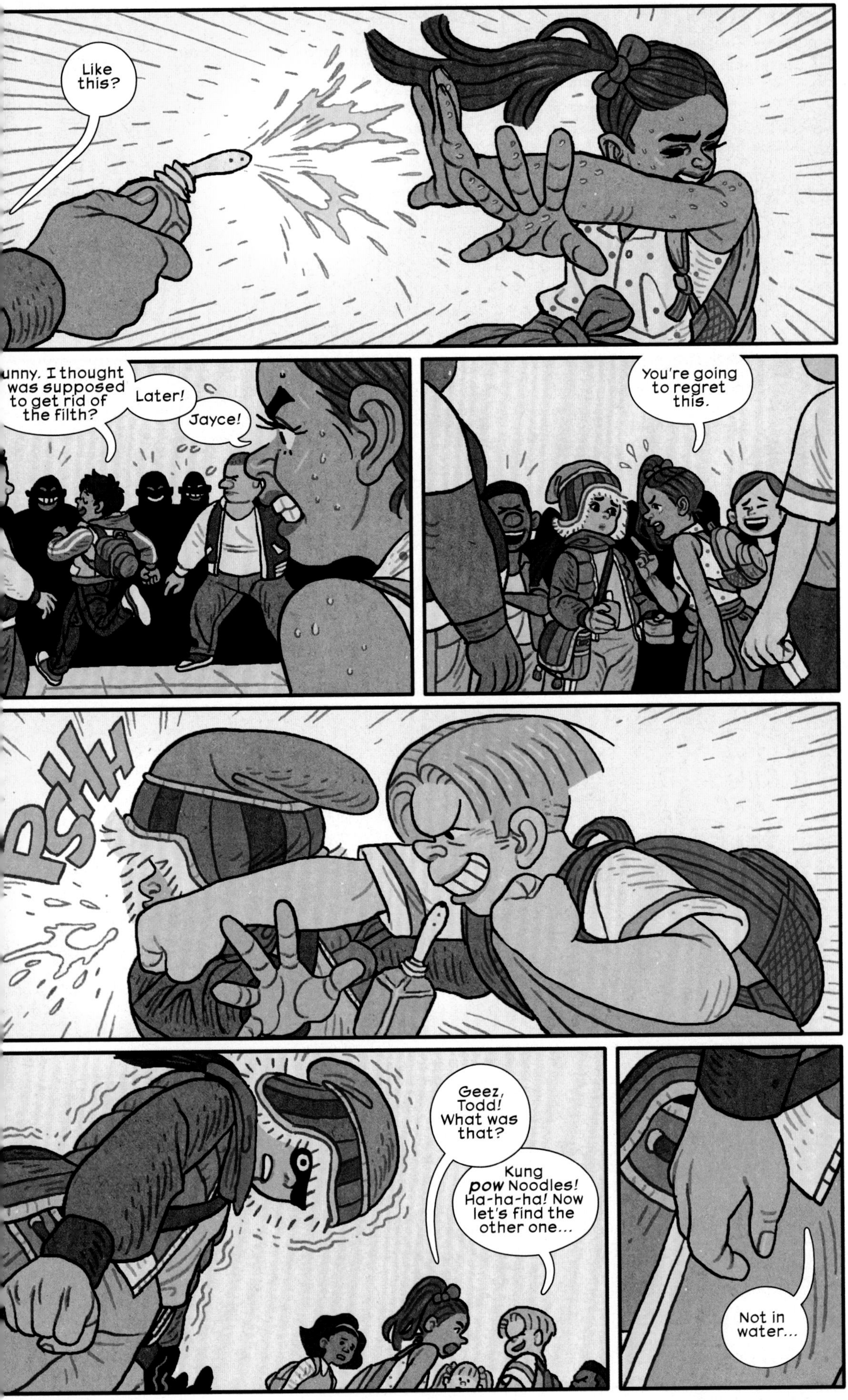
Like this?
unny. I thought was supposed to get rid of the filth?
Later!
Jayce!
You're going to regret this.
PSHH
Geez, Todd! What was that?
Kung *pow* Noodles! Ha-ha-ha! Now let's find the other one...
Not in water...

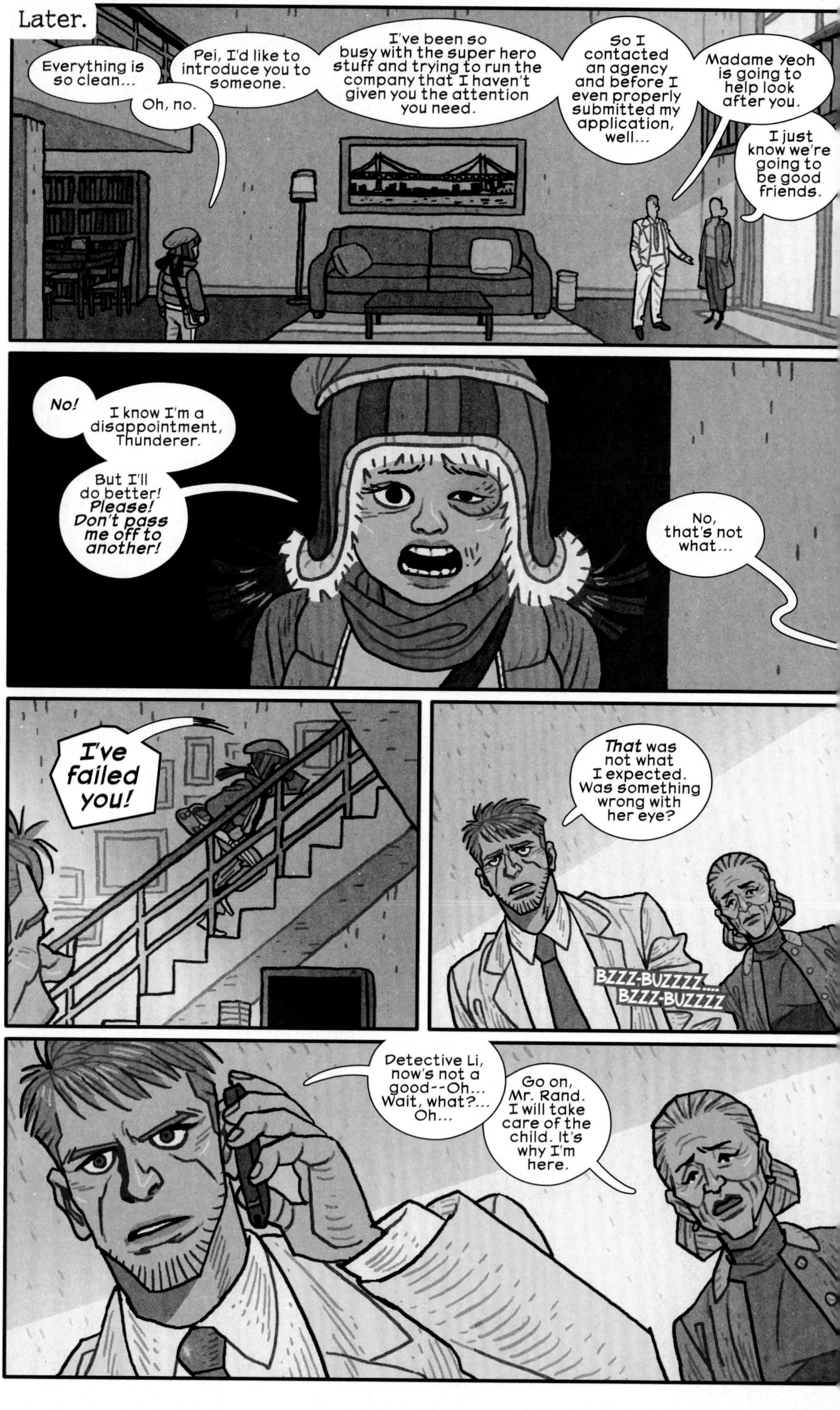
Later.
Everything is so clean...
Oh, no.
Pei, I'd like to introduce you to someone.
I've been so busy with the super hero stuff and trying to run the company that I haven't given you the attention you need.
So I contacted an agency and before I even properly submitted my application, well...
Madame Yeoh is going to help look after you.
I just know we're going to be good friends.
No!
I know I'm a disappointment, Thunderer.
But I'll do better! *Please! Don't pass me off to another!*
No, that's not what...
I've failed you!
That was not what I expected. Was something wrong with her eye?
BZZZ-BUZZZZ.... BZZZ-BUZZZZ
Detective Li, now's not a good--Oh... Wait, what?... Oh...
Go on, Mr. Rand. I will take care of the child. It's why I'm here.

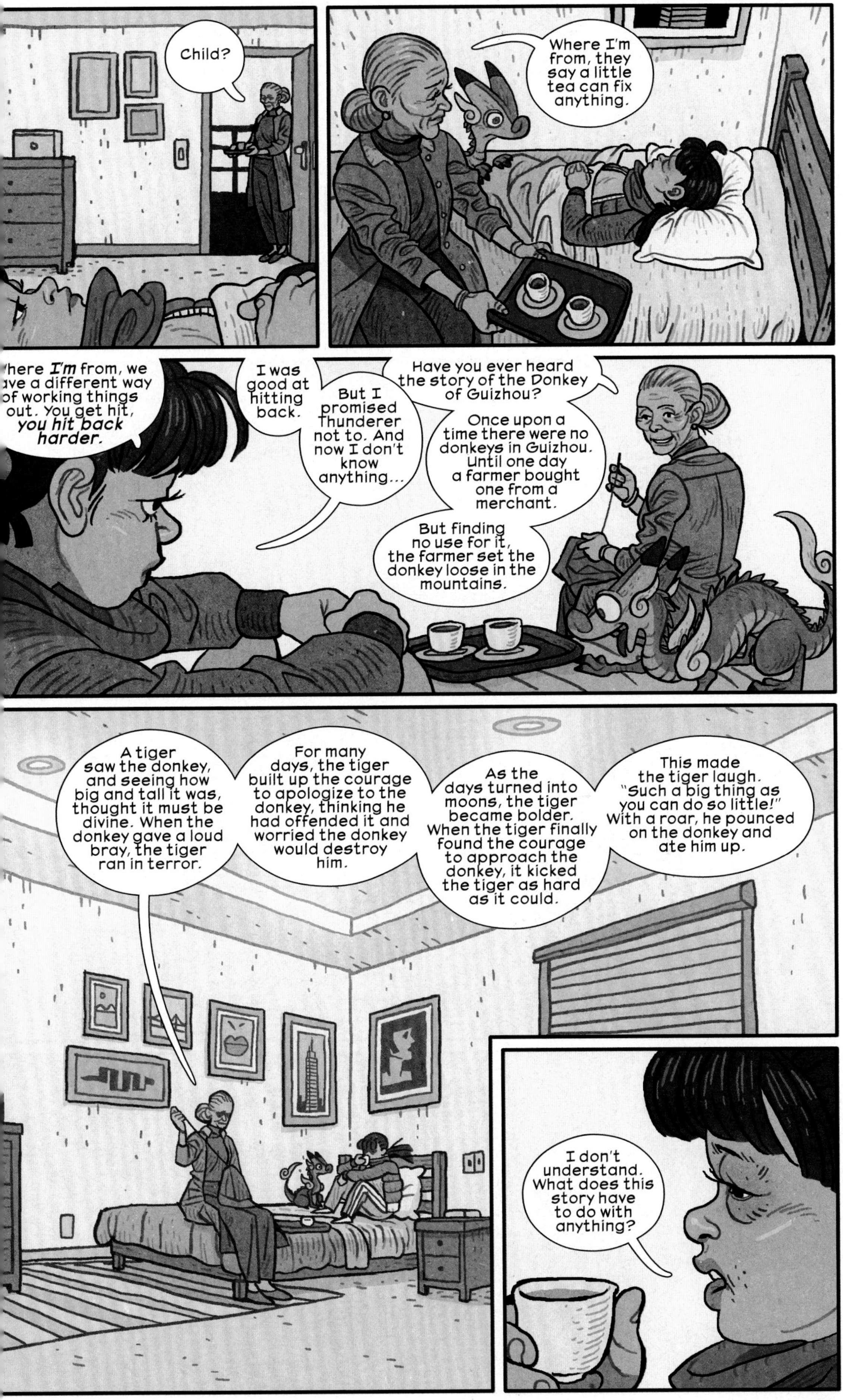

Child?
Where I'm from, they say a little tea can fix anything.
here I'm from, we ave a different way of working things out. You get hit, you hit back harder.
I was good at hitting back.
But I promised Thunderer not to. And now I don't know anything...
Have you ever heard the story of the Donkey of Guizhou?
Once upon a time there were no donkeys in Guizhou. Until one day a farmer bought one from a merchant.
But finding no use for it, the farmer set the donkey loose in the mountains.
A tiger saw the donkey, and seeing how big and tall it was, thought it must be divine. When the donkey gave a loud bray, the tiger ran in terror.
For many days, the tiger built up the courage to apologize to the donkey, thinking he had offended it and worried the donkey would destroy him.
As the days turned into moons, the tiger became bolder. When the tiger finally found the courage to approach the donkey, it kicked the tiger as hard as it could.
This made the tiger laugh. "Such a big thing as you can do so little!" With a roar, he pounced on the donkey and ate him up.
I don't understand. What does this story have to do with anything?

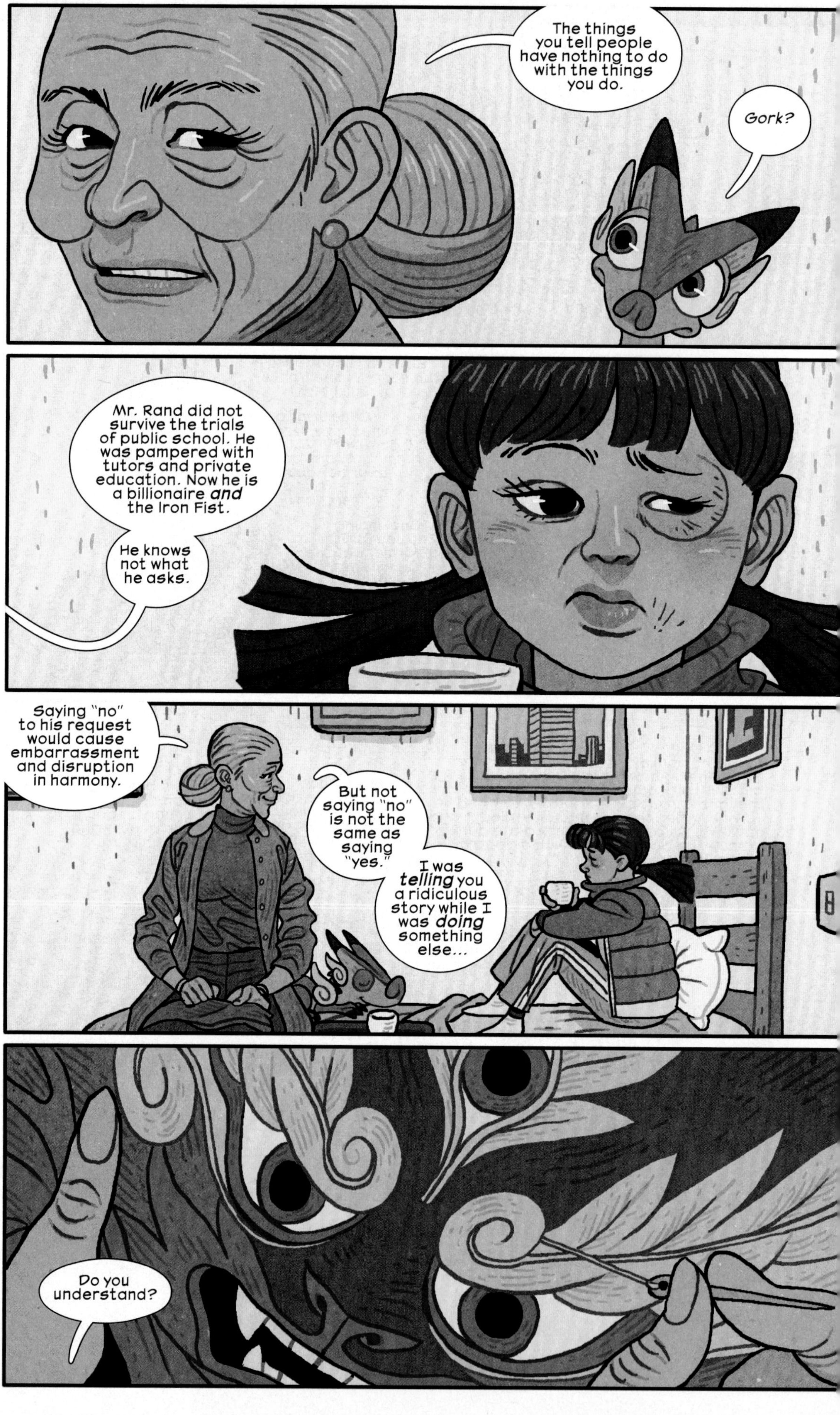
The things you tell people have nothing to do with the things you do.
Gork?
Mr. Rand did not survive the trials of public school. He was pampered with tutors and private education. Now he is a billionaire *and* the Iron Fist.
He knows not what he asks.
Saying "no" to his request would cause embarrassment and disruption in harmony.
But not saying "no" is not the same as saying "yes."
I was *telling* you a ridiculous story while I was *doing* something else...
Do you understand?

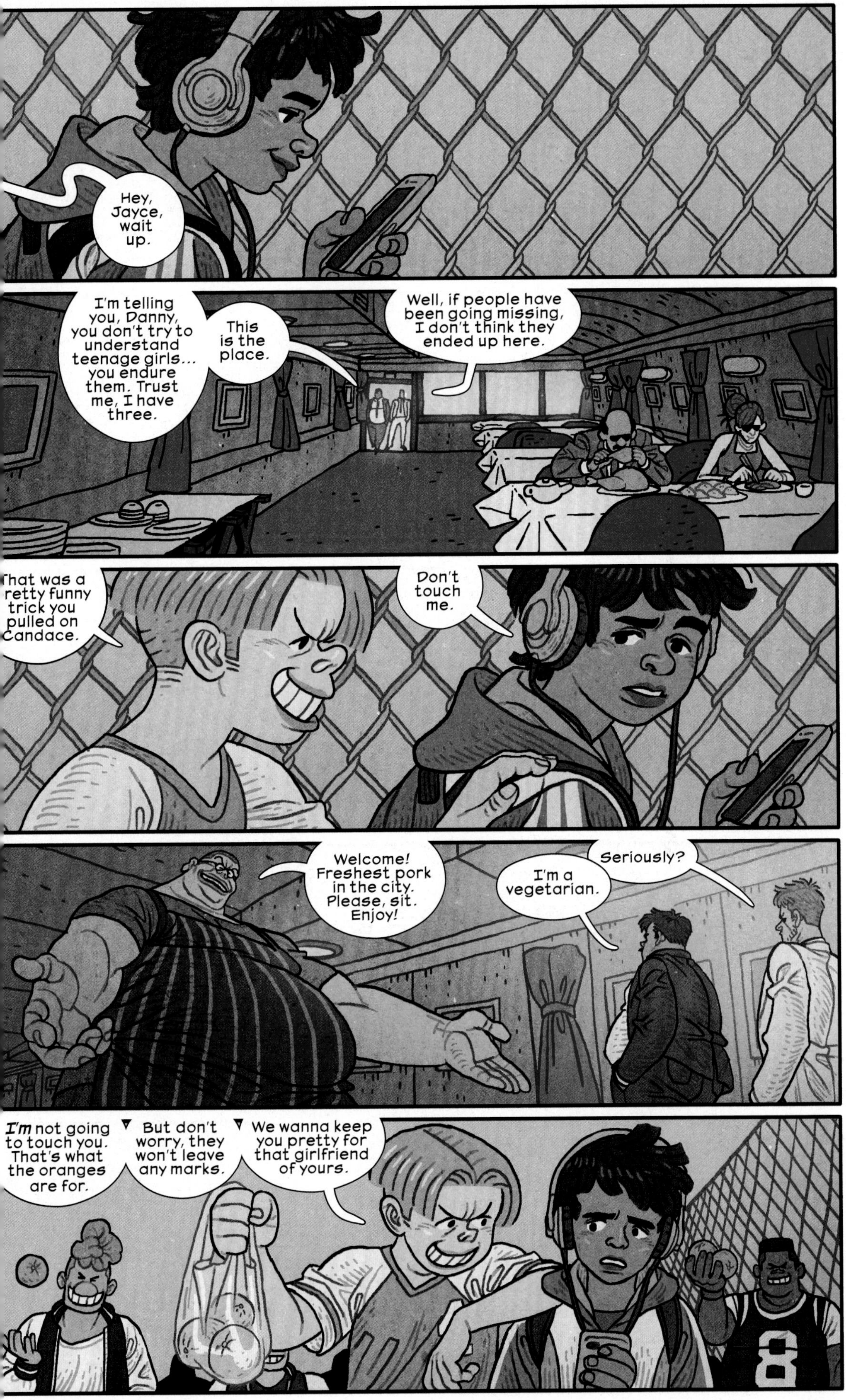
Hey, Jayce, wait up.
I'm telling you, Danny, you don't try to understand teenage girls... you endure them. Trust me, I have three.
This is the place.
Well, if people have been going missing, I don't think they ended up here.
That was a retty funny trick you pulled on Candace.
Don't touch me.
Welcome! Freshest pork in the city. Please, sit. Enjoy!
I'm a vegetarian.
Seriously?
I'm not going to touch you. That's what the oranges are for.
But don't worry, they won't leave any marks.
We wanna keep you pretty for that girlfriend of yours.

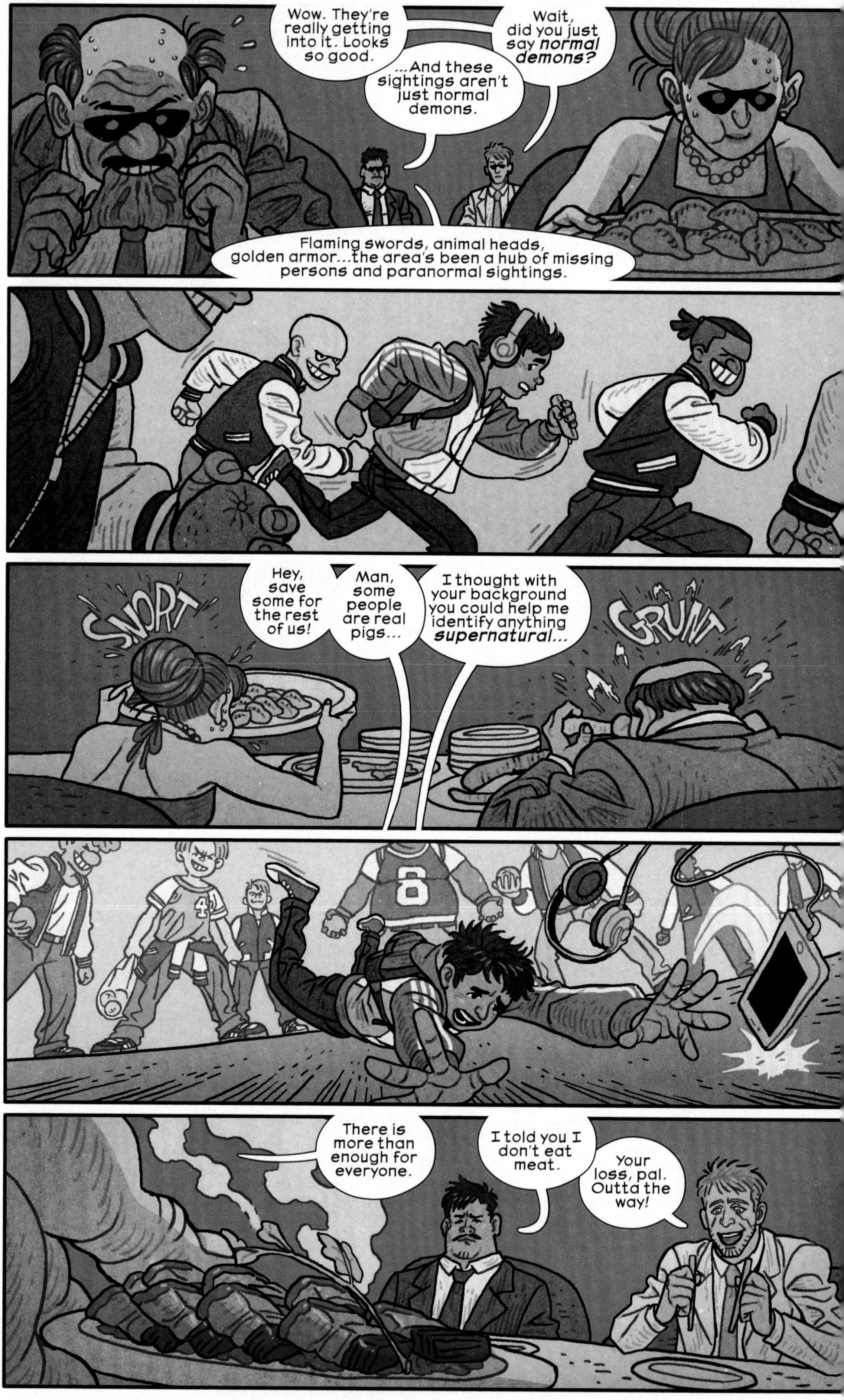

Wow. They're really getting into it. Looks so good.
Wait, did you just say *normal demons?*
...And these sightings aren't just normal demons.
Flaming swords, animal heads, golden armor...the area's been a hub of missing persons and paranormal sightings.
SNORT
Hey, save some for the rest of us!
Man, some people are real pigs...
I thought with your background you could help me identify anything *supernatural*...
GRUNT
8
There is more than enough for everyone.
I told you I don't eat meat.
Your loss, pal. Outta the way!

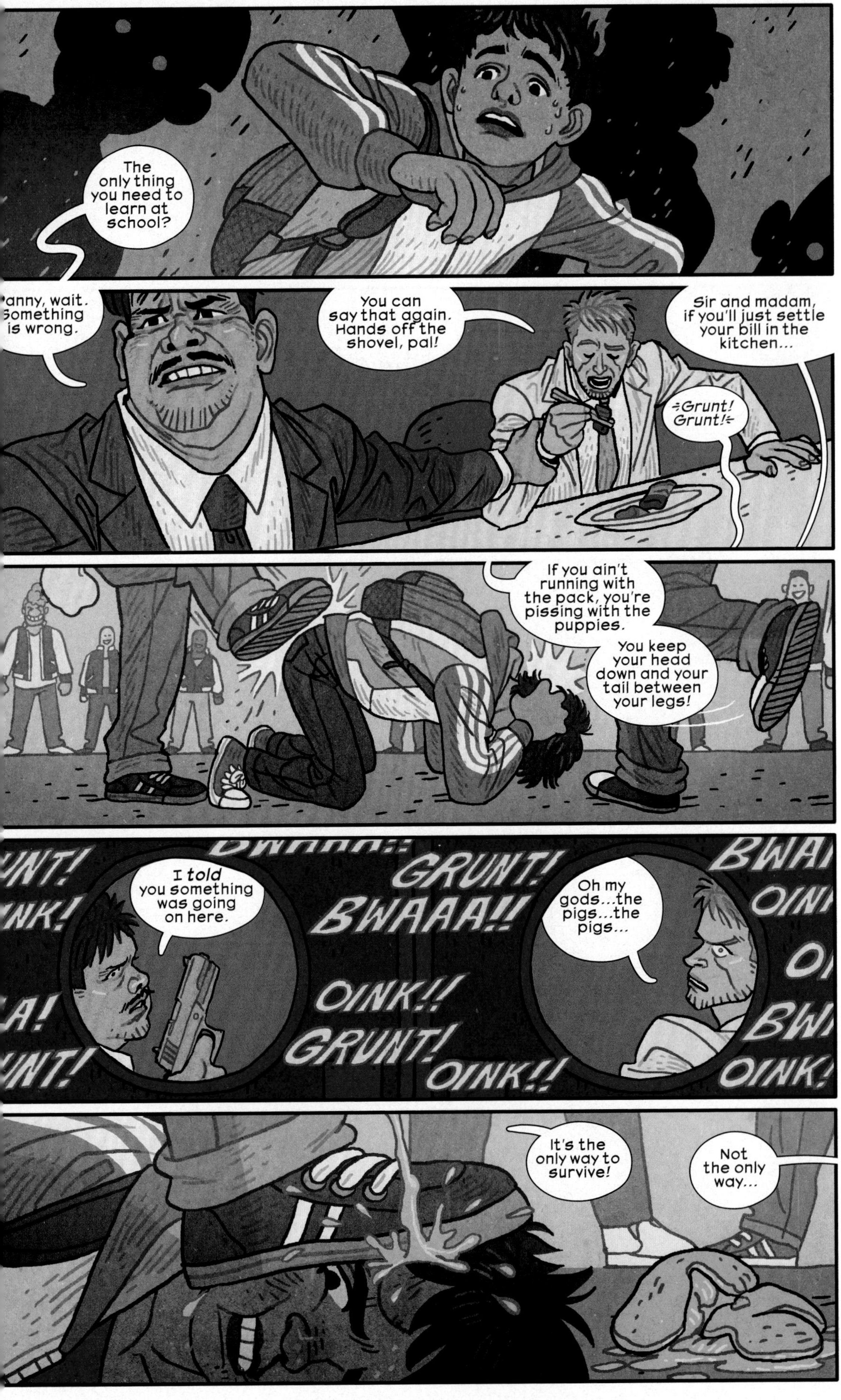
The only thing you need to learn at school?
Danny, wait. Something is wrong.
You can say that again. Hands off the shovel, pal!
Sir and madam, if you'll just settle your bill in the kitchen...
Grunt! Grunt!
If you ain't running with the pack, you're pissing with the puppies.
You keep your head down and your tail between your legs!
I told you something was going on here.
GRUNT!
BWAAA!!
OINK!!
GRUNT!
OINK!!
Oh my gods...the pigs...the pigs...
OINK!
It's the only way to survive!
Not the only way...

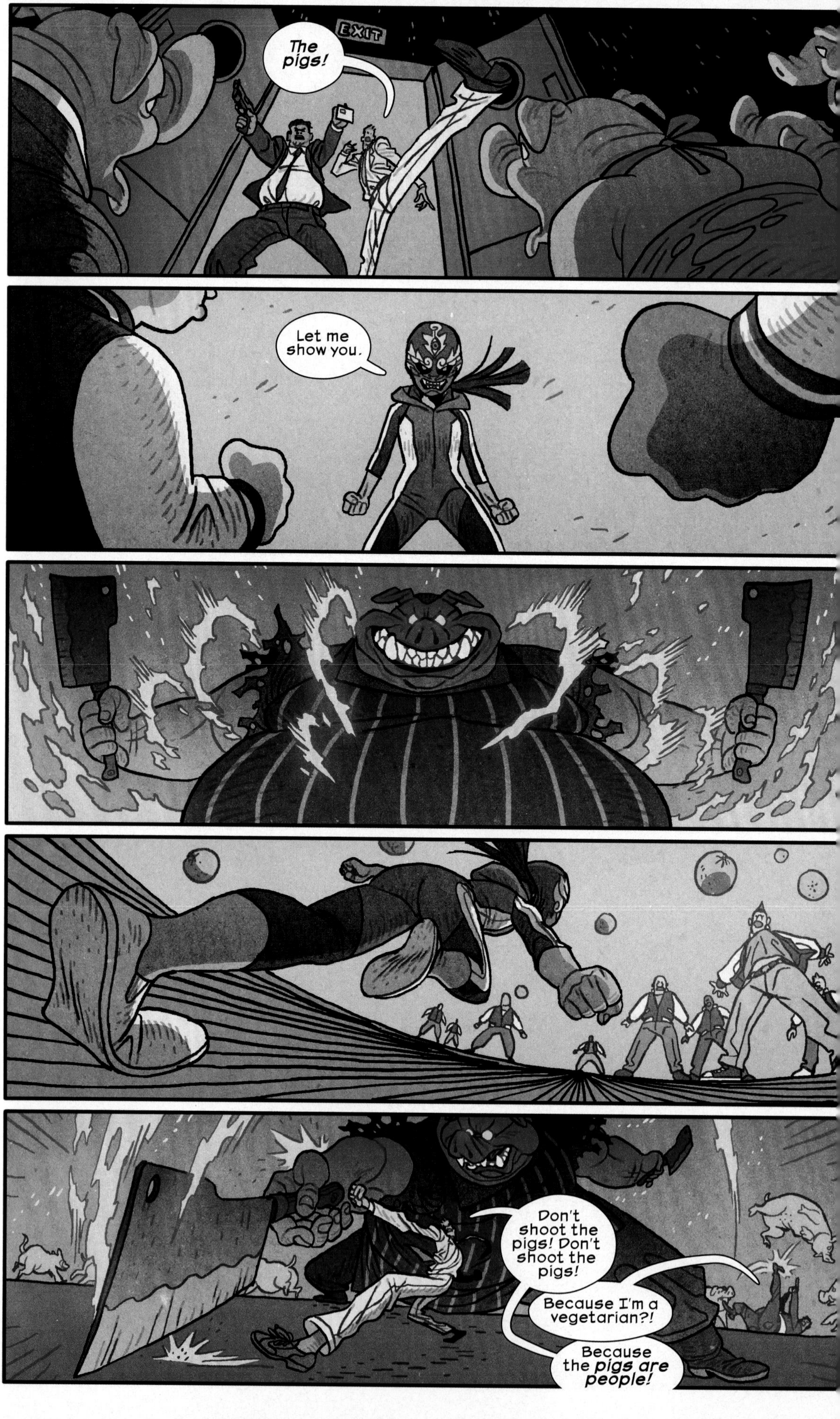
The pigs!
Let me show you.
Don't shoot the pigs! Don't shoot the pigs!
Because I'm a vegetarian?!
Because the *pigs are people!*

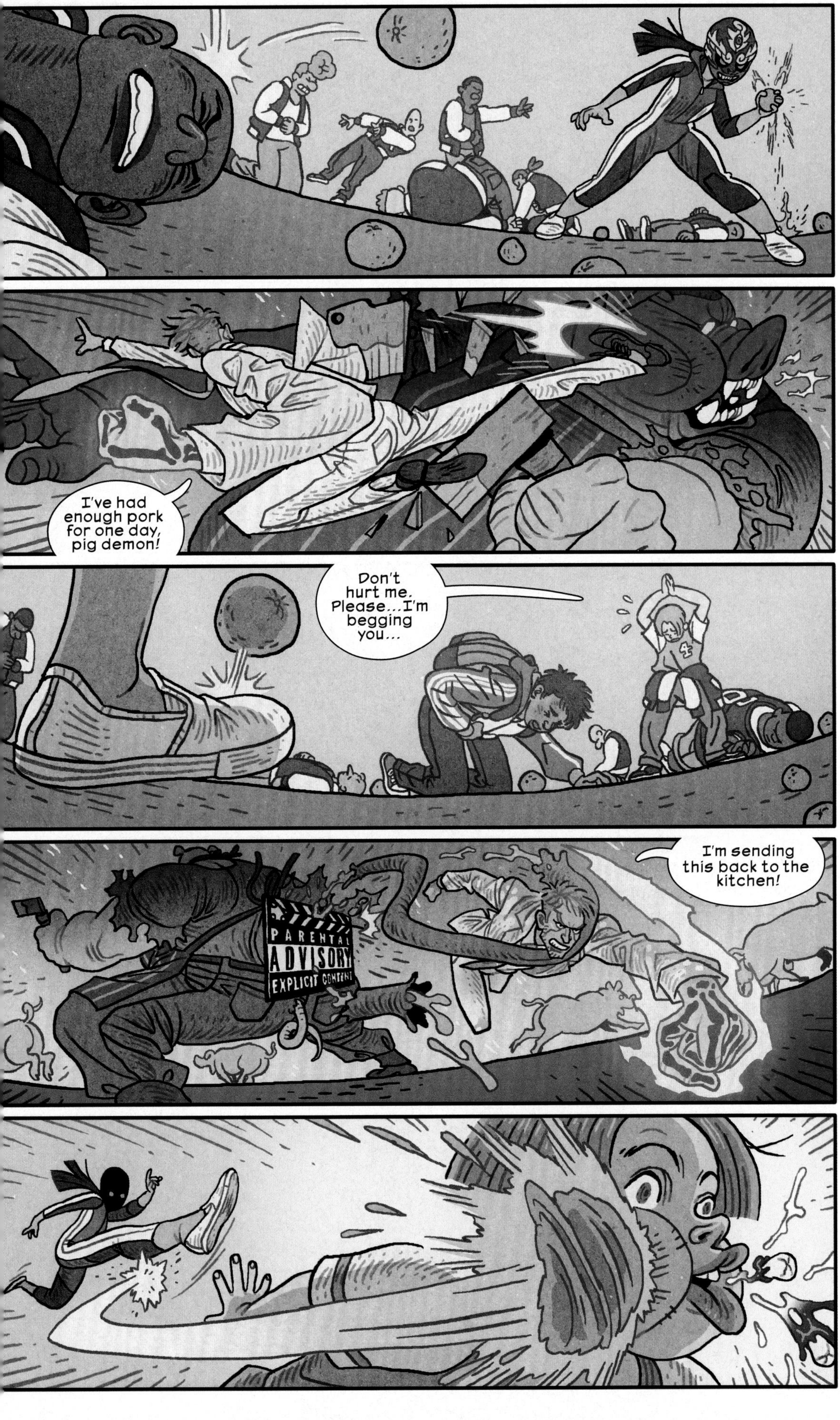
I've had enough pork for one day, pig demon!
Don't hurt me. Please...I'm begging you...
4
I'm sending this back to the kitchen!
PARENTAL ADVISORY EXPLICIT CONTENT

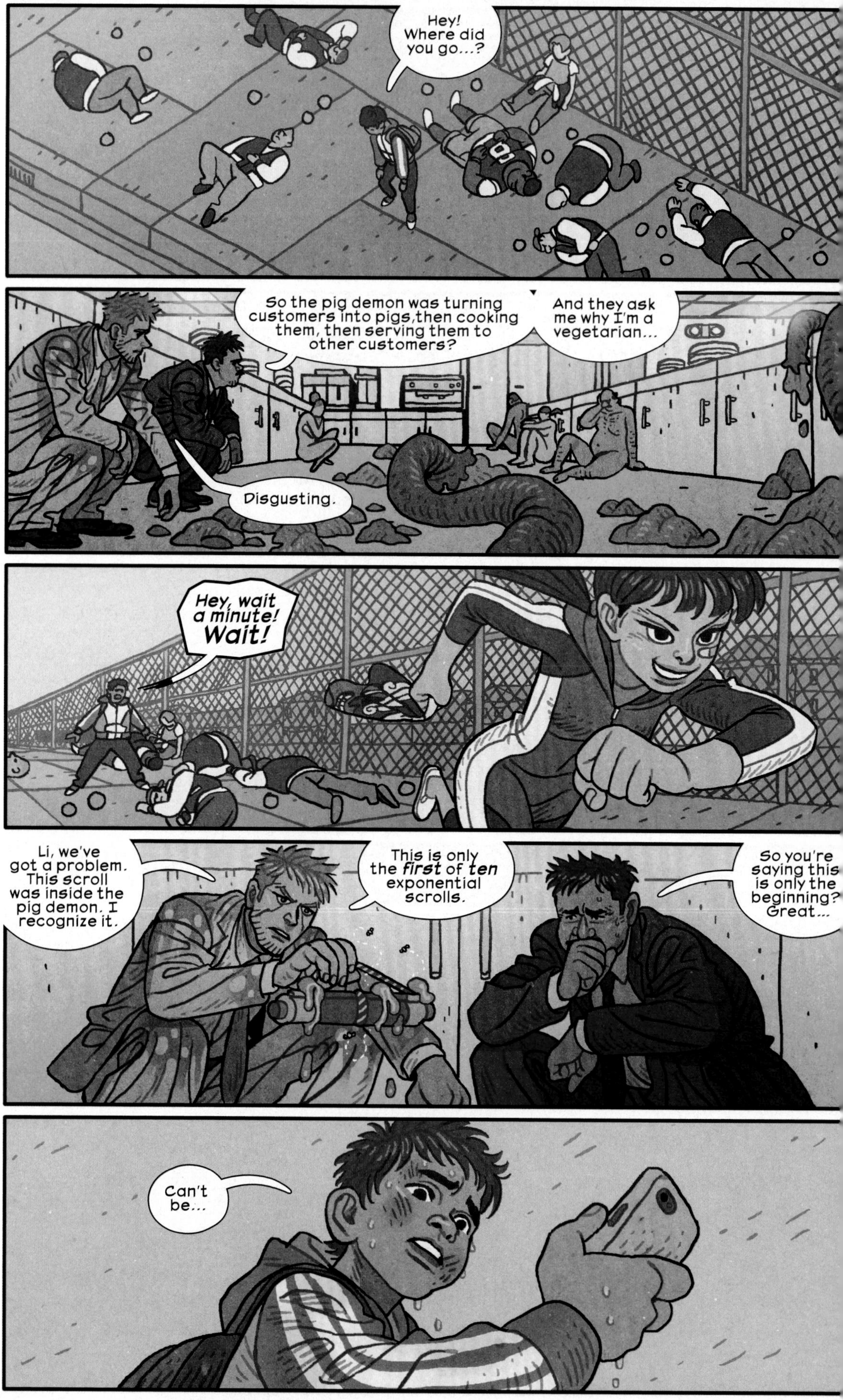
Hey! Where did you go...?
So the pig demon was turning customers into pigs, then cooking them, then serving them to other customers?
And they ask me why I'm a vegetarian...
Disgusting.
Hey, wait a minute! Wait!
Li, we've got a problem. This scroll was inside the pig demon. I recognize it.
This is only the *first* of *ten* exponential scrolls.
So you're saying this is only the beginning? Great...
Can't be...

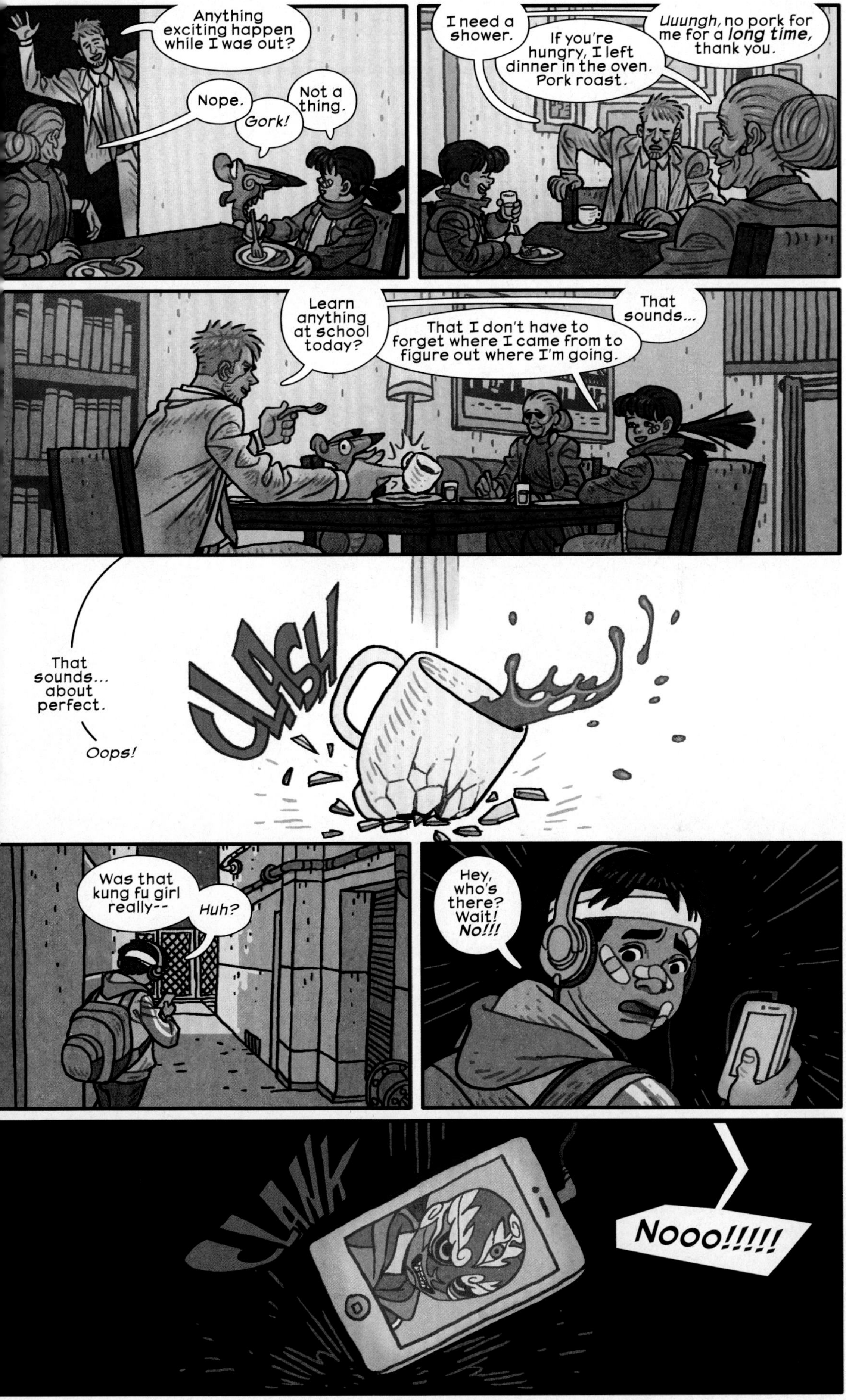

Anything exciting happen while I was out?
Nope.
Gork!
Not a thing.
I need a shower.
If you're hungry, I left dinner in the oven. Pork roast.
Uuungh, no pork for me for a ***long time***, thank you.
Learn anything at school today?
That I don't have to forget where I came from to figure out where I'm going.
That sounds...
That sounds... about perfect.
Oops!
CLASH
Was that kung fu girl really--
Huh?
Hey, who's there? Wait! ***No!!!***
CLANK
Nooo!!!!!

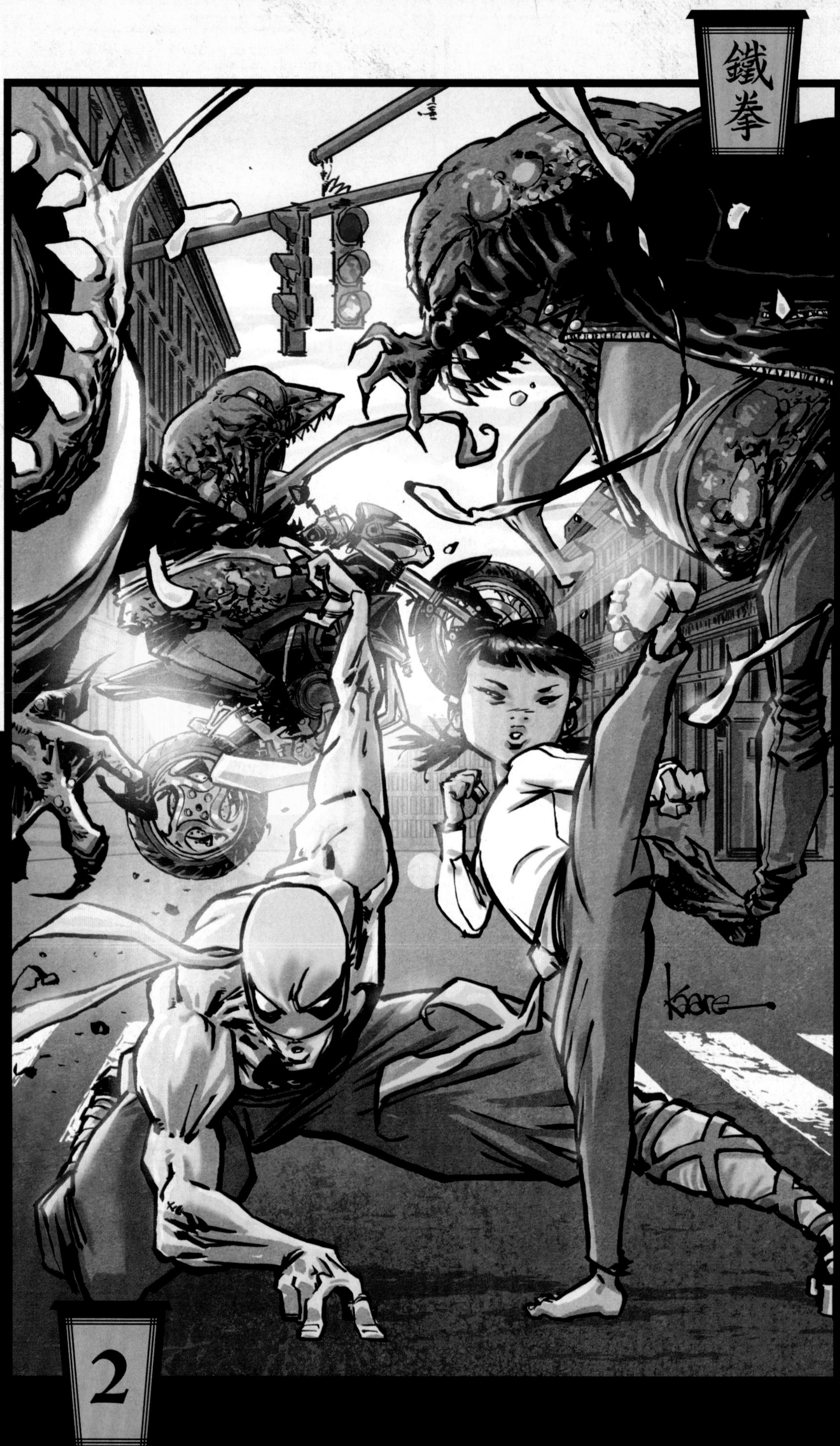
鐵拳
2

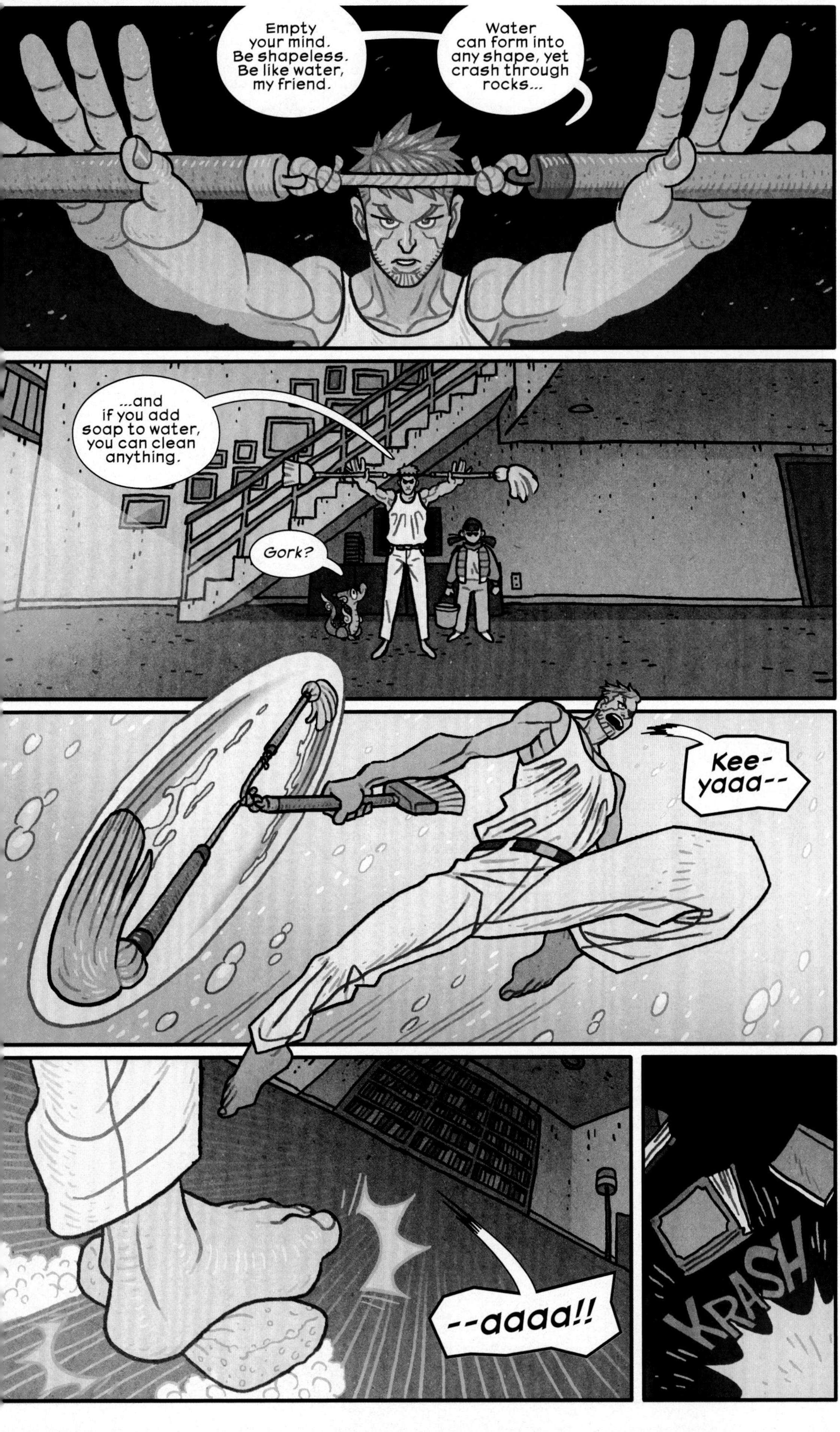
Empty your mind. Be shapeless. Be like water, my friend.
Water can form into any shape, yet crash through rocks...
...and if you add soap to water, you can clean anything.
Gork?
Kee-yaaa--
--aaaa!!
KRASH

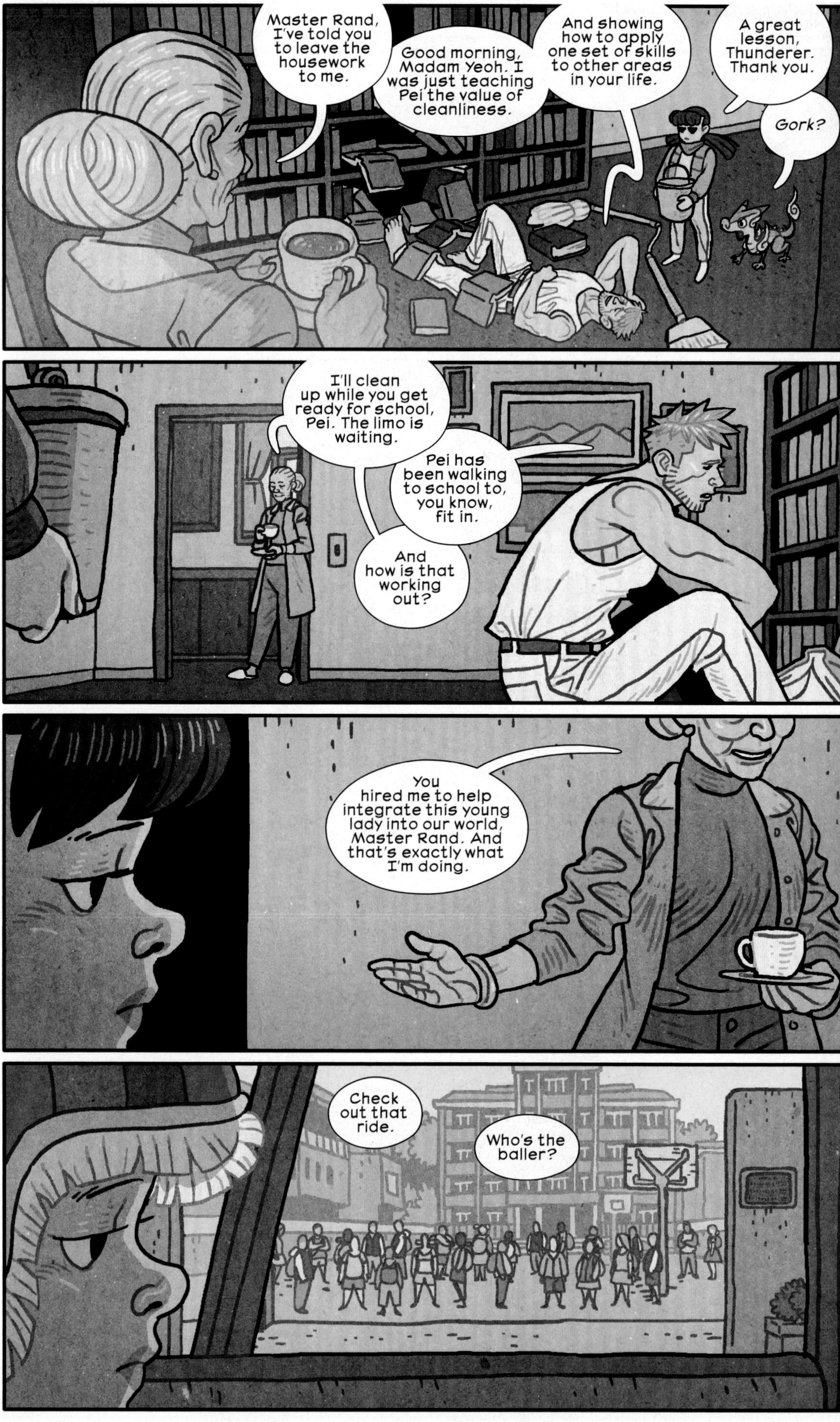
Master Rand, I've told you to leave the housework to me.
Good morning, Madam Yeoh. I was just teaching Pei the value of cleanliness.
And showing how to apply one set of skills to other areas in your life.
A great lesson, Thunderer. Thank you.
Gork?
I'll clean up while you get ready for school, Pei. The limo is waiting.
Pei has been walking to school to, you know, fit in.
And how is that working out?
You hired me to help integrate this young lady into our world, Master Rand. And that's exactly what I'm doing.
Check out that ride.
Who's the baller?

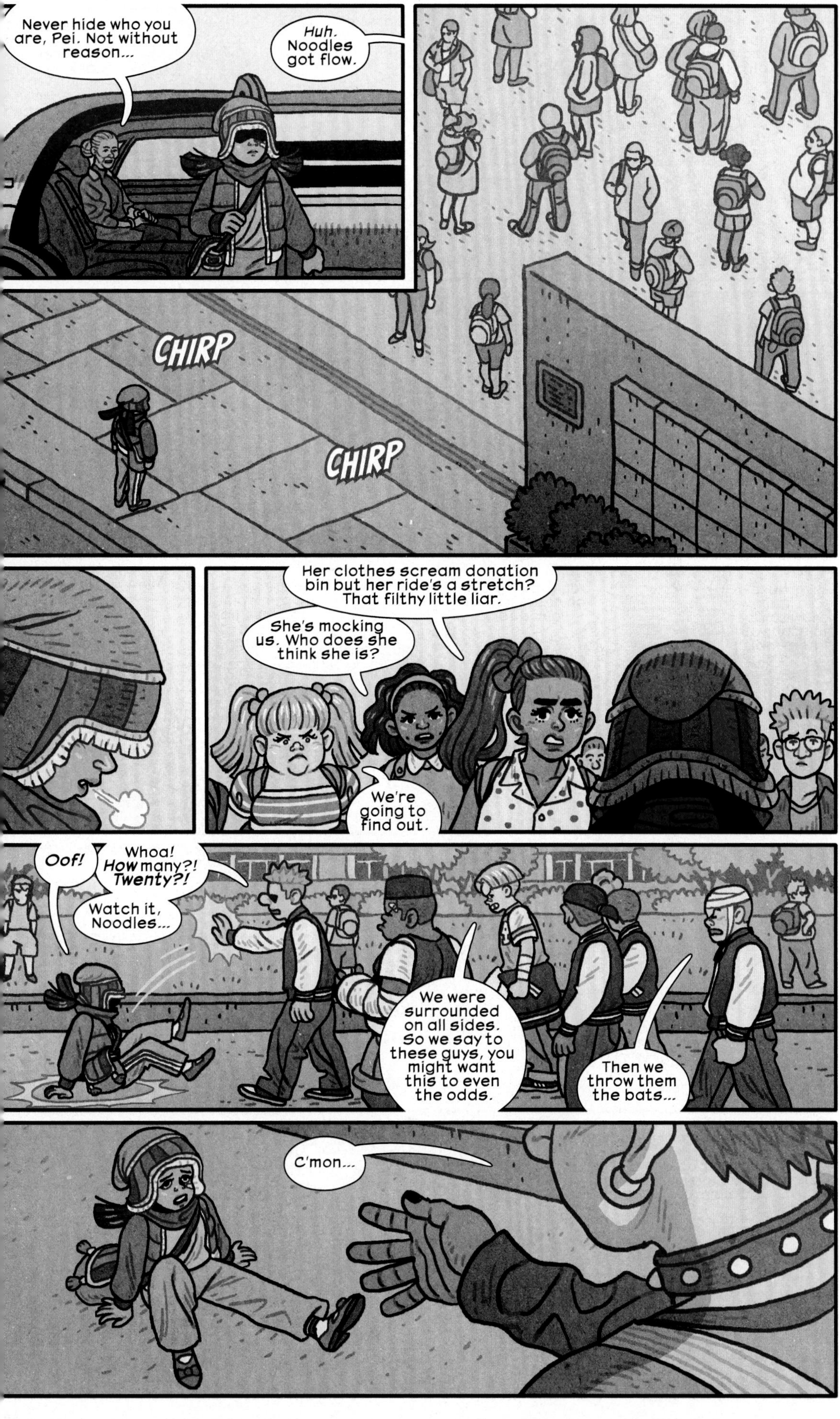
Never hide who you are, Pei. Not without reason...
Huh. Noodles got flow.
CHIRP
CHIRP
Her clothes scream donation bin but her ride's a stretch? That filthy little liar.
She's mocking us. Who does she think she is?
We're going to find out.
Oof!
Whoa! How many?! Twenty?!
Watch it, Noodles...
We were surrounded on all sides. So we say to these guys, you might want this to even the odds.
Then we throw them the bats...
C'mon...

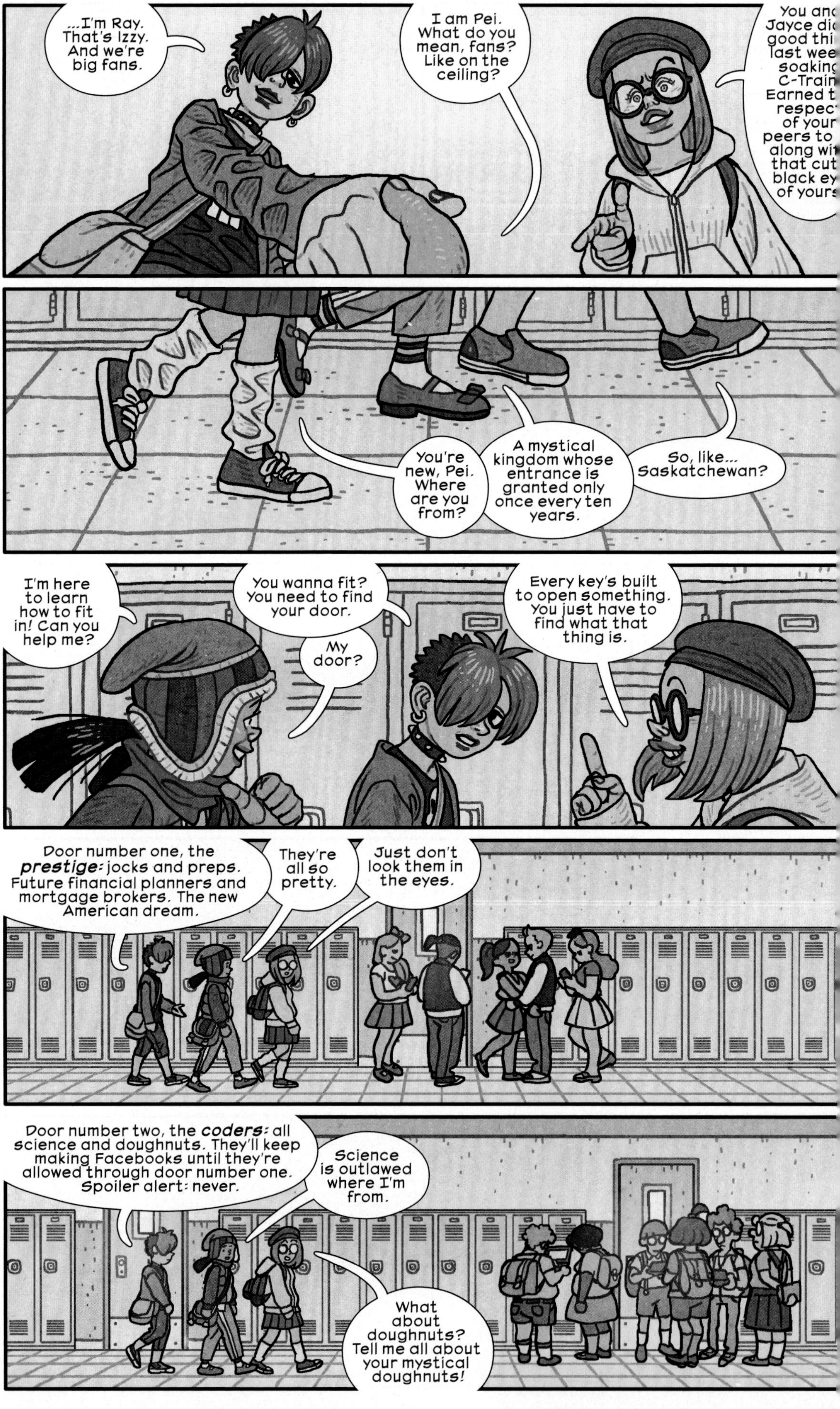

...I'm Ray. That's Izzy. And we're big fans.
I am Pei. What do you mean, fans? Like on the ceiling?
You're new, Pei. Where are you from?
A mystical kingdom whose entrance is granted only once every ten years.
So, like... Saskatchewan?
I'm here to learn how to fit in! Can you help me?
You wanna fit? You need to find your door.
My door?
Every key's built to open something. You just have to find what that thing is.
Door number one, the *prestige:* jocks and preps. Future financial planners and mortgage brokers. The new American dream.
They're all so pretty.
Just don't look them in the eyes.
Door number two, the *coders:* all science and doughnuts. They'll keep making Facebooks until they're allowed through door number one. Spoiler alert: never.
Science is outlawed where I'm from.
What about doughnuts? Tell me all about your mystical doughnuts!

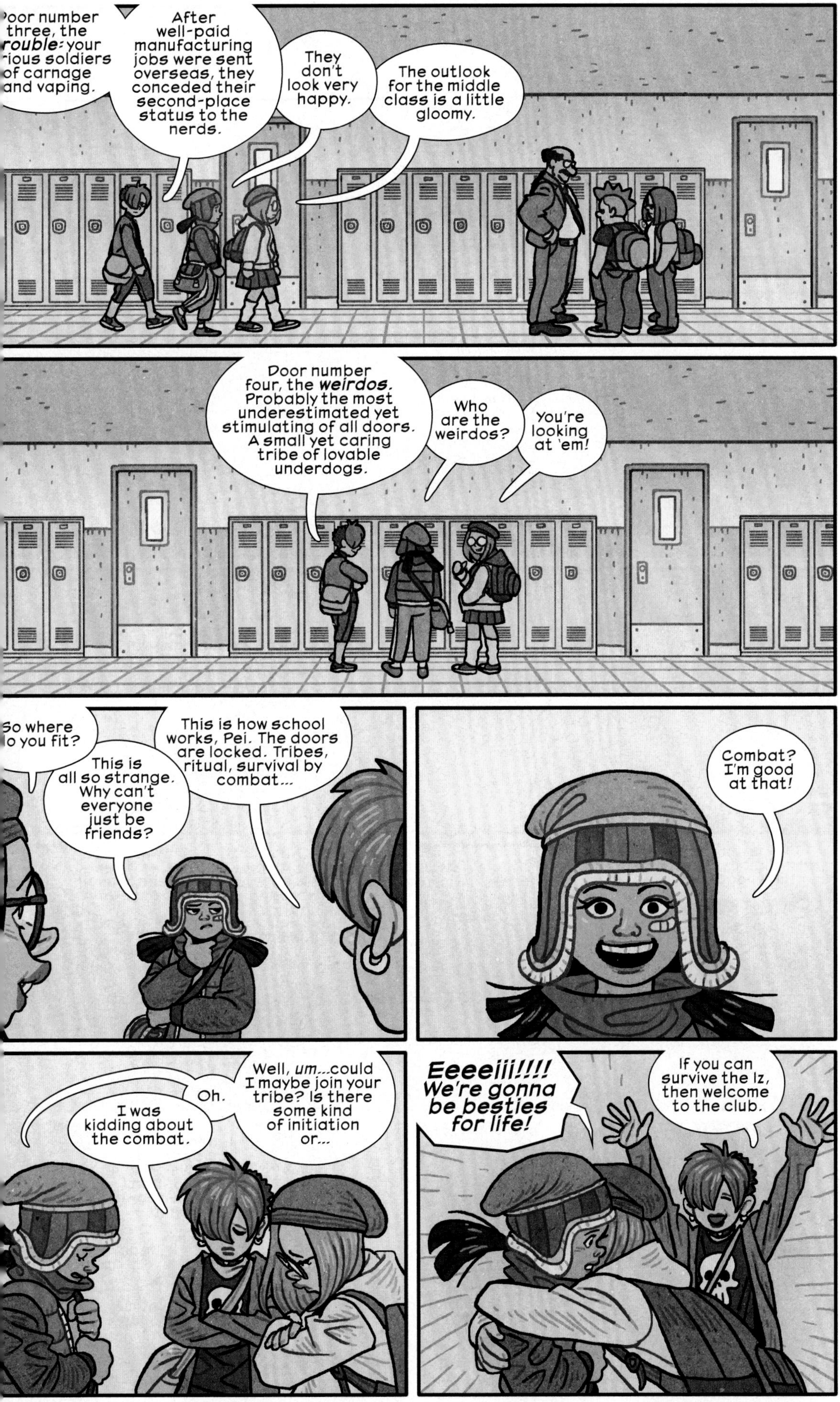

Door number three, the trouble: your rious soldiers of carnage and vaping.
After well-paid manufacturing jobs were sent overseas, they conceded their second-place status to the nerds.
They don't look very happy.
The outlook for the middle class is a little gloomy.
Door number four, the weirdos. Probably the most underestimated yet stimulating of all doors. A small yet caring tribe of lovable underdogs.
Who are the weirdos?
You're looking at 'em!
So where do you fit?
This is all so strange. Why can't everyone just be friends?
This is how school works, Pei. The doors are locked. Tribes, ritual, survival by combat...
Combat? I'm good at that!
I was kidding about the combat.
Oh.
Well, um...could I maybe join your tribe? Is there some kind of initiation or...
Eeeiiii!!!! We're gonna be besties for life!
If you can survive the Iz, then welcome to the club.

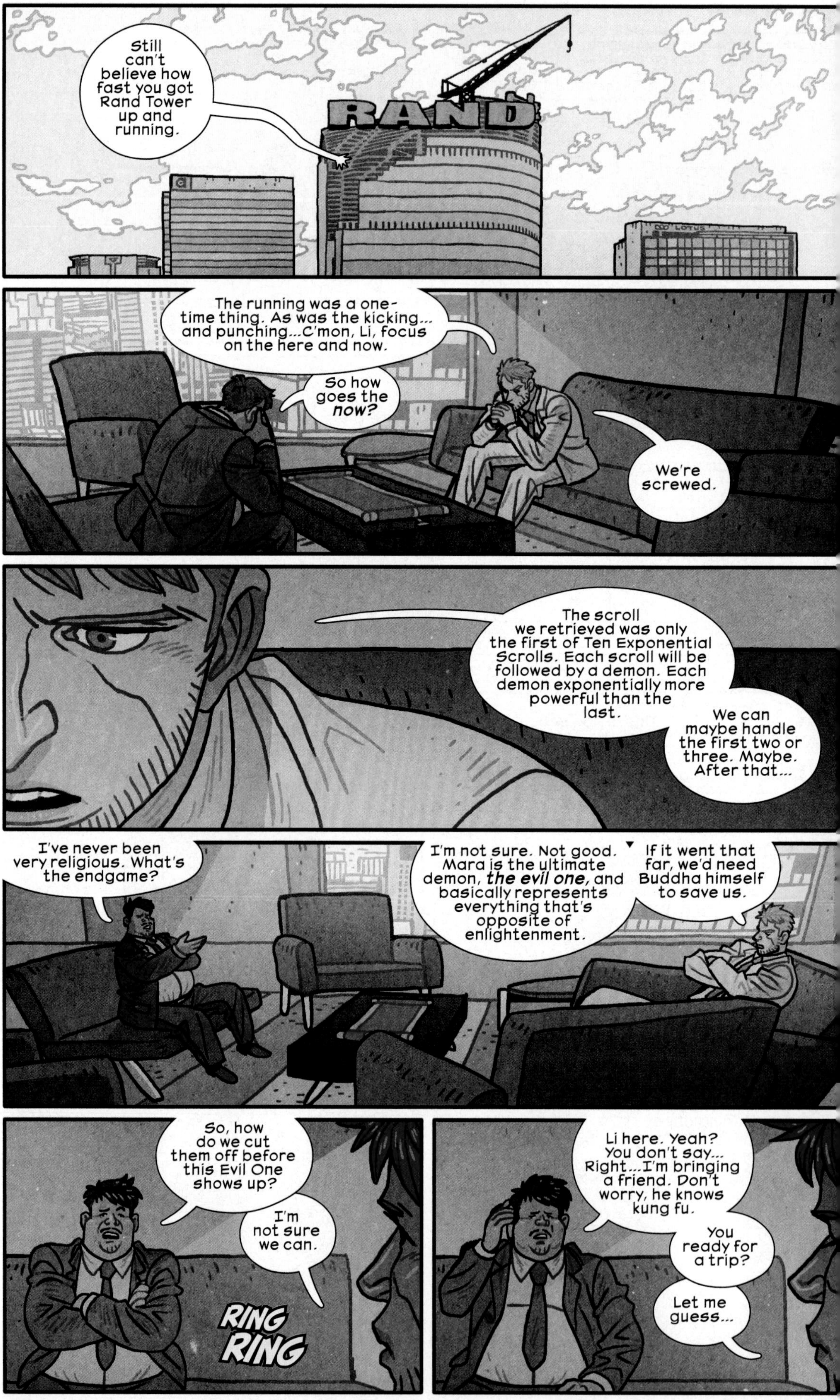

Still can't believe how fast you got Rand Tower up and running.
RAND
The running was a one-time thing. As was the kicking... and punching... C'mon, Li, focus on the here and now.
So how goes the *now?*
We're screwed.
The scroll we retrieved was only the first of Ten Exponential Scrolls. Each scroll will be followed by a demon. Each demon exponentially more powerful than the last.
We can maybe handle the first two or three. Maybe. After that...
I've never been very religious. What's the endgame?
I'm not sure. Not good. Mara is the ultimate demon, *the evil one,* and basically represents everything that's opposite of enlightenment.
If it went that far, we'd need Buddha himself to save us.
So, how do we cut them off before this Evil One shows up?
I'm not sure we can.
RING RING
Li here. Yeah? You don't say... Right... I'm bringing a friend. Don't worry, he knows kung fu.
You ready for a trip?
Let me guess...

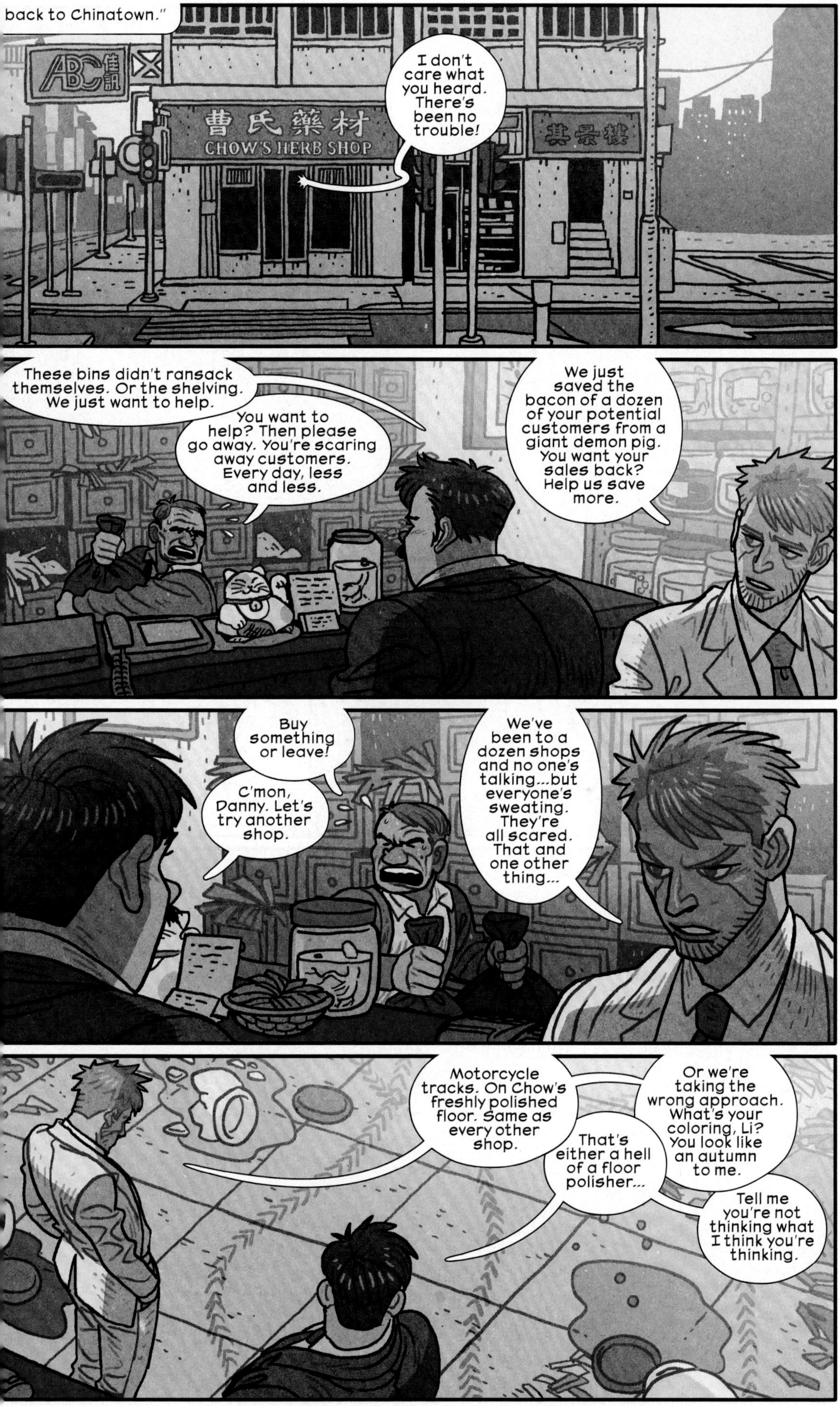

back to Chinatown."
ABC 佳訊
曹氏藥材
CHOW'S HERB SHOP
I don't care what you heard. There's been no trouble!
These bins didn't ransack themselves. Or the shelving. We just want to help.
You want to help? Then please go away. You're scaring away customers. Every day, less and less.
We just saved the bacon of a dozen of your potential customers from a giant demon pig. You want your sales back? Help us save more.
Buy something or leave!
C'mon, Danny. Let's try another shop.
We've been to a dozen shops and no one's talking...but everyone's sweating. They're all scared. That and one other thing...
Motorcycle tracks. On Chow's freshly polished floor. Same as every other shop.
That's either a hell of a floor polisher...
Or we're taking the wrong approach. What's your coloring, Li? You look like an autumn to me.
Tell me you're not thinking what I think you're thinking.

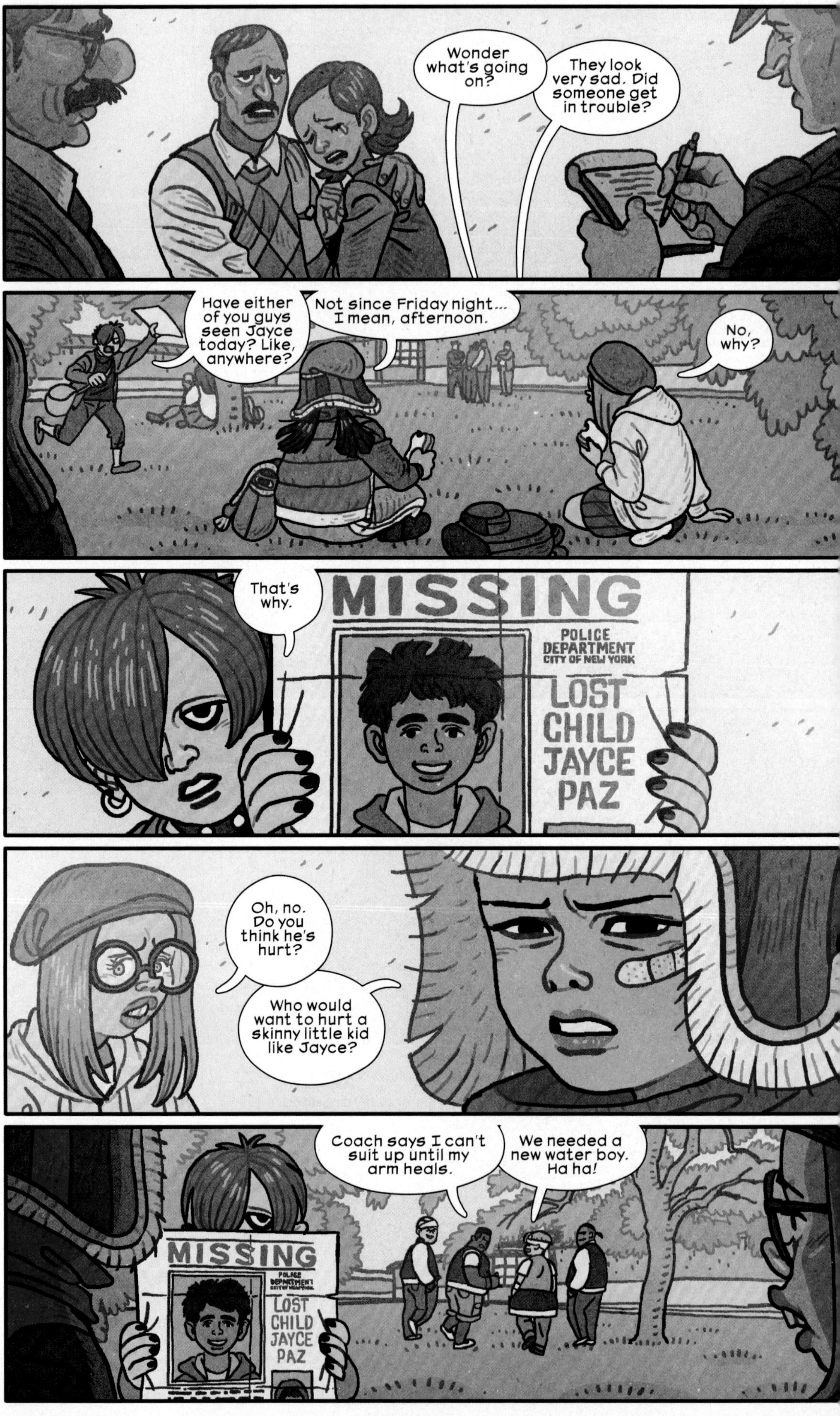

Wonder what's going on?
They look very sad. Did someone get in trouble?
Have either of you guys seen Jayce today? Like, anywhere?
Not since Friday night... I mean, afternoon.
No, why?
That's why.
MISSING
POLICE DEPARTMENT CITY OF NEW YORK
LOST CHILD JAYCE PAZ
Oh, no. Do you think he's hurt?
Who would want to hurt a skinny little kid like Jayce?
Coach says I can't suit up until my arm heals.
We needed a new water boy. Ha ha!
MISSING
LOST CHILD JAYCE PAZ

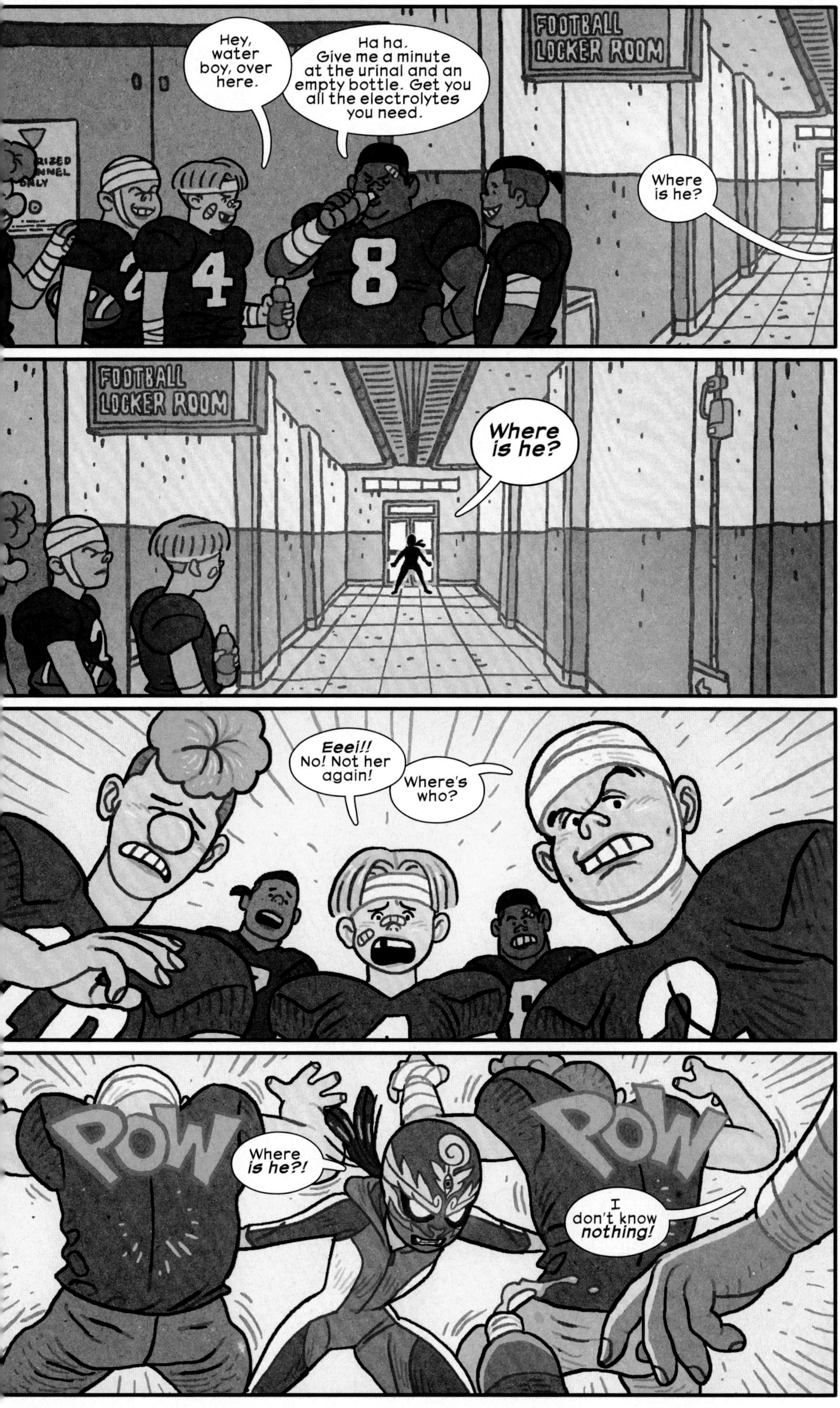

Hey, water boy, over here.
Ha ha. Give me a minute at the urinal and an empty bottle. Get you all the electrolytes you need.
FOOTBALL LOCKER ROOM
Where is he?
FOOTBALL LOCKER ROOM
Where is he?
Eeei!! No! Not her again!
Where's who?
POW
POW
Where *is he?!*
I don't know *nothing!*

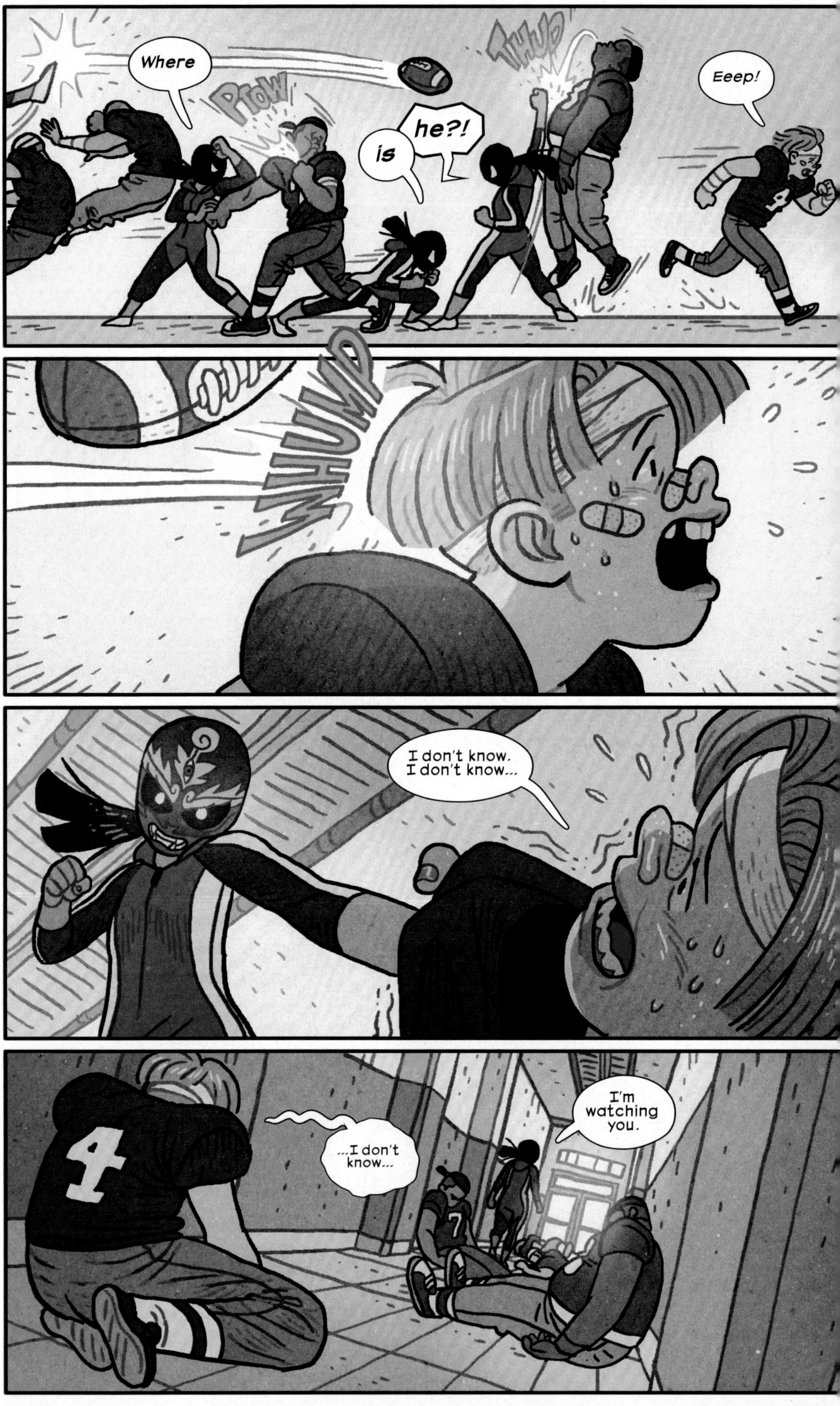

Where
PTOW
THUP
is
he?!
Eeep!
WHUMP
I don't know.
I don't know...
...I don't know...
I'm watching you.

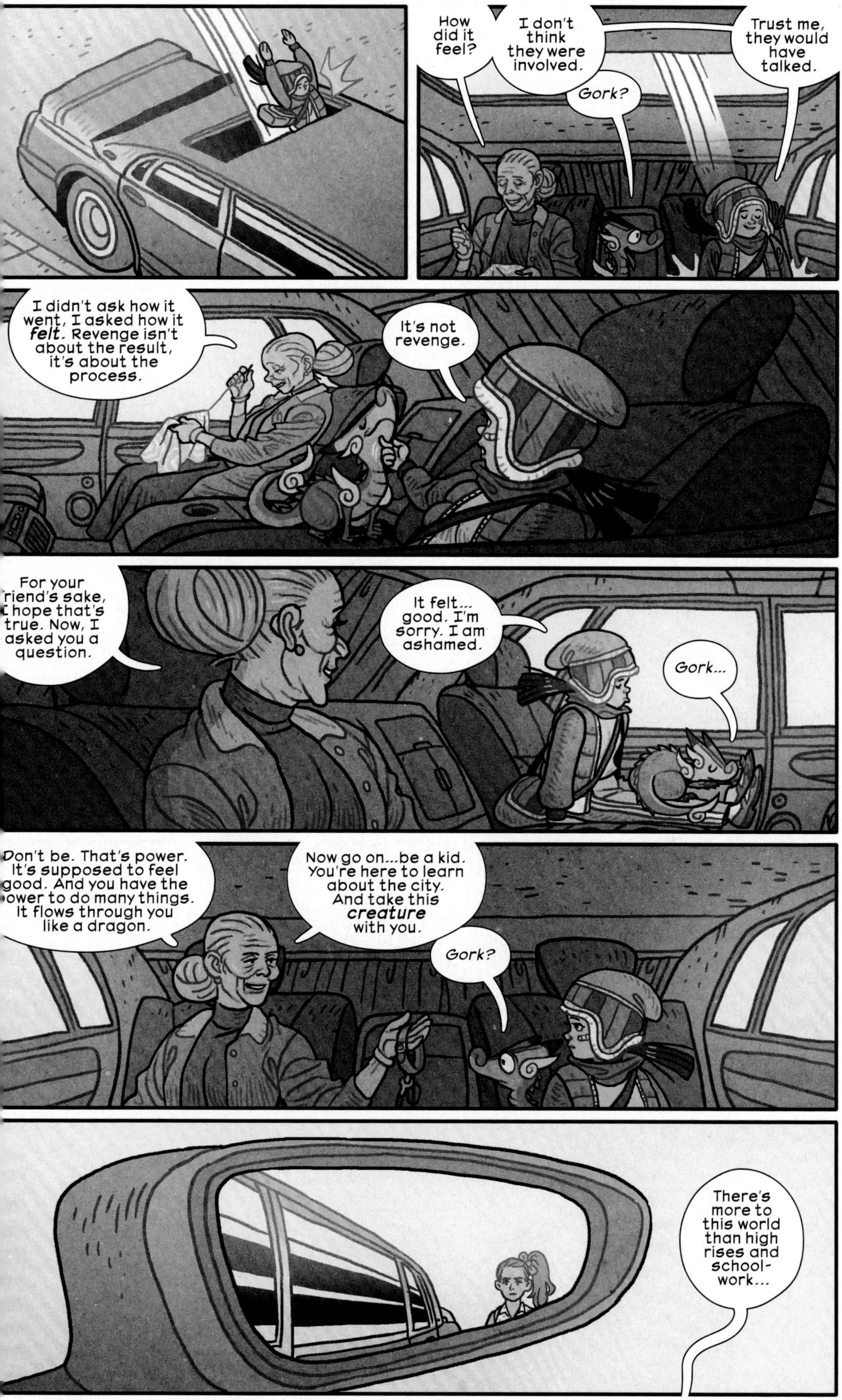
How did it feel?
I don't think they were involved.
Trust me, they would have talked.
Gork?
I didn't ask how it went, I asked how it **felt**. Revenge isn't about the result, it's about the process.
It's not revenge.
For your friend's sake, I hope that's true. Now, I asked you a question.
It felt... good. I'm sorry. I am ashamed.
Gork...
Don't be. That's power. It's supposed to feel good. And you have the power to do many things. It flows through you like a dragon.
Now go on...be a kid. You're here to learn about the city. And take this **creature** with you.
Gork?
There's more to this world than high rises and school-work...

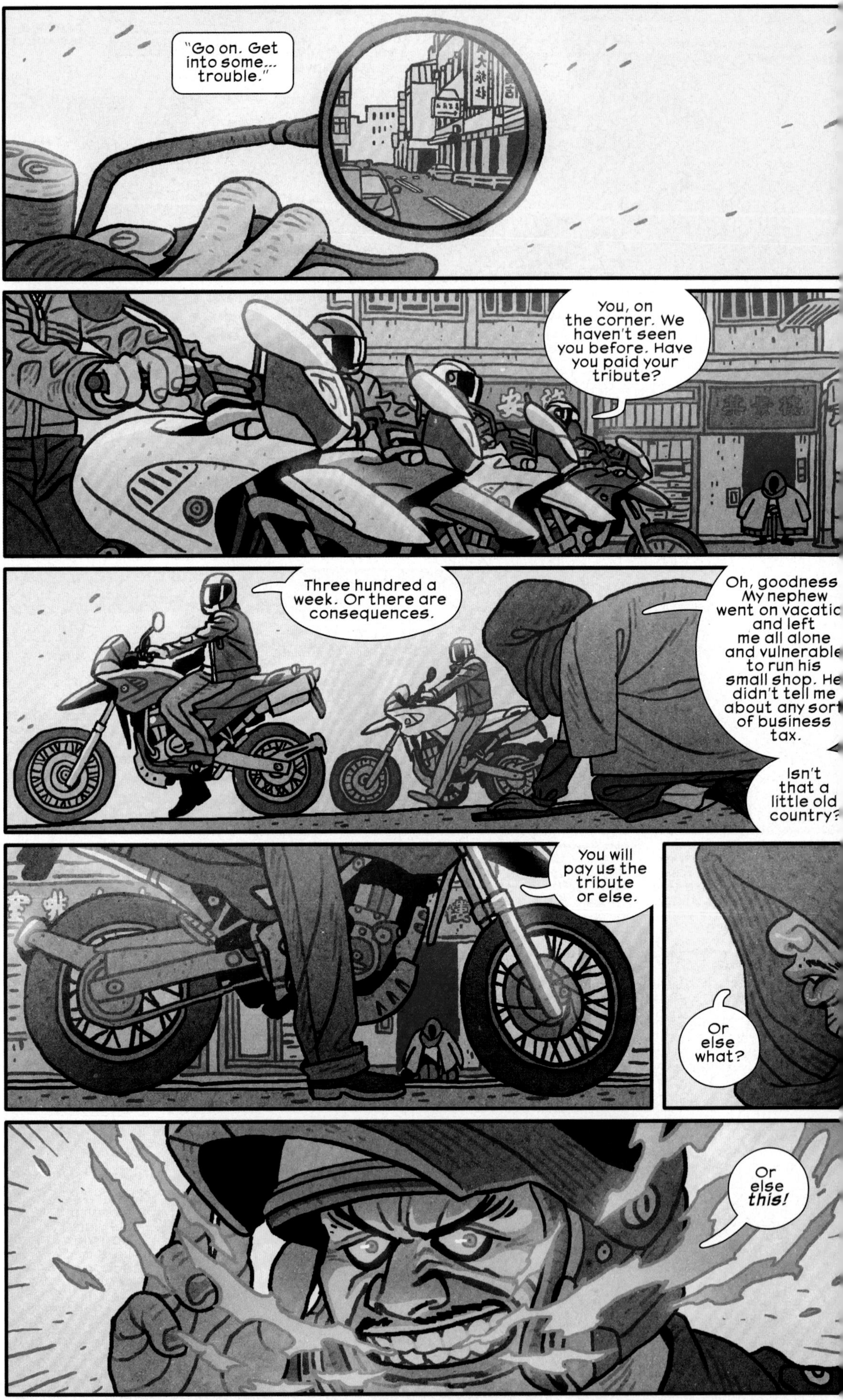
"Go on. Get into some... trouble."
You, on the corner. We haven't seen you before. Have you paid your tribute?
Three hundred a week. Or there are consequences.
Oh, goodness My nephew went on vacatio and left me all alone and vulnerable to run his small shop. He didn't tell me about any sort of business tax.
Isn't that a little old country?
You will pay us the tribute or else.
Or else what?
Or else this!

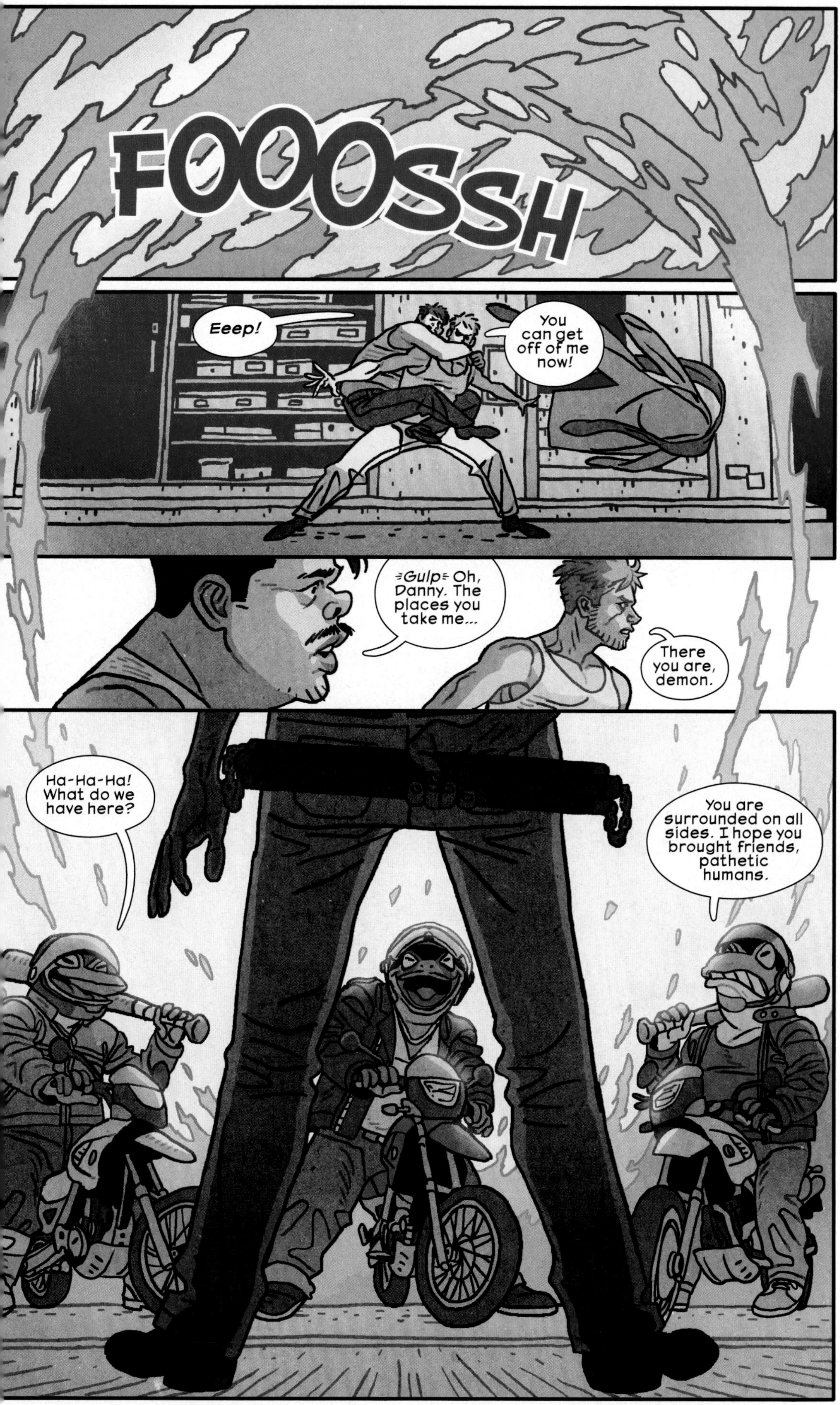
FOOOSSH
Eeep!
You can get off of me now!
=Gulp= Oh, Danny. The places you take me...
There you are, demon.
Ha-Ha-Ha! What do we have here?
You are surrounded on all sides. I hope you brought friends, pathetic humans.

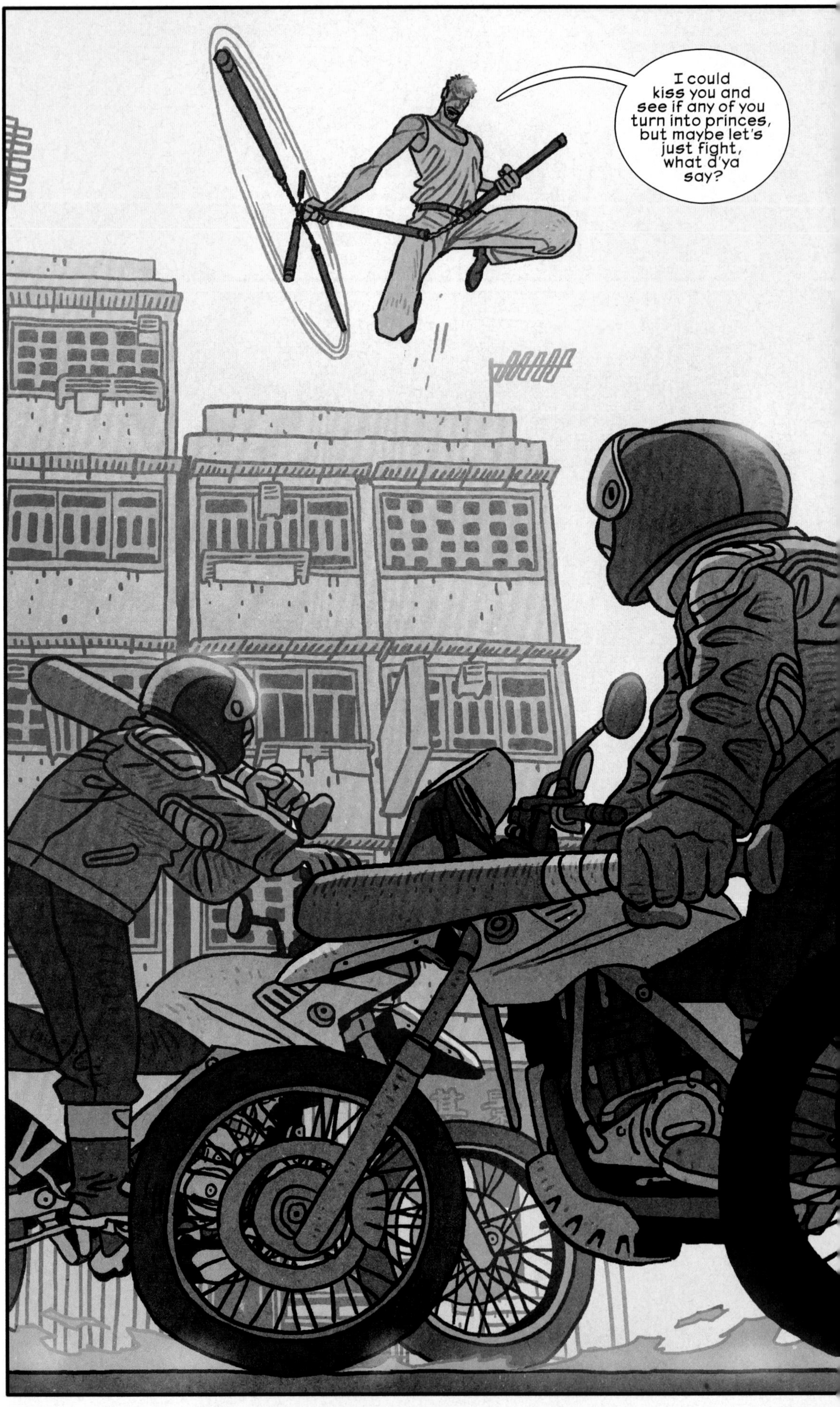
I could kiss you and see if any of you turn into princes, but maybe let's just fight, what d'ya say?

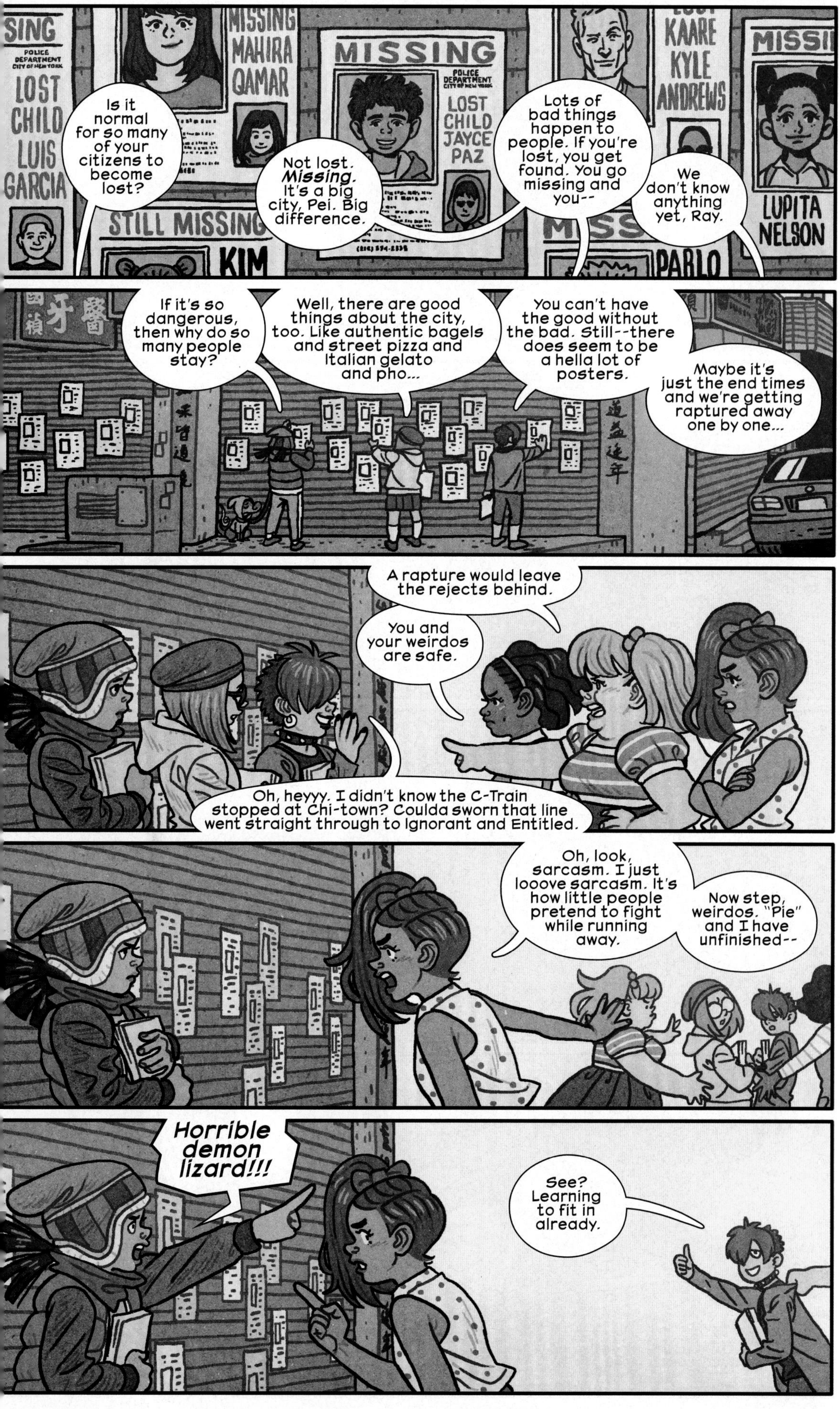

MISSING
MAHIRA QAMAR
MISSING
POLICE DEPARTMENT CITY OF NEW YORK
LOST CHILD JAYCE PAZ
KAARE KYLE ANDREWS
MISSI
LUPITA NELSON
SING
POLICE DEPARTMENT CITY OF NEW YORK
LOST CHILD LUIS GARCIA
STILL MISSING
KIM
PABLO
Is it normal for so many of your citizens to become lost?
Not lost. *Missing.* It's a big city, Pei. Big difference.
Lots of bad things happen to people. If you're lost, you get found. You go missing and you--
We don't know anything yet, Ray.
If it's so dangerous, then why do so many people stay?
Well, there are good things about the city, too. Like authentic bagels and street pizza and Italian gelato and pho...
You can't have the good without the bad. Still--there does seem to be a hella lot of posters.
Maybe it's just the end times and we're getting raptured away one by one...
A rapture would leave the rejects behind.
You and your weirdos are safe.
Oh, heyyy. I didn't know the C-Train stopped at Chi-town? Coulda sworn that line went straight through to Ignorant and Entitled.
Oh, look, sarcasm. I just looove sarcasm. It's how little people pretend to fight while running away.
Now step, weirdos. "Pie" and I have unfinished--
Horrible demon lizard!!!
See? Learning to fit in already.

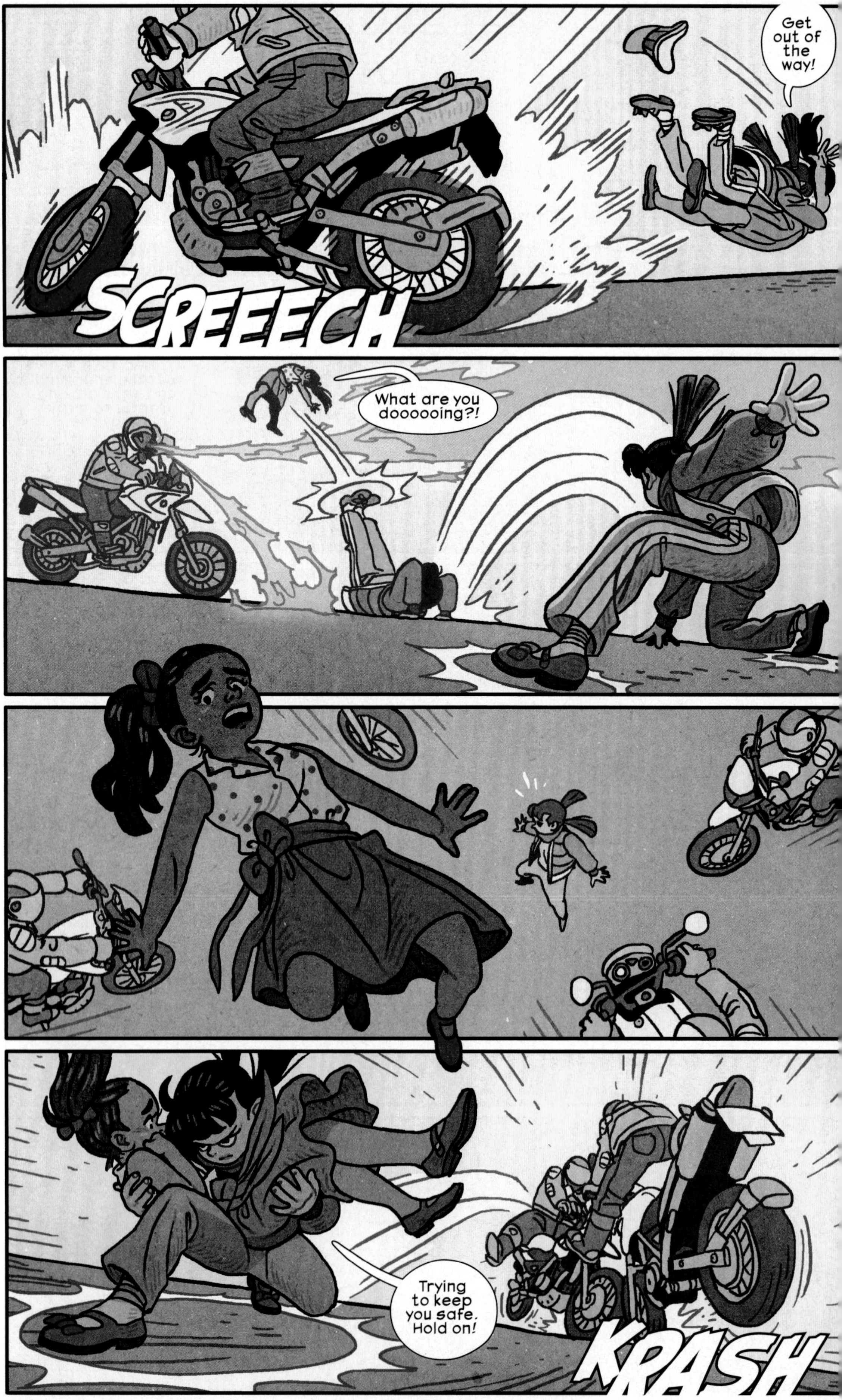
Get out of the way!
SCREEECH
What are you doooooing?!
Trying to keep you safe. Hold on!
KRASH

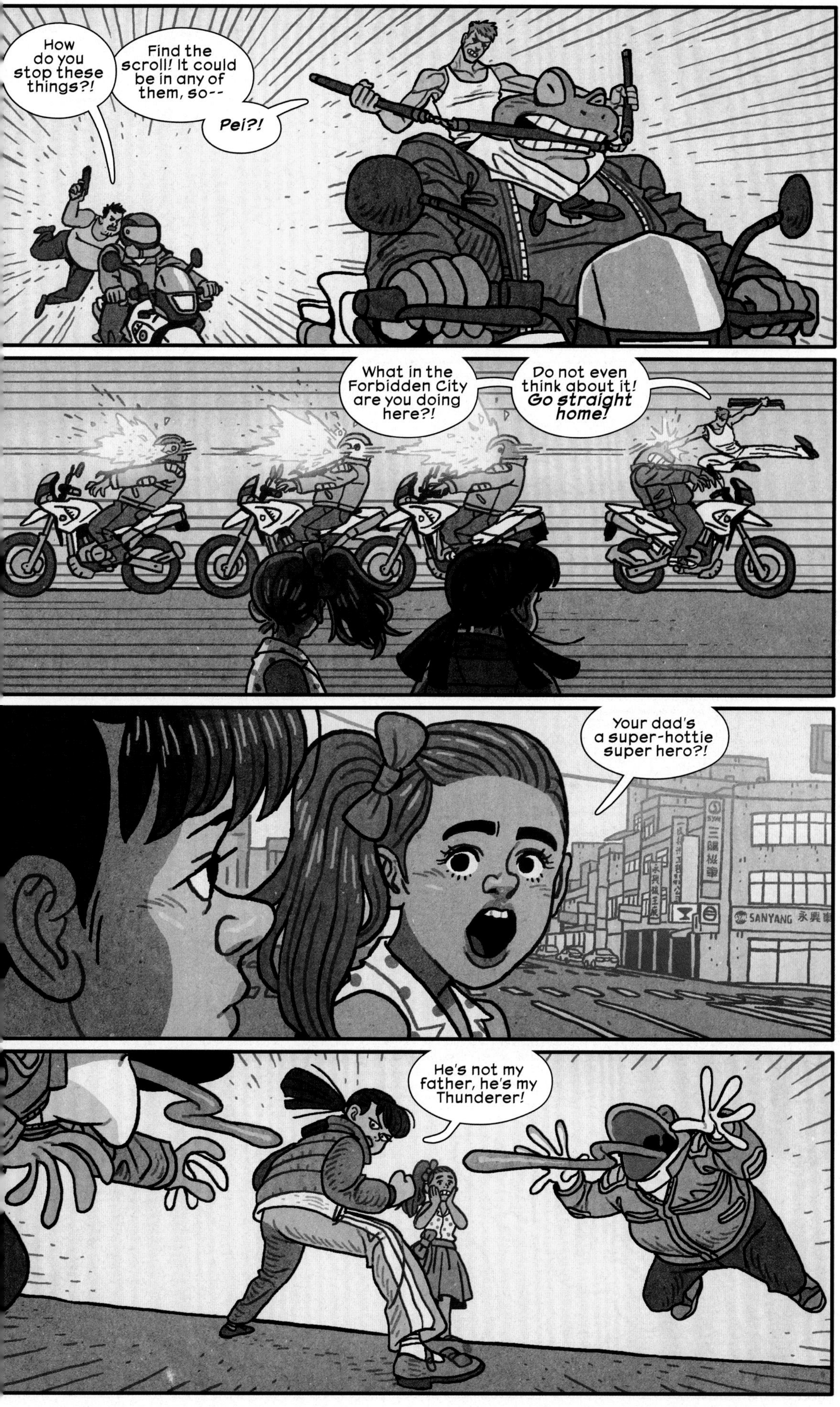
How do you stop these things?!
Find the scroll! It could be in any of them, so--
Pei?!
What in the Forbidden City are you doing here?!
Do not even think about it! Go straight home!
Your dad's a super-hottie super hero?!
SANYANG 永興車
He's not my father, he's my Thunderer!

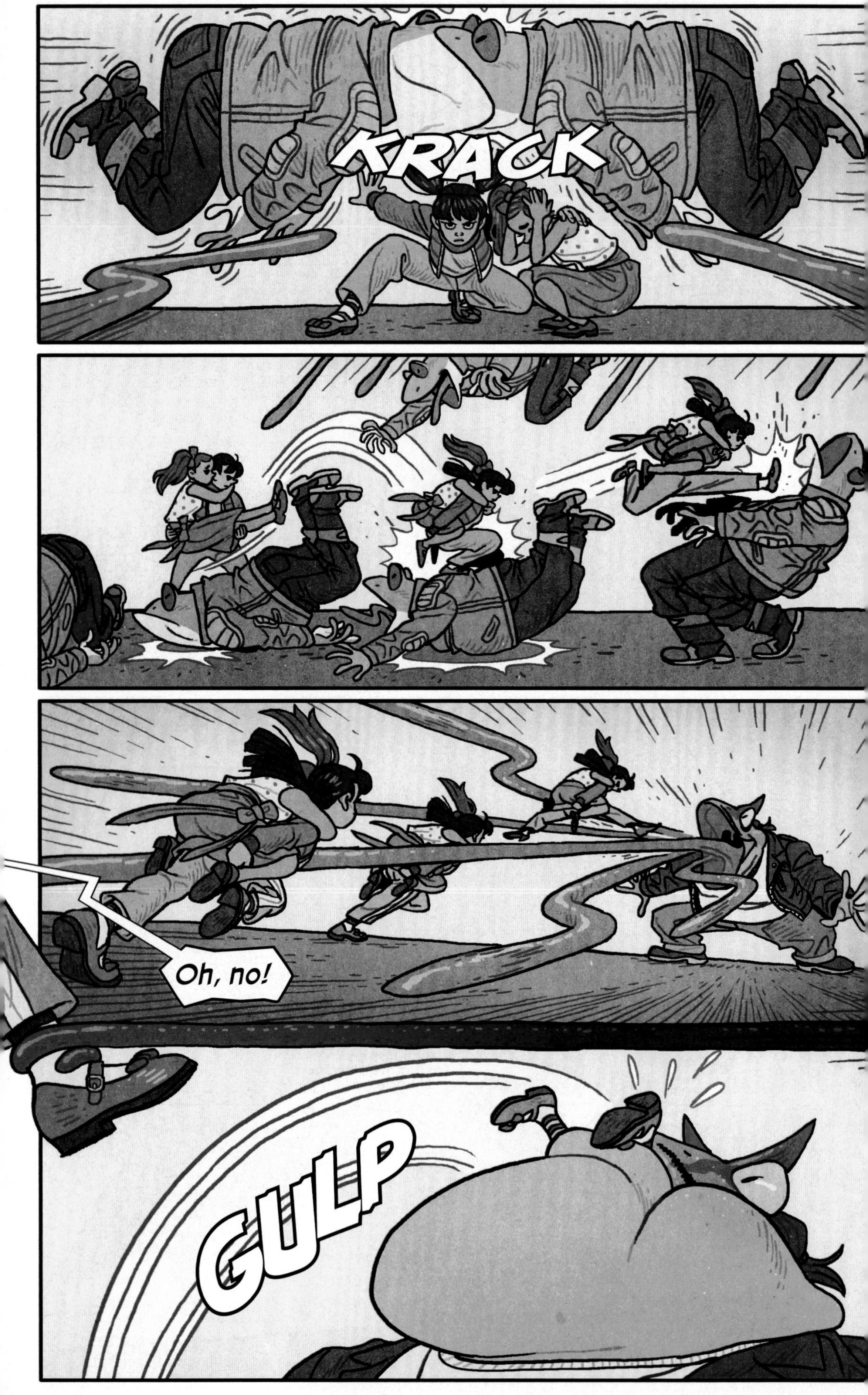
KRACK
Oh, no!
GULP

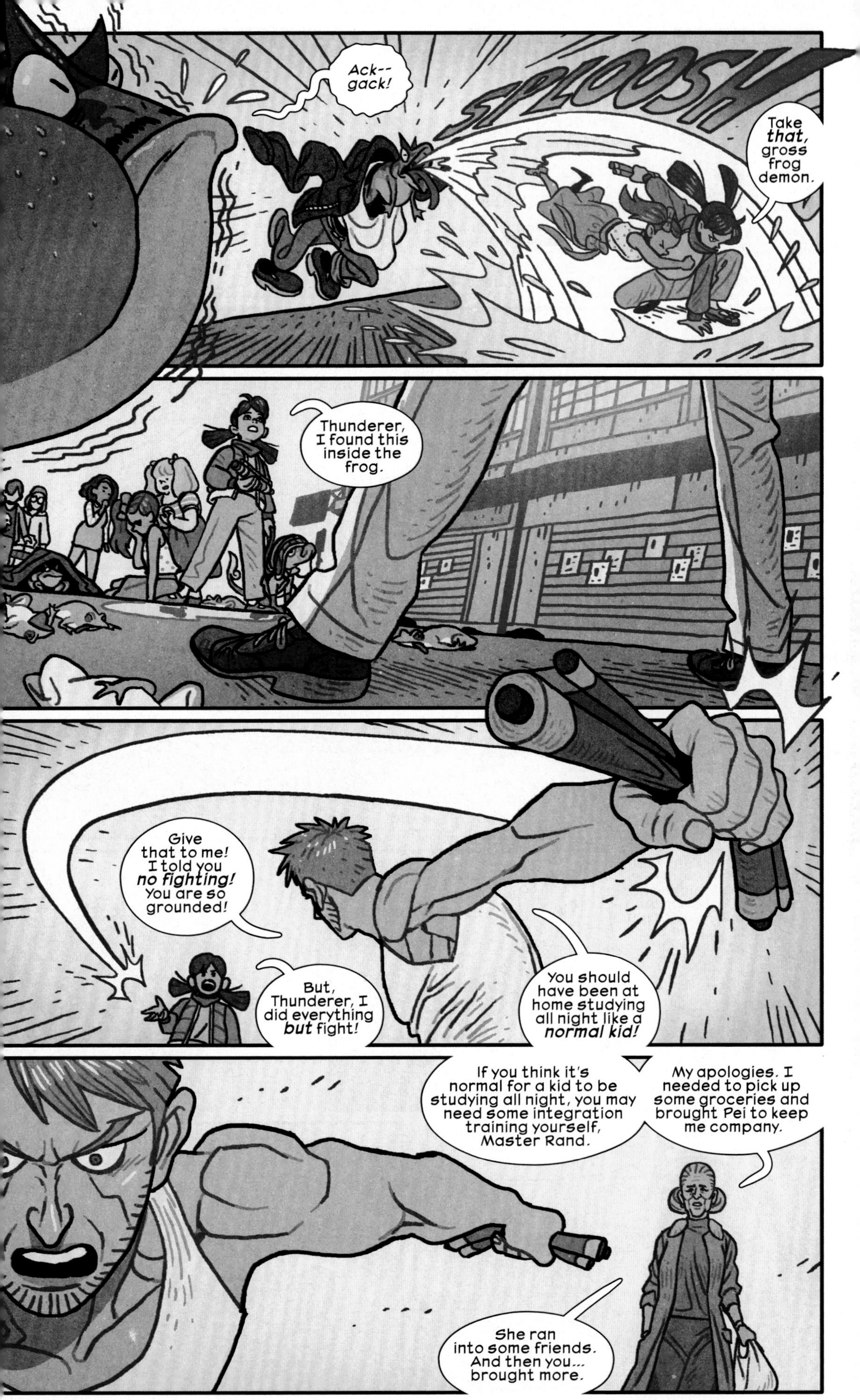

Ack--gack!
SPLOOSH
Take *that*, gross frog demon.
Thunderer, I found this inside the frog.
Give that to me! I told you *no fighting!* You are so grounded!
But, Thunderer, I did everything *but* fight!
You should have been at home studying all night like a *normal kid!*
If you think it's normal for a kid to be studying all night, you may need some integration training yourself, Master Rand.
My apologies. I needed to pick up some groceries and brought Pei to keep me company.
She ran into some friends. And then you... brought more.

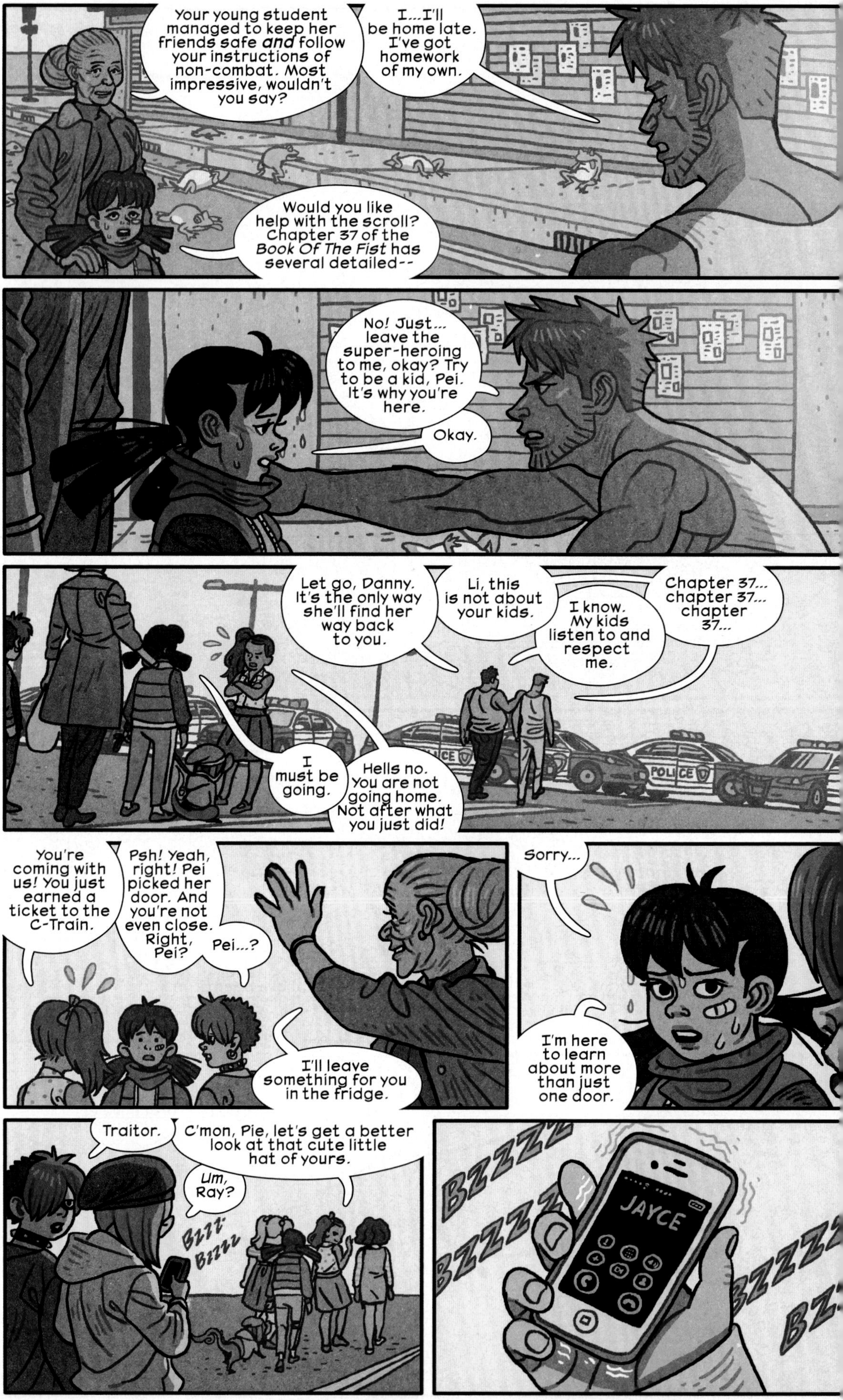

Your young student managed to keep her friends safe *and* follow your instructions of non-combat. Most impressive, wouldn't you say?
I...I'll be home late. I've got homework of my own.
Would you like help with the scroll? Chapter 37 of the *Book Of The Fist* has several detailed--
No! Just... leave the super-heroing to me, okay? Try to be a kid, Pei. It's why you're here.
Okay.
Let go, Danny. It's the only way she'll find her way back to you.
Li, this is not about your kids.
I know. My kids listen to and respect me.
Chapter 37... chapter 37... chapter 37...
I must be going.
Hells no. You are not going home. Not after what you just did!
You're coming with us! You just earned a ticket to the C-Train.
Psh! Yeah, right! Pei picked her door. And you're not even close. Right, Pei?
Pei...?
I'll leave something for you in the fridge.
Sorry...
I'm here to learn about more than just one door.
Traitor.
C'mon, Pie, let's get a better look at that cute little hat of yours.
Um, Ray?
Bzzz Bzzz
BZZZZ BZZZZ BZZZZ
JAYCE

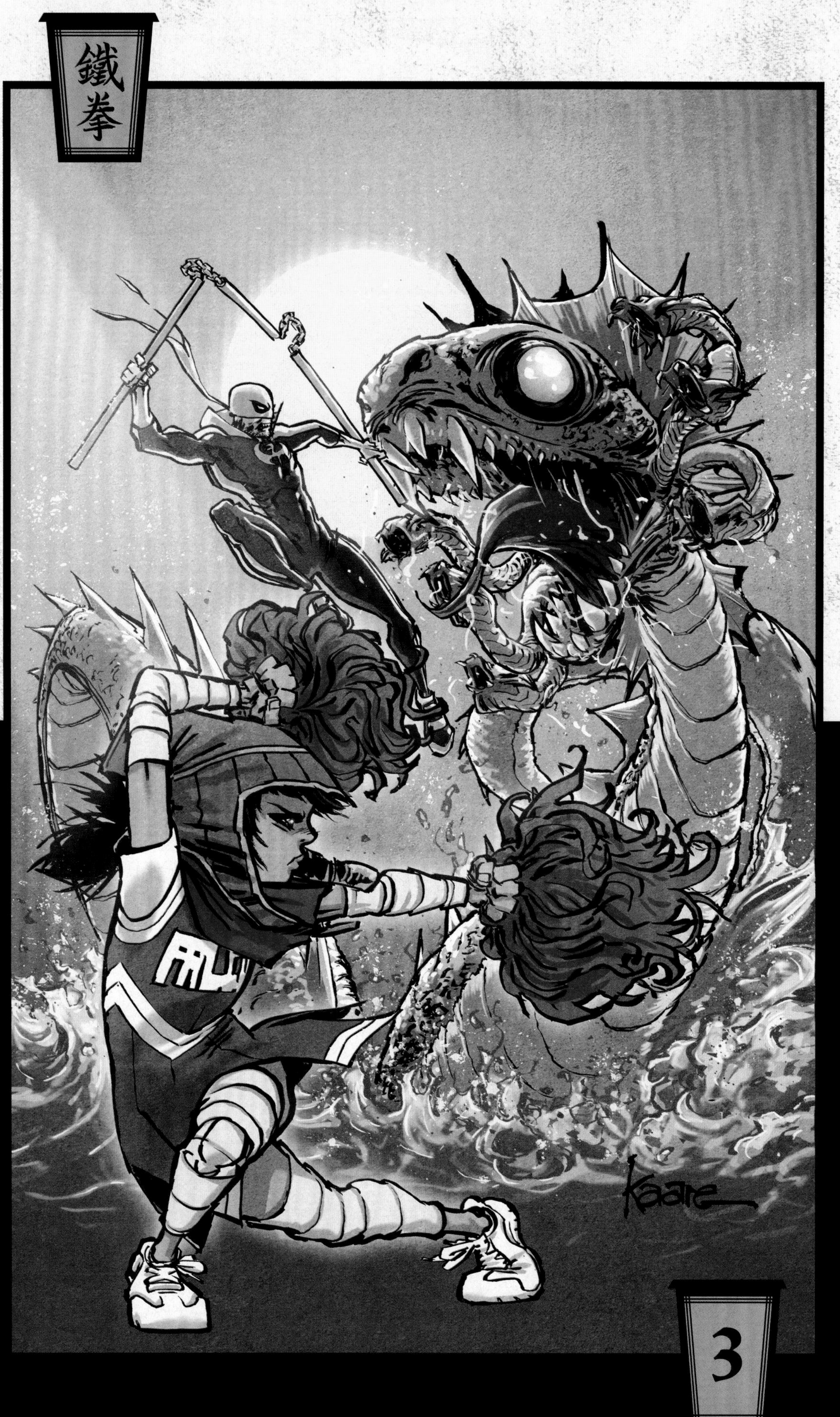
鐵拳
kaare
3

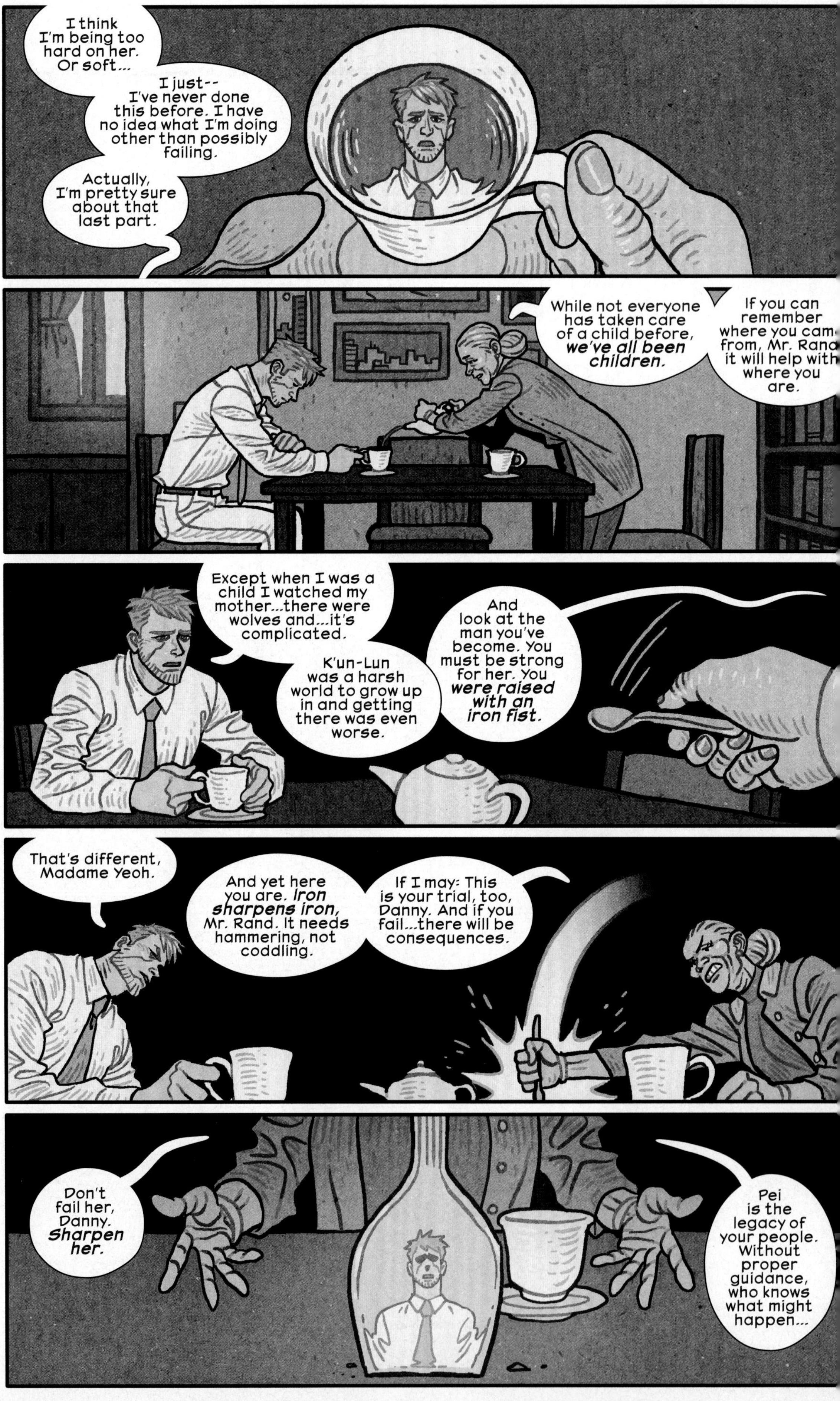
I think I'm being too hard on her. Or soft...
I just-- I've never done this before. I have no idea what I'm doing other than possibly failing.
Actually, I'm pretty sure about that last part.
While not everyone has taken care of a child before, we've all been children.
If you can remember where you cam from, Mr. Rand it will help with where you are.
Except when I was a child I watched my mother...there were wolves and...it's complicated.
K'un-Lun was a harsh world to grow up in and getting there was even worse.
And look at the man you've become. You must be strong for her. You were raised with an iron fist.
That's different, Madame Yeoh.
And yet here you are. Iron sharpens iron, Mr. Rand. It needs hammering, not coddling.
If I may: This is your trial, too, Danny. And if you fail...there will be consequences.
Don't fail her, Danny. Sharpen her.
Pei is the legacy of your people. Without proper guidance, who knows what might happen...

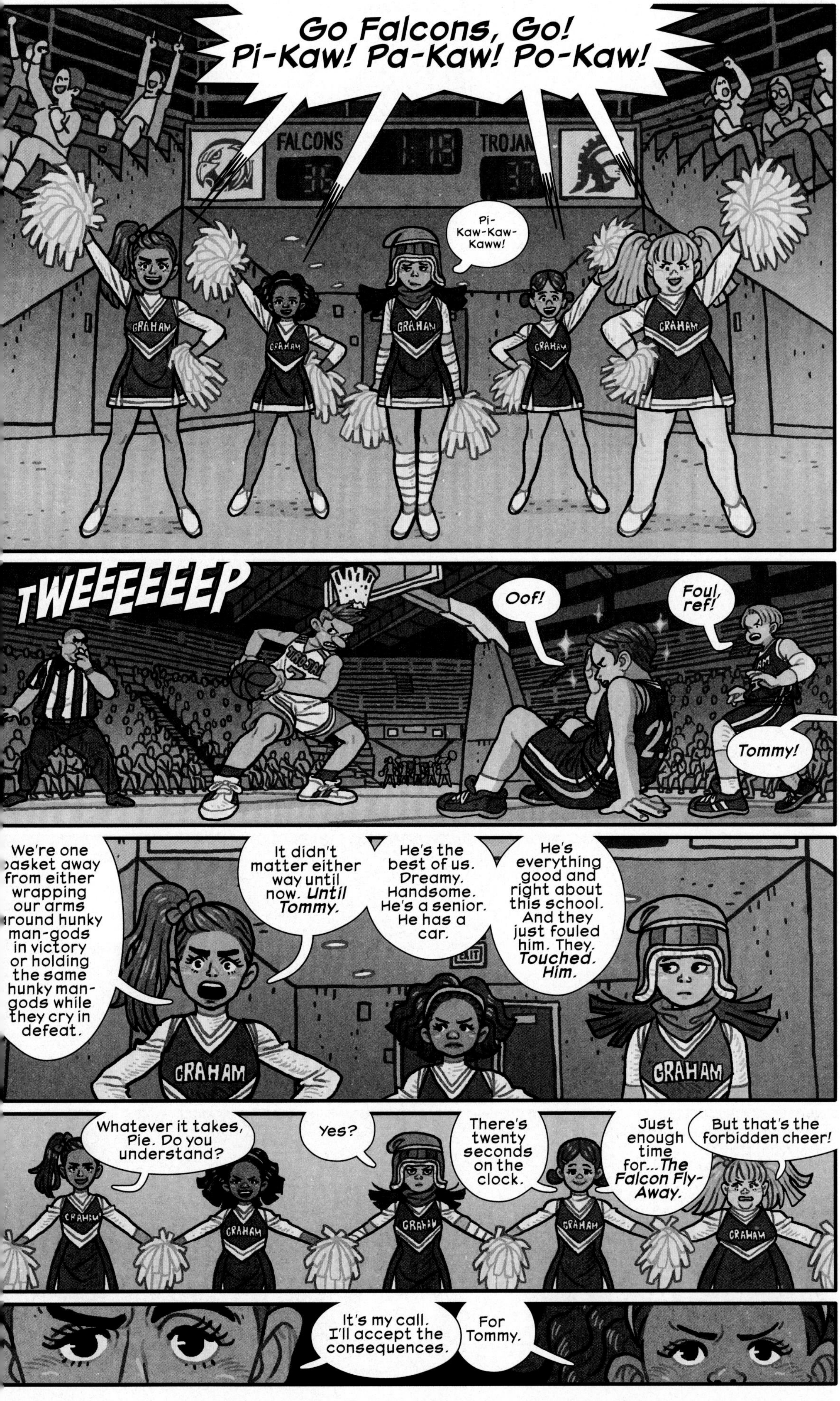

Go Falcons, Go! Pi-Kaw! Pa-Kaw! Po-Kaw!
FALCONS
TROJAN
Pi-Kaw-Kaw-Kaww!
TWEEEEEEP
Oof!
Foul, ref!
Tommy!
We're one asket away from either wrapping our arms round hunky man-gods in victory or holding the same hunky man-gods while they cry in defeat.
It didn't matter either way until now. *Until Tommy.*
He's the best of us. Dreamy. Handsome. He's a senior. He has a car.
He's everything good and right about this school. And they just fouled him. They. *Touched. Him.*
Whatever it takes, Pie. Do you understand?
Yes?
There's twenty seconds on the clock.
Just enough time for... *The Falcon Fly-Away.*
But that's the forbidden cheer!
It's my call. I'll accept the consequences.
For Tommy.

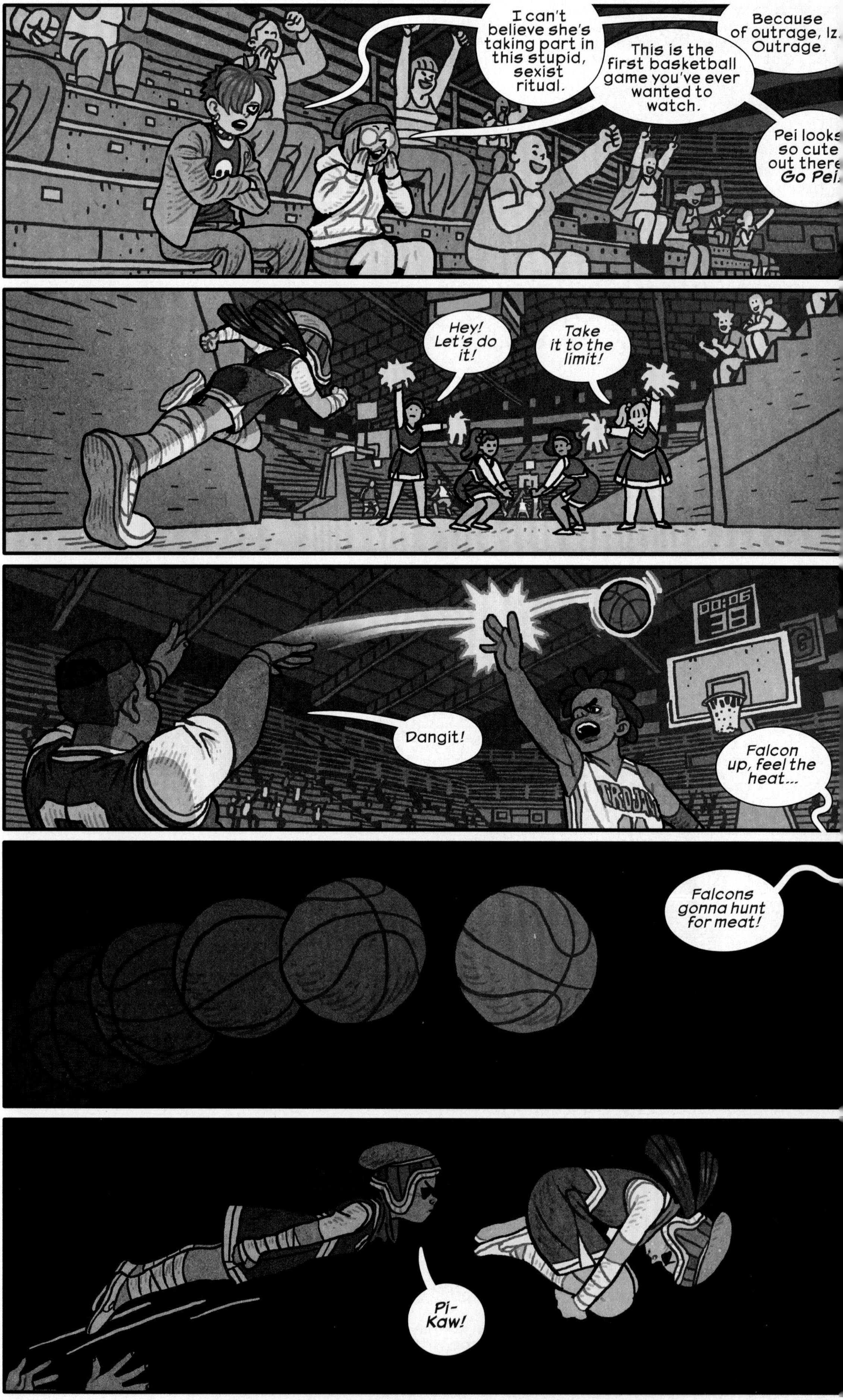
I can't believe she's taking part in this stupid, sexist ritual.
This is the first basketball game you've ever wanted to watch.
Because of outrage, Iz. Outrage.
Pei looks so cute out there Go Pei.
Hey! Let's do it!
Take it to the limit!
00:06
38
Dangit!
Falcon up, feel the heat...
Falcons gonna hunt for meat!
Pi-Kaw!

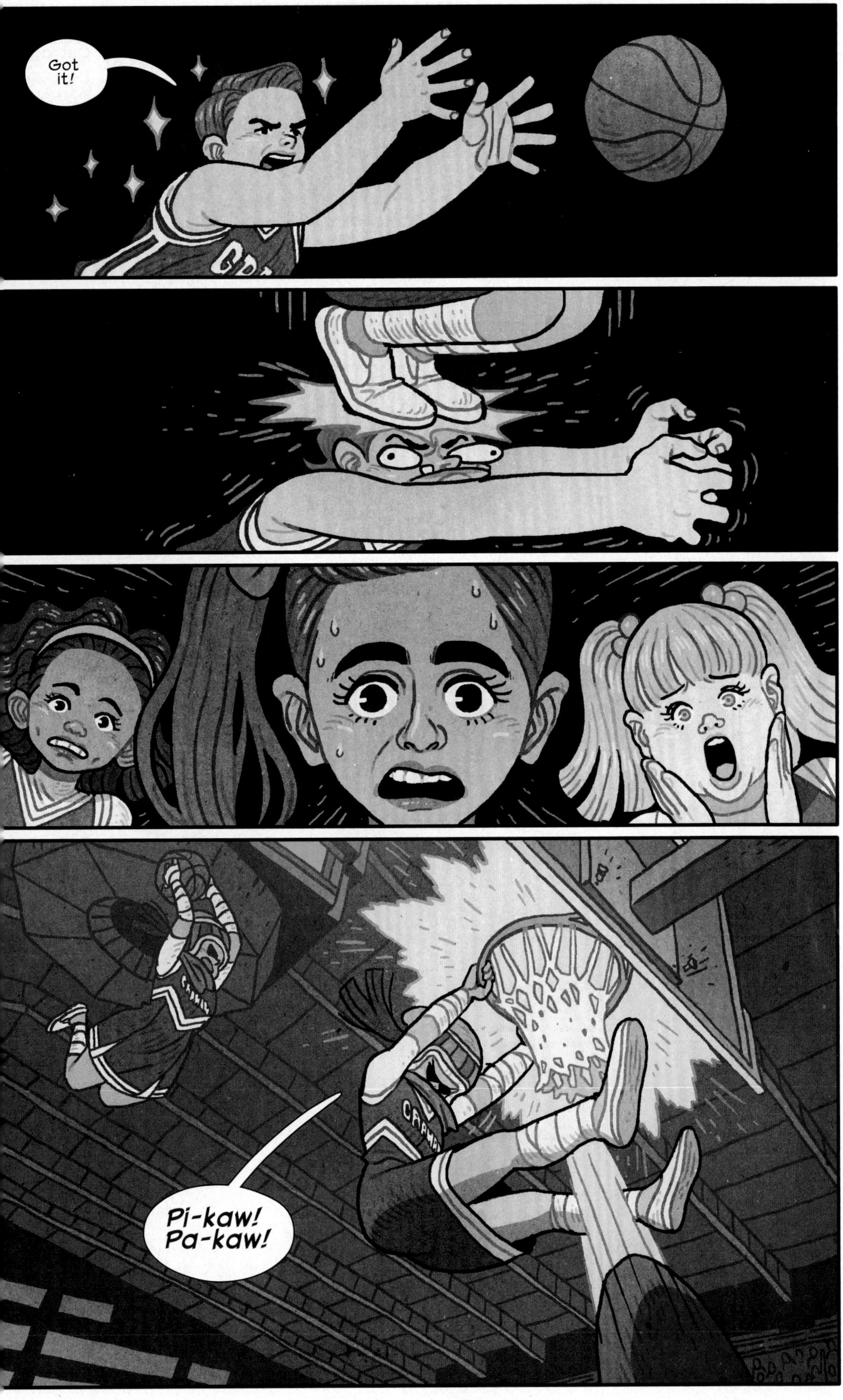
Got it!
Pi-kaw! Pa-kaw!

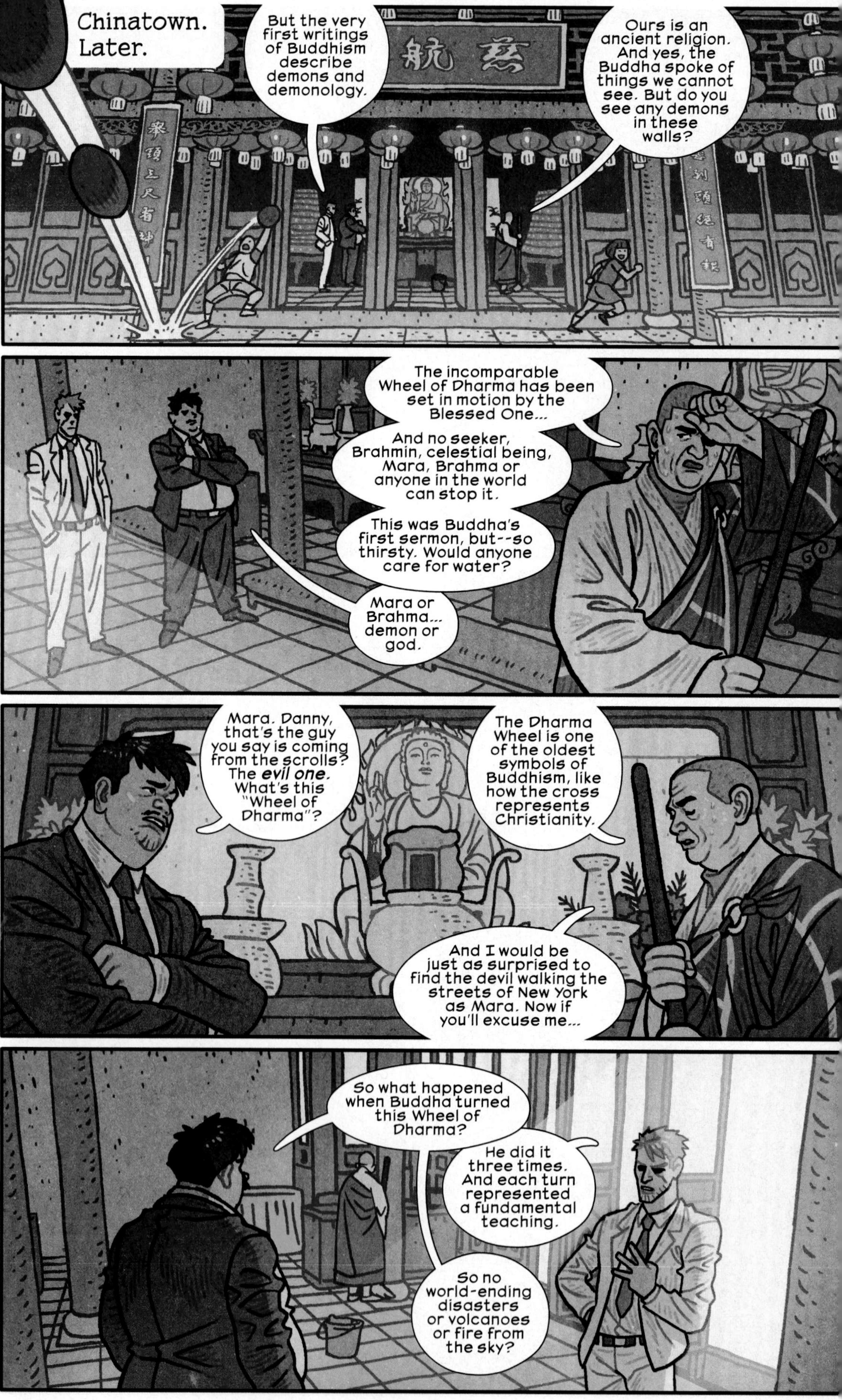
Chinatown. Later.
But the very first writings of Buddhism describe demons and demonology.
慈航
Ours is an ancient religion. And yes, the Buddha spoke of things we cannot see. But do you see any demons in these walls?
The incomparable Wheel of Dharma has been set in motion by the Blessed One...
And no seeker, Brahmin, celestial being, Mara, Brahma or anyone in the world can stop it.
This was Buddha's first sermon, but--so thirsty. Would anyone care for water?
Mara or Brahma... demon or god.
Mara. Danny, that's the guy you say is coming from the scrolls? The *evil one.* What's this "Wheel of Dharma"?
The Dharma Wheel is one of the oldest symbols of Buddhism, like how the cross represents Christianity.
And I would be just as surprised to find the devil walking the streets of New York as Mara. Now if you'll excuse me...
So what happened when Buddha turned this Wheel of Dharma?
He did it three times. And each turn represented a fundamental teaching.
So no world-ending disasters or volcanoes or fire from the sky?

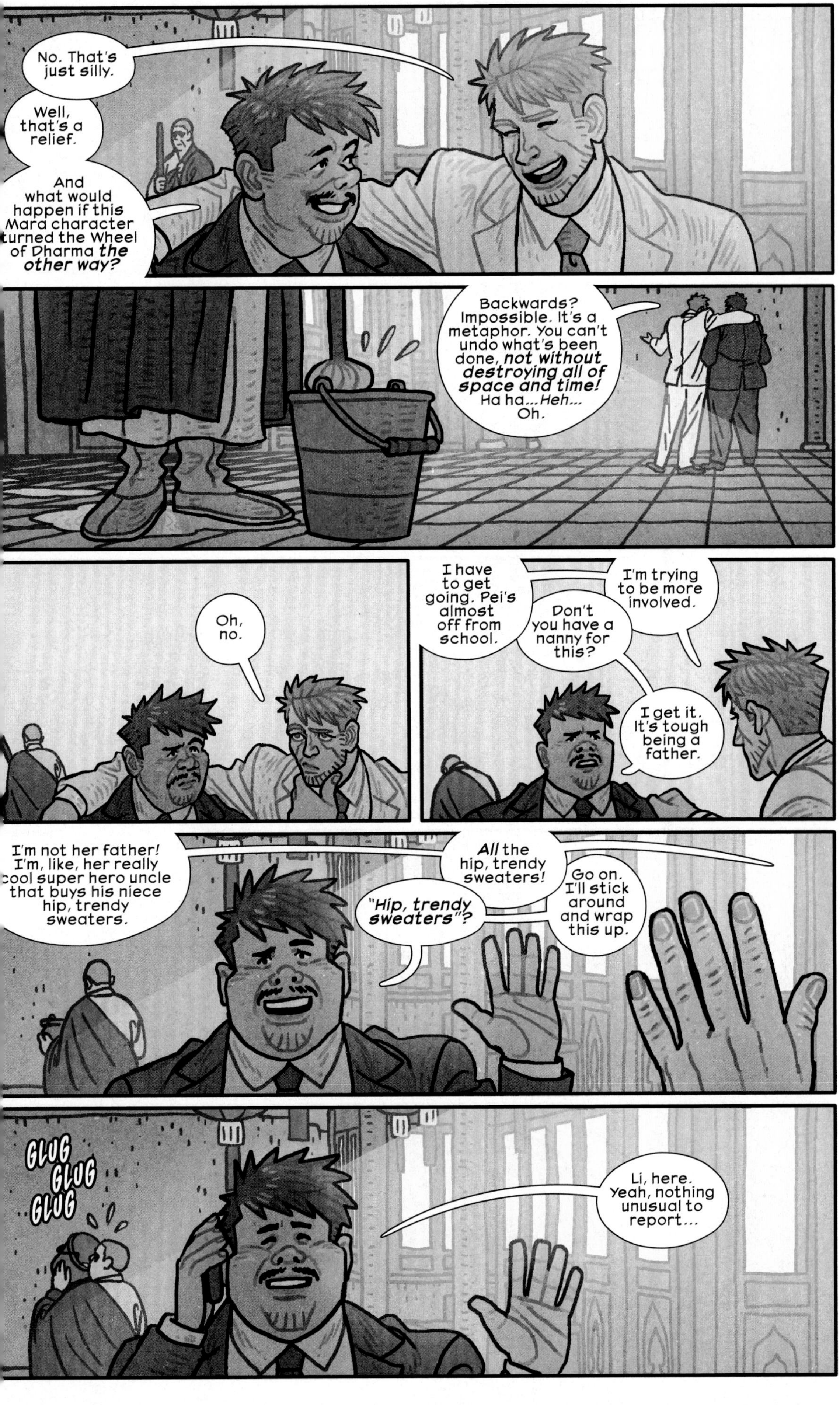
No. That's just silly.
Well, that's a relief.
And what would happen if this Mara character turned the Wheel of Dharma *the other way?*
Backwards? Impossible. It's a metaphor. You can't undo what's been done, *not without destroying all of space and time!* Ha ha... *Heh...* Oh.
Oh, no.
I have to get going. Pei's almost off from school.
I'm trying to be more involved.
Don't you have a nanny for this?
I get it. It's tough being a father.
I'm not her father! I'm, like, her really cool super hero uncle that buys his niece hip, trendy sweaters.
All the hip, trendy sweaters!
"Hip, trendy sweaters"?
Go on. I'll stick around and wrap this up.
GLUG GLUG GLUG
Li, here. Yeah, nothing unusual to report...

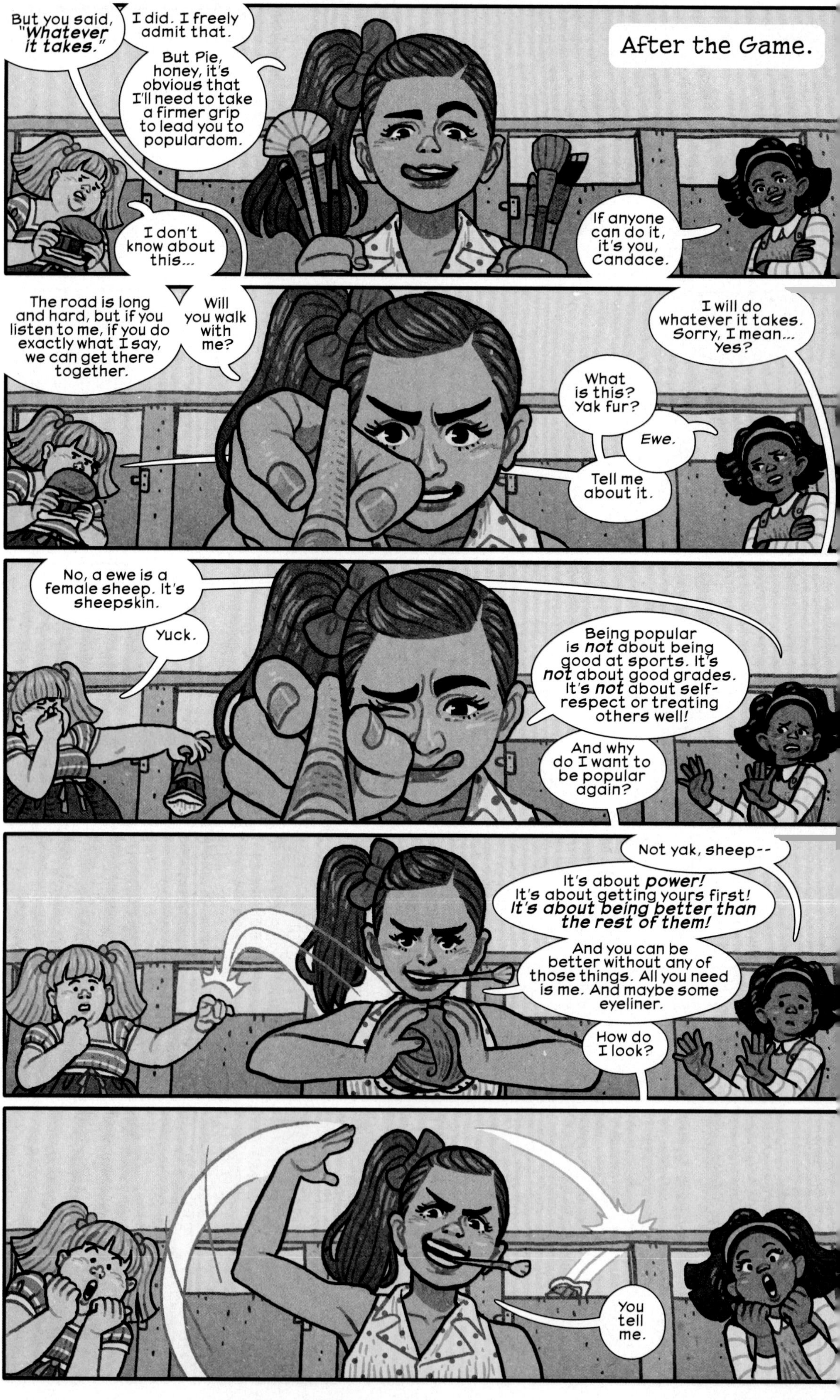
After the Game.
But you said, "*Whatever it takes.*"
I did. I freely admit that.
But Pie, honey, it's obvious that I'll need to take a firmer grip to lead you to populardom.
I don't know about this...
If anyone can do it, it's you, Candace.
The road is long and hard, but if you listen to me, if you do exactly what I say, we can get there together.
Will you walk with me?
I will do whatever it takes. Sorry, I mean... Yes?
What is this? Yak fur?
Ewe.
Tell me about it.
No, a ewe is a female sheep. It's sheepskin.
Yuck.
Being popular is ***not*** about being good at sports. It's ***not*** about good grades. It's ***not*** about self-respect or treating others well!
And why do I want to be popular again?
Not yak, sheep--
It's about ***power!*** It's about getting yours first! ***It's about being better than the rest of them!***
And you can be better without any of those things. All you need is me. And maybe some eyeliner.
How do I look?
You tell me.

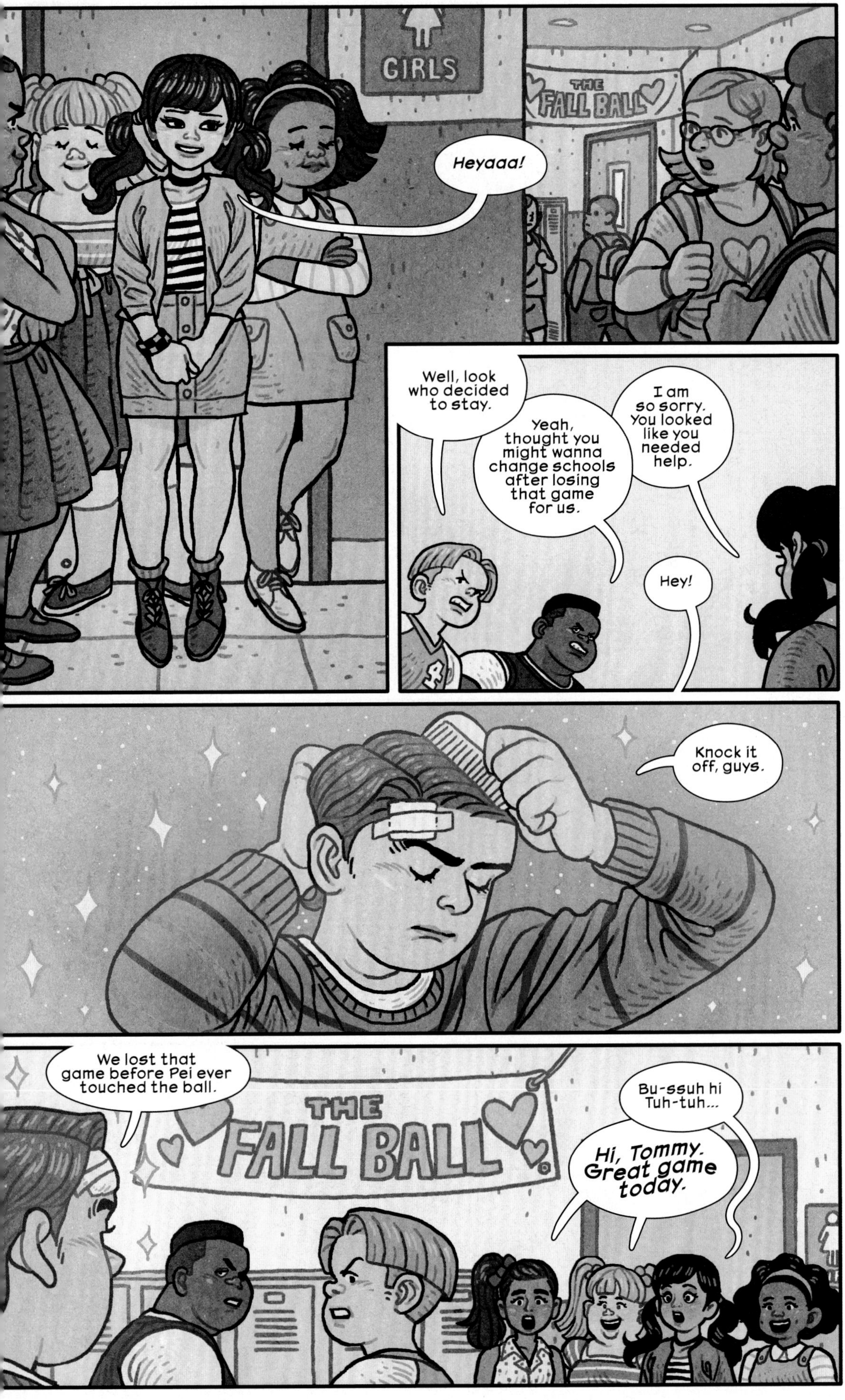
GIRLS
Heyaaa!
THE FALL BALL
Well, look who decided to stay.
Yeah, thought you might wanna change schools after losing that game for us.
I am so sorry. You looked like you needed help.
Hey!
Knock it off, guys.
We lost that game before Pei ever touched the ball.
THE FALL BALL
Bu-ssuh hi Tuh-tuh...
Hi, Tommy. Great game today.

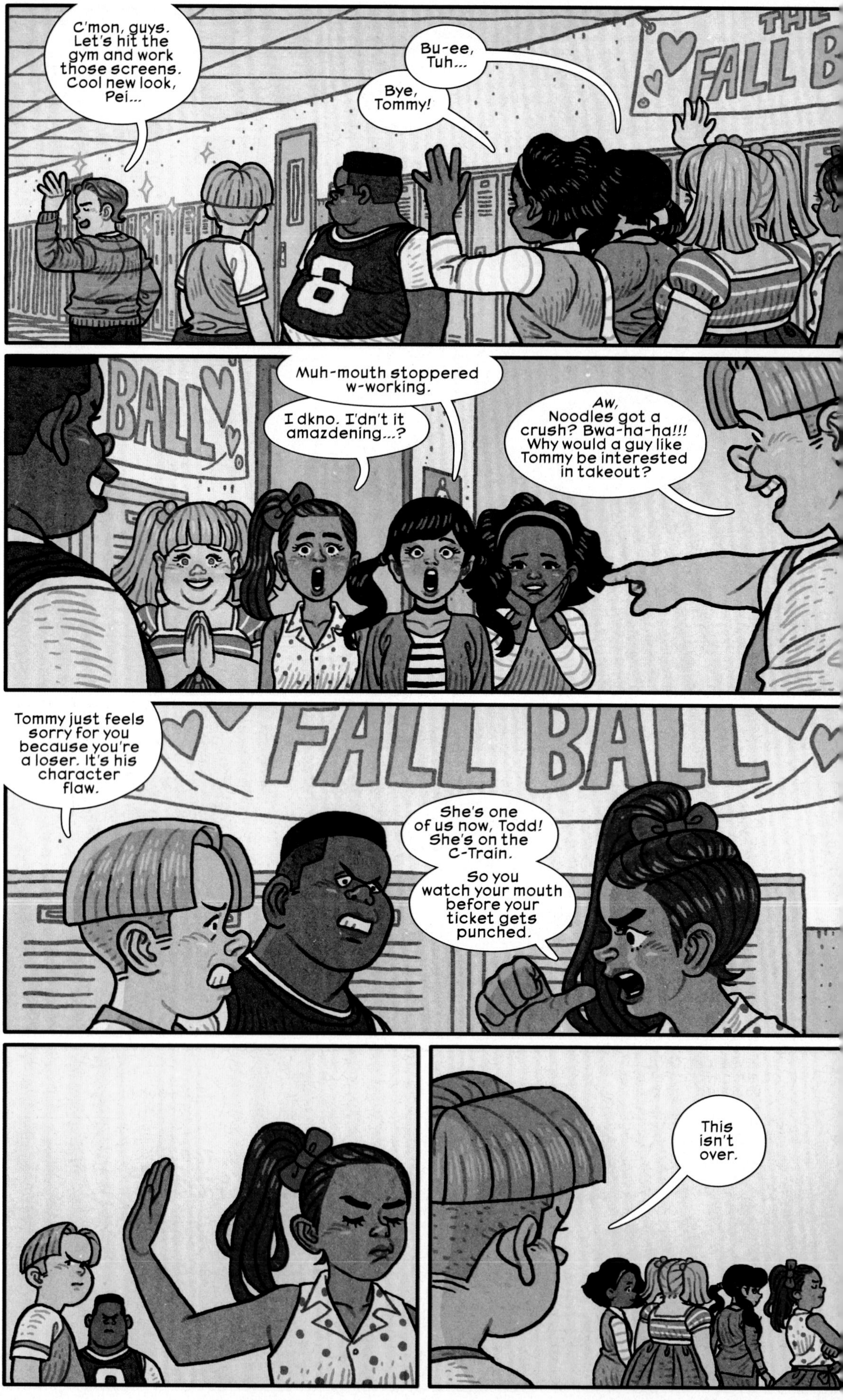

C'mon, guys. Let's hit the gym and work those screens. Cool new look, Pei...
Bu-ee, Tuh...
Bye, Tommy!
THE FALL B
BALL
Muh-mouth stoppered w-working.
I dkno. I'dn't it amazdening...?
Aw, Noodles got a crush? Bwa-ha-ha!!! Why would a guy like Tommy be interested in takeout?
FALL BALL
Tommy just feels sorry for you because you're a loser. It's his character flaw.
She's one of us now, Todd! She's on the C-Train.
So you watch your mouth before your ticket gets punched.
This isn't over.

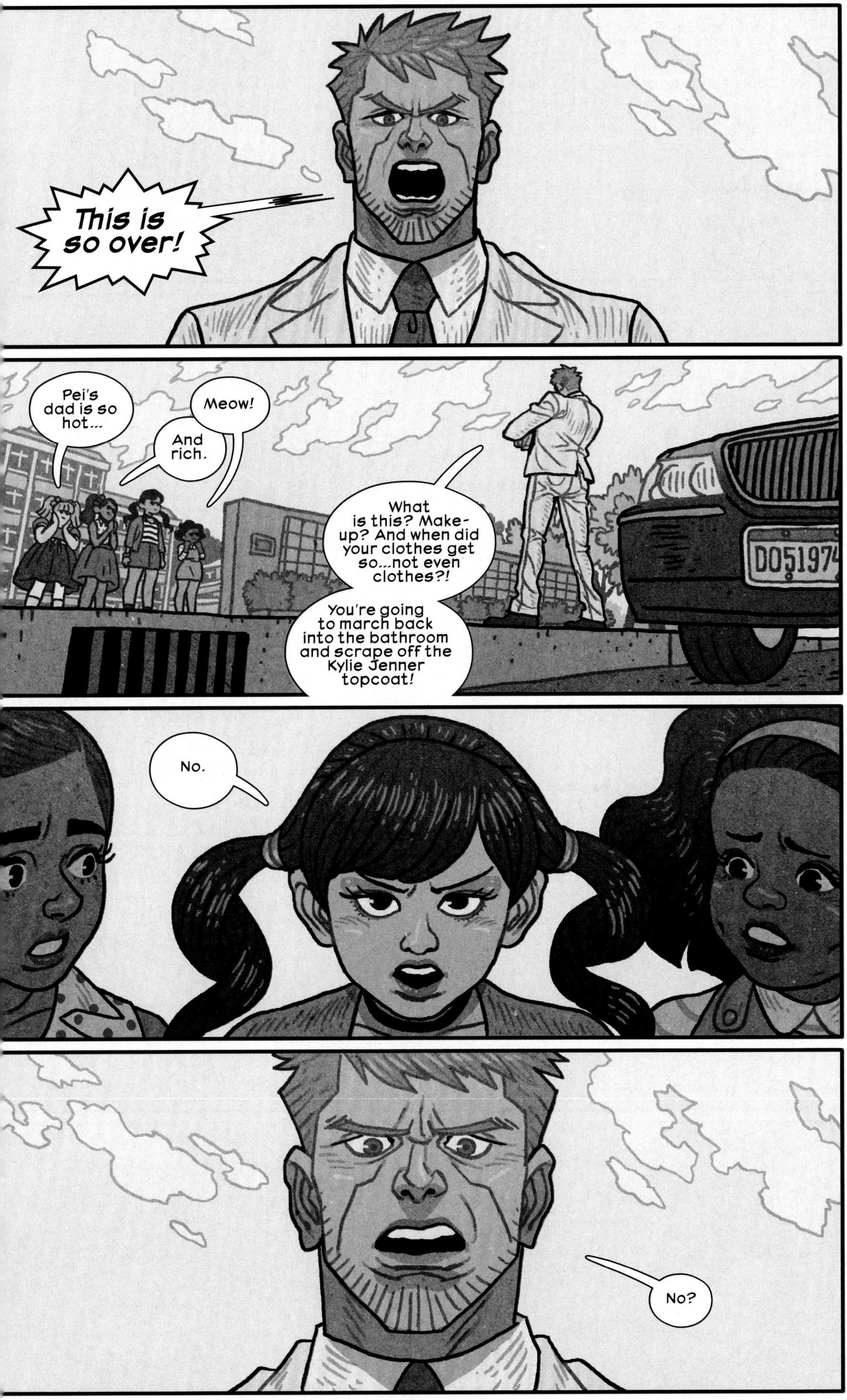
This is so over!
Pei's dad is so hot...
And rich.
Meow!
What is this? Make-up? And when did your clothes get so...not even clothes?!
You're going to march back into the bathroom and scrape off the Kylie Jenner topcoat!
DO51974
No.
No?

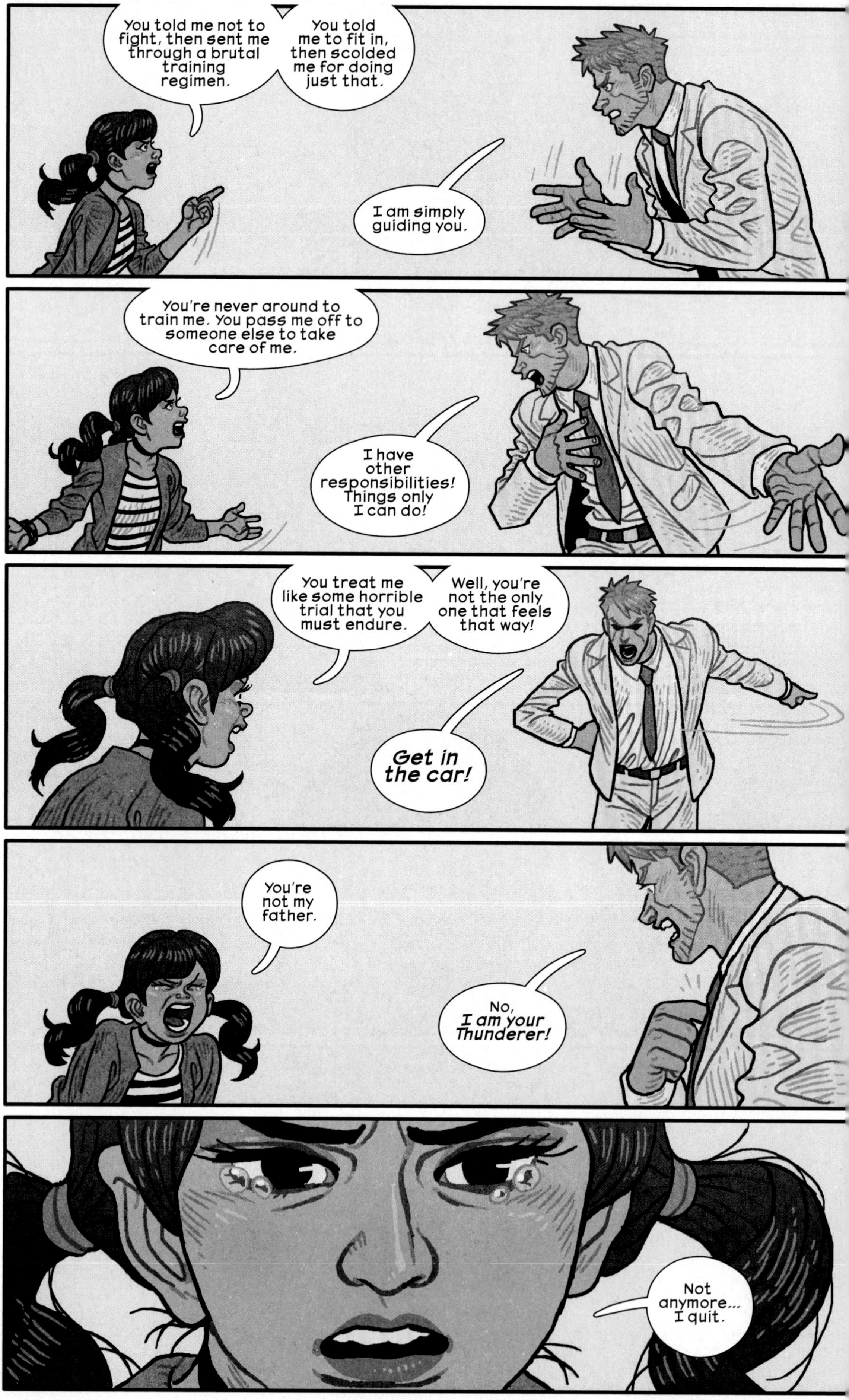
You told me not to fight, then sent me through a brutal training regimen.
You told me to fit in, then scolded me for doing just that.
I am simply guiding you.
You're never around to train me. You pass me off to someone else to take care of me.
I have other responsibilities! Things only I can do!
You treat me like some horrible trial that you must endure.
Well, you're not the only one that feels that way!
Get in the car!
You're not my father.
No, I am your Thunderer!
Not anymore... I quit.

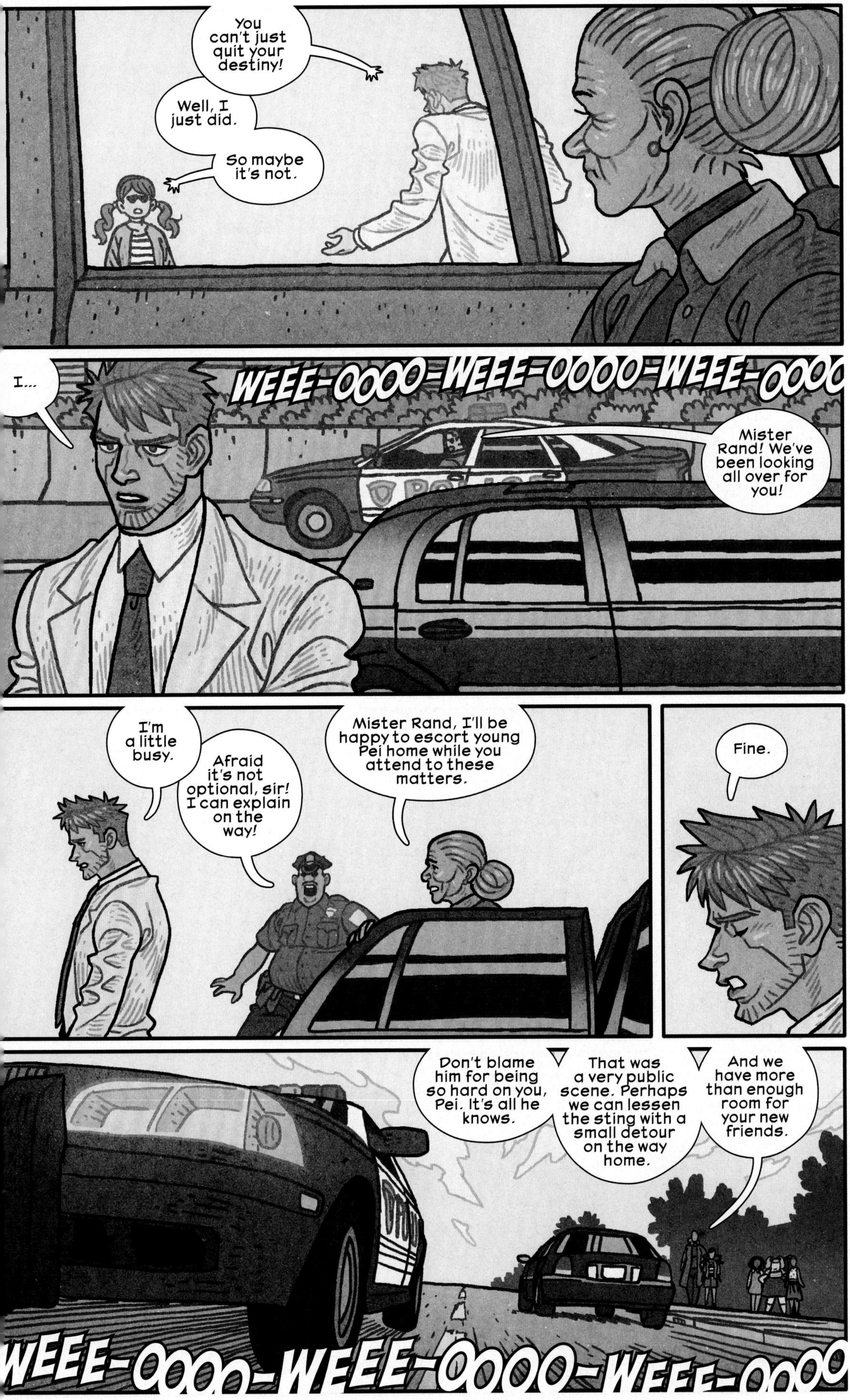
You can't just quit your destiny!
Well, I just did.
So maybe it's not.
I...
WEEE-OOOO-WEEE-OOOO-WEEE-OOOO
Mister Rand! We've been looking all over for you!
I'm a little busy.
Afraid it's not optional, sir! I can explain on the way!
Mister Rand, I'll be happy to escort young Pei home while you attend to these matters.
Fine.
Don't blame him for being so hard on you, Pei. It's all he knows.
That was a very public scene. Perhaps we can lessen the sting with a small detour on the way home.
And we have more than enough room for your new friends.
WEEE-OOOO-WEEE-OOOO-WEEE-OOOO

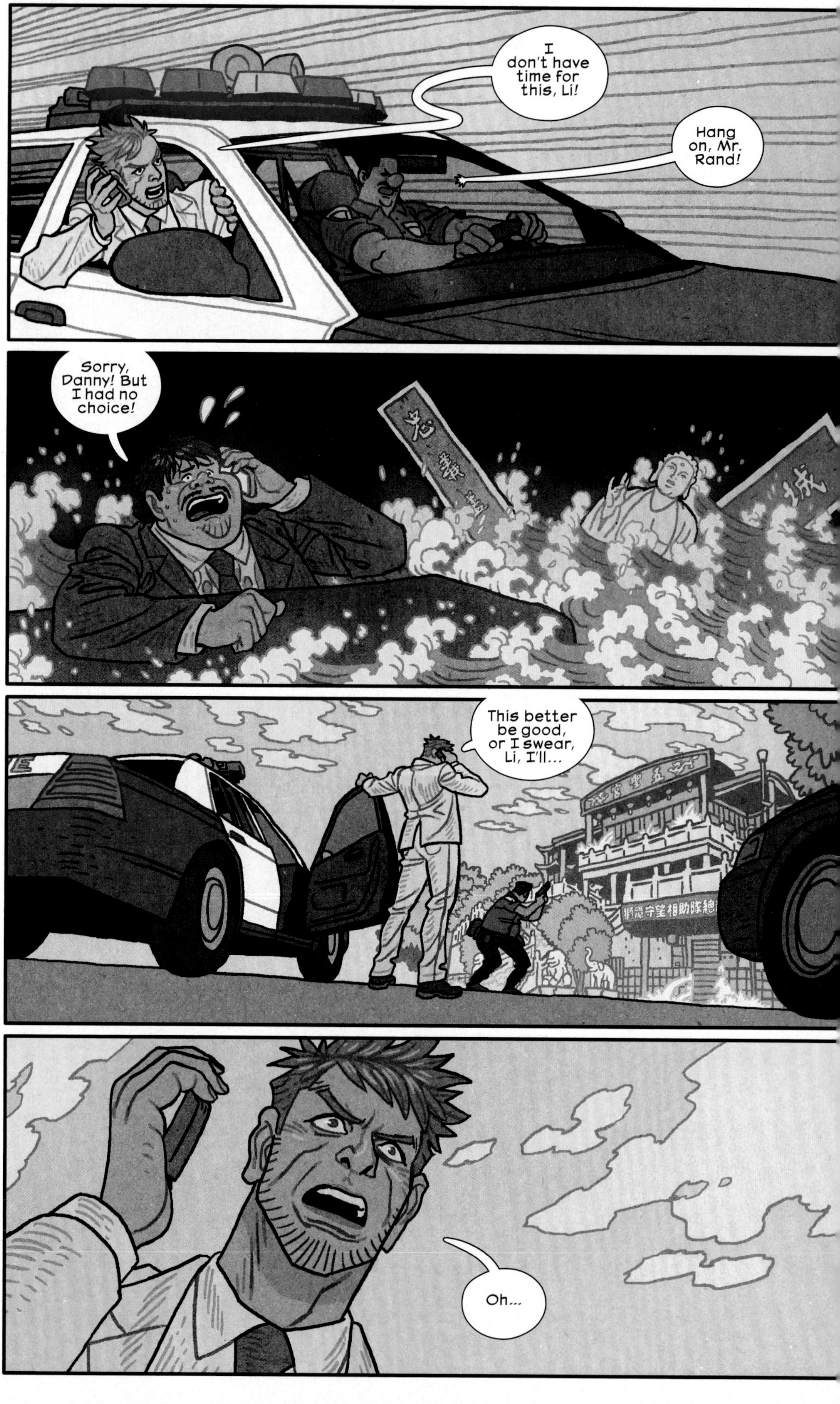

I don't have time for this, Li!
Hang on, Mr. Rand!
Sorry, Danny! But I had no choice!
This better be good, or I swear, Li, I'll...
Oh...

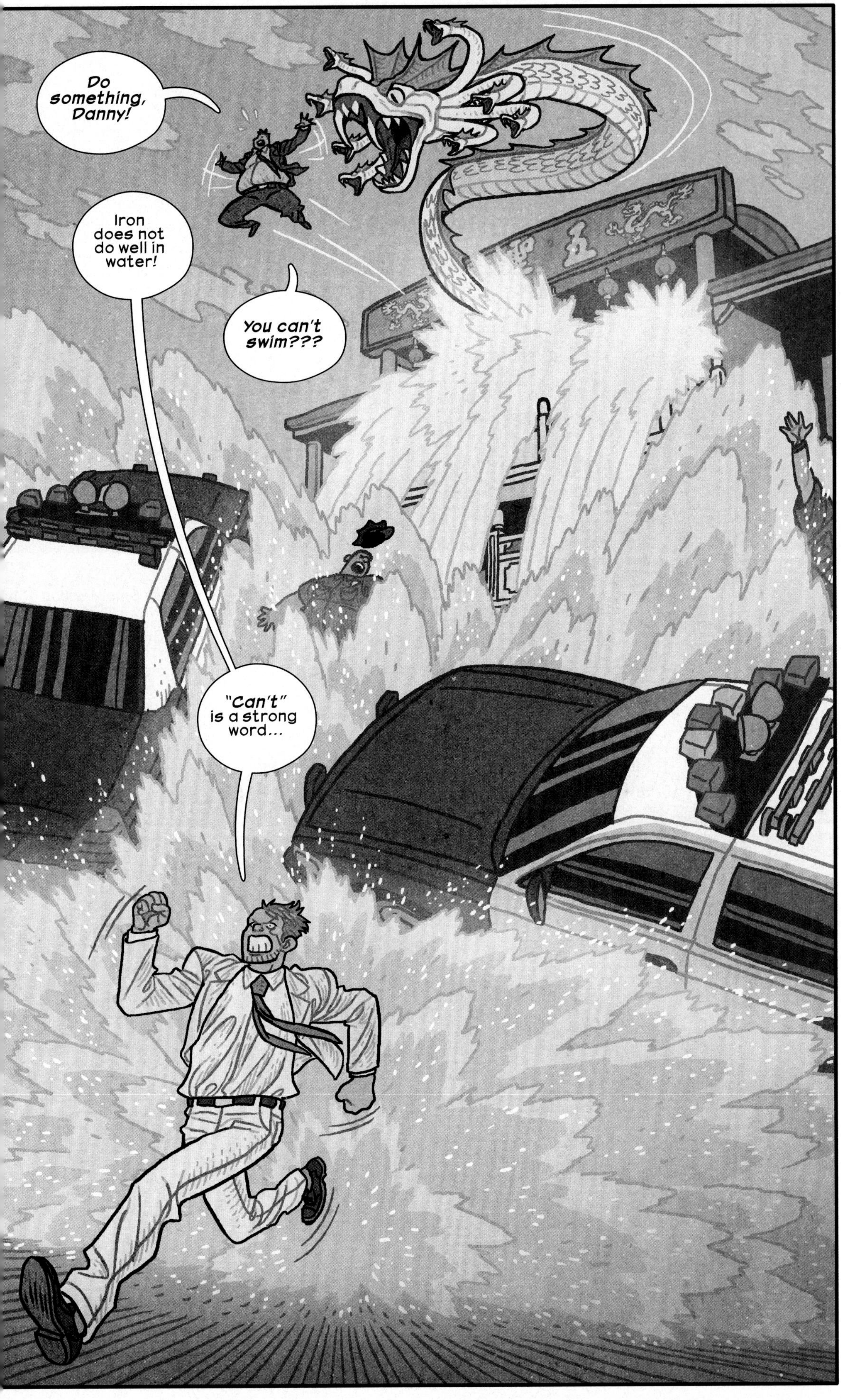
Do something, Danny!
Iron does not do well in water!
You can't swim???
"Can't" is a strong word...

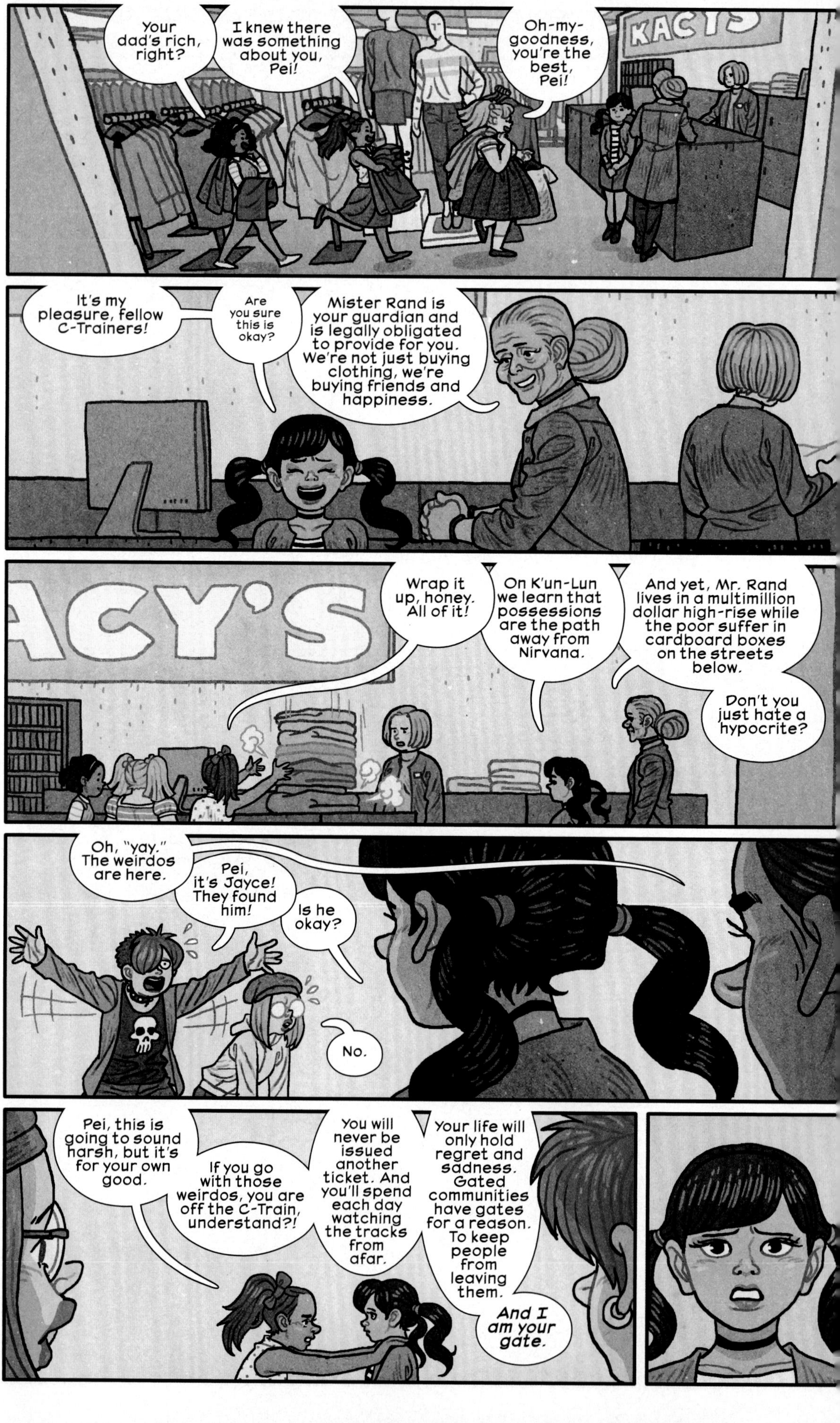

Your dad's rich, right?
I knew there was something about you, Pei!
Oh-my-goodness, you're the best, Pei!
KACYS
It's my pleasure, fellow C-Trainers!
Are you sure this is okay?
Mister Rand is your guardian and is legally obligated to provide for you. We're not just buying clothing, we're buying friends and happiness.
ACY'S
Wrap it up, honey. All of it!
On K'un-Lun we learn that possessions are the path away from Nirvana.
And yet, Mr. Rand lives in a multimillion dollar high-rise while the poor suffer in cardboard boxes on the streets below.
Don't you just hate a hypocrite?
Oh, "yay." The weirdos are here.
Pei, it's Jayce! They found him!
Is he okay?
No.
Pei, this is going to sound harsh, but it's for your own good.
If you go with those weirdos, you are off the C-Train, understand?!
You will never be issued another ticket. And you'll spend each day watching the tracks from afar.
Your life will only hold regret and sadness. Gated communities have gates for a reason. To keep people from leaving them.
And I am your gate.

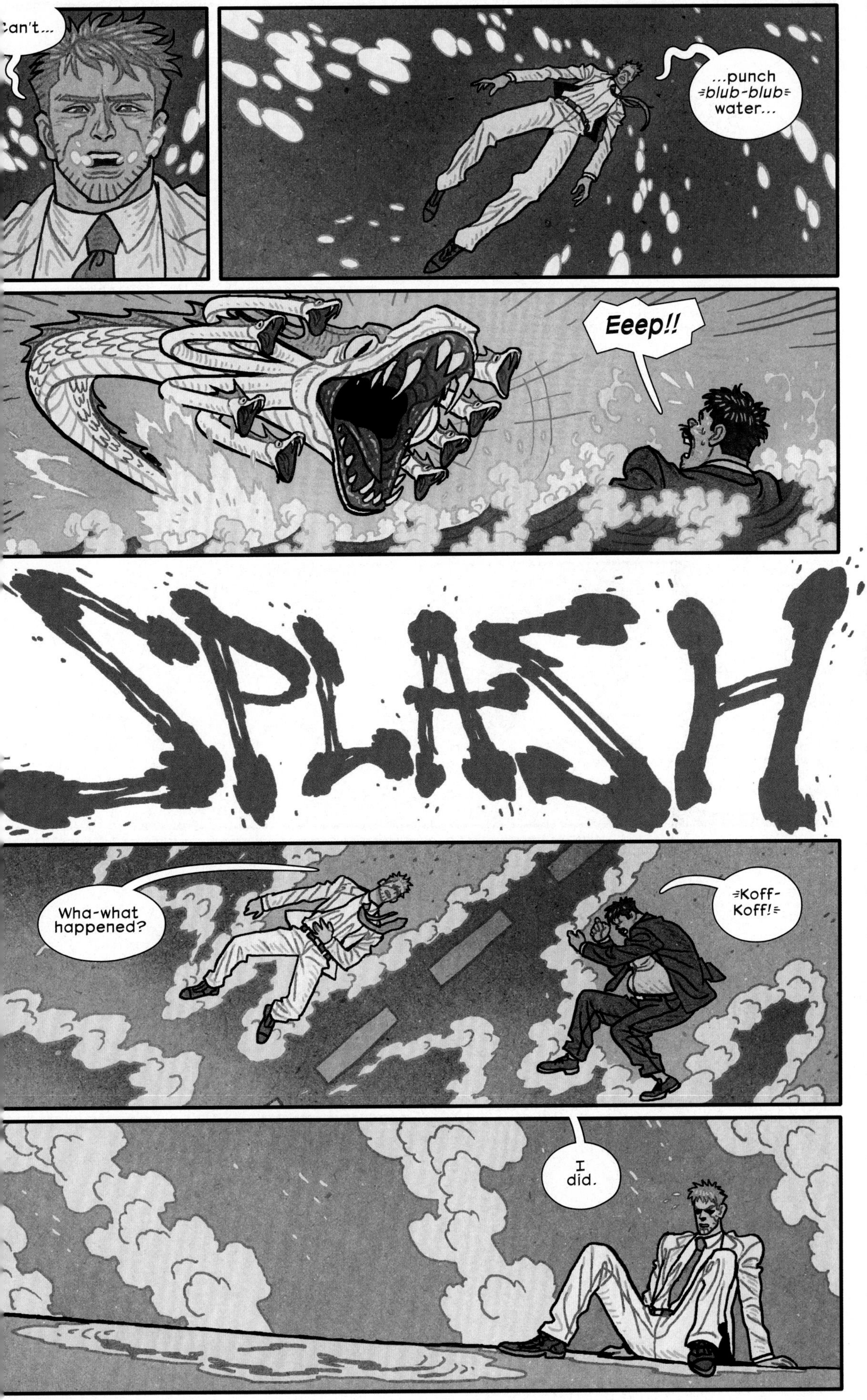
can't...
...punch =blub-blub= water...
Eeep!!
SPLASH
Wha-what happened?
=Koff-Koff!=
I did.

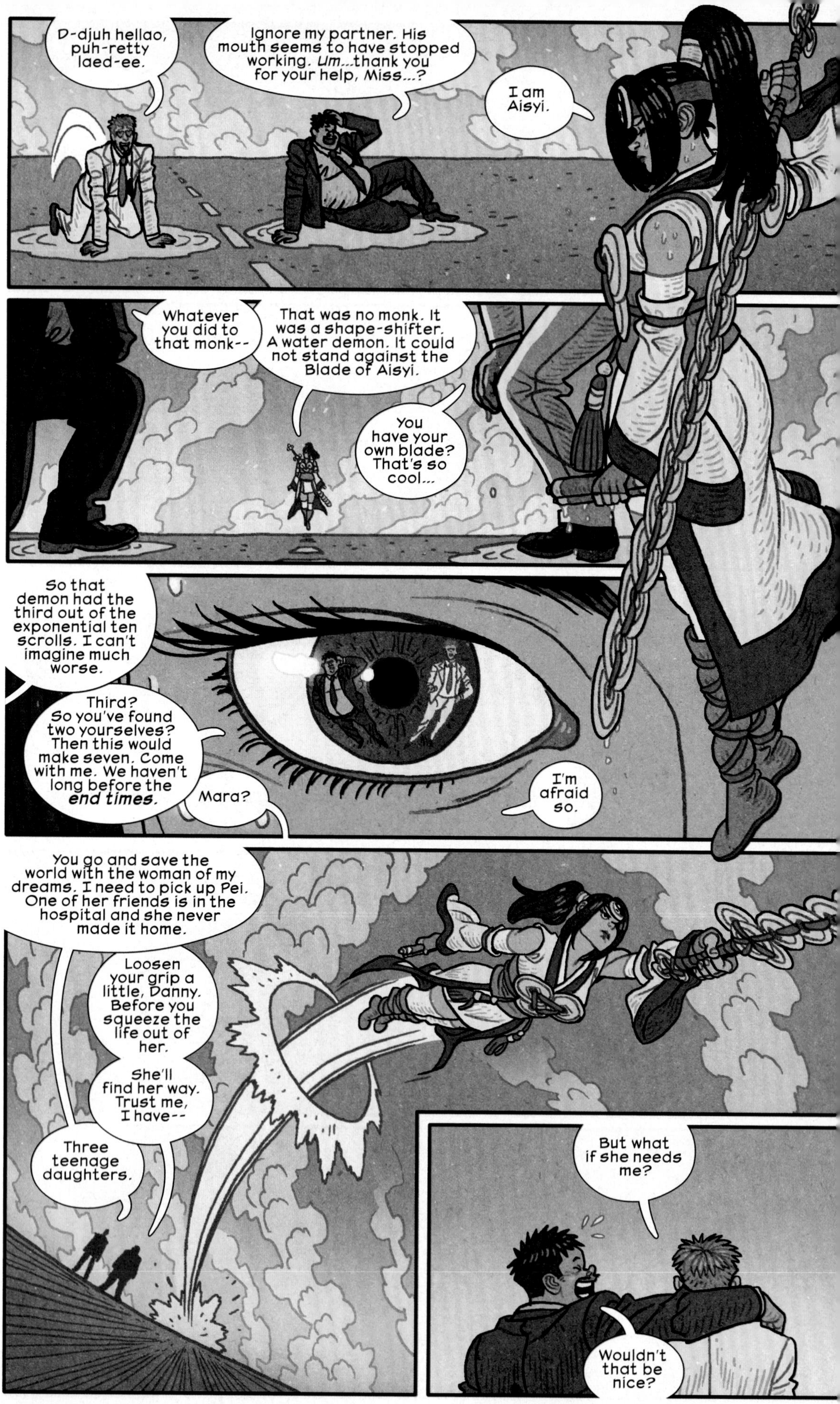
D-djuh hellao, puh-retty laed-ee.
Ignore my partner. His mouth seems to have stopped working. *Um...*thank you for your help, Miss...?
I am Aisyi.
Whatever you did to that monk--
That was no monk. It was a shape-shifter. A water demon. It could not stand against the Blade of Aisyi.
You have your own blade? That's so cool...
So that demon had the third out of the exponential ten scrolls. I can't imagine much worse.
Third? So you've found two yourselves? Then this would make seven. Come with me. We haven't long before the *end times.*
Mara?
I'm afraid so.
You go and save the world with the woman of my dreams. I need to pick up Pei. One of her friends is in the hospital and she never made it home.
Loosen your grip a little, Danny. Before you squeeze the life out of her.
She'll find her way. Trust me, I have--
Three teenage daughters.
But what if she needs me?
Wouldn't that be nice?

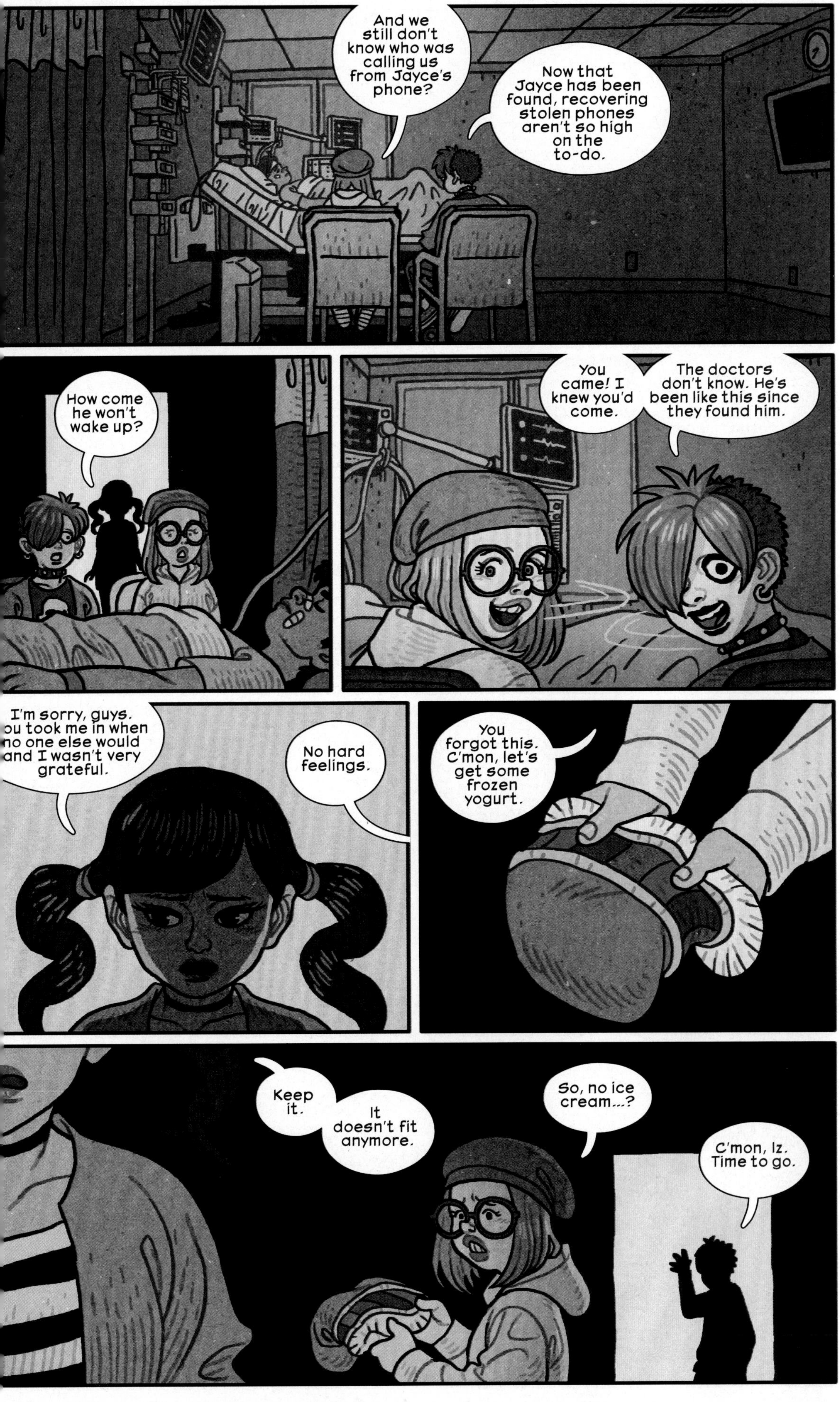
And we still don't know who was calling us from Jayce's phone?
Now that Jayce has been found, recovering stolen phones aren't so high on the to-do.
How come he won't wake up?
You came! I knew you'd come.
The doctors don't know. He's been like this since they found him.
I'm sorry, guys. ou took me in when no one else would and I wasn't very grateful.
No hard feelings.
You forgot this. C'mon, let's get some frozen yogurt.
Keep it.
It doesn't fit anymore.
So, no ice cream...?
C'mon, Iz. Time to go.

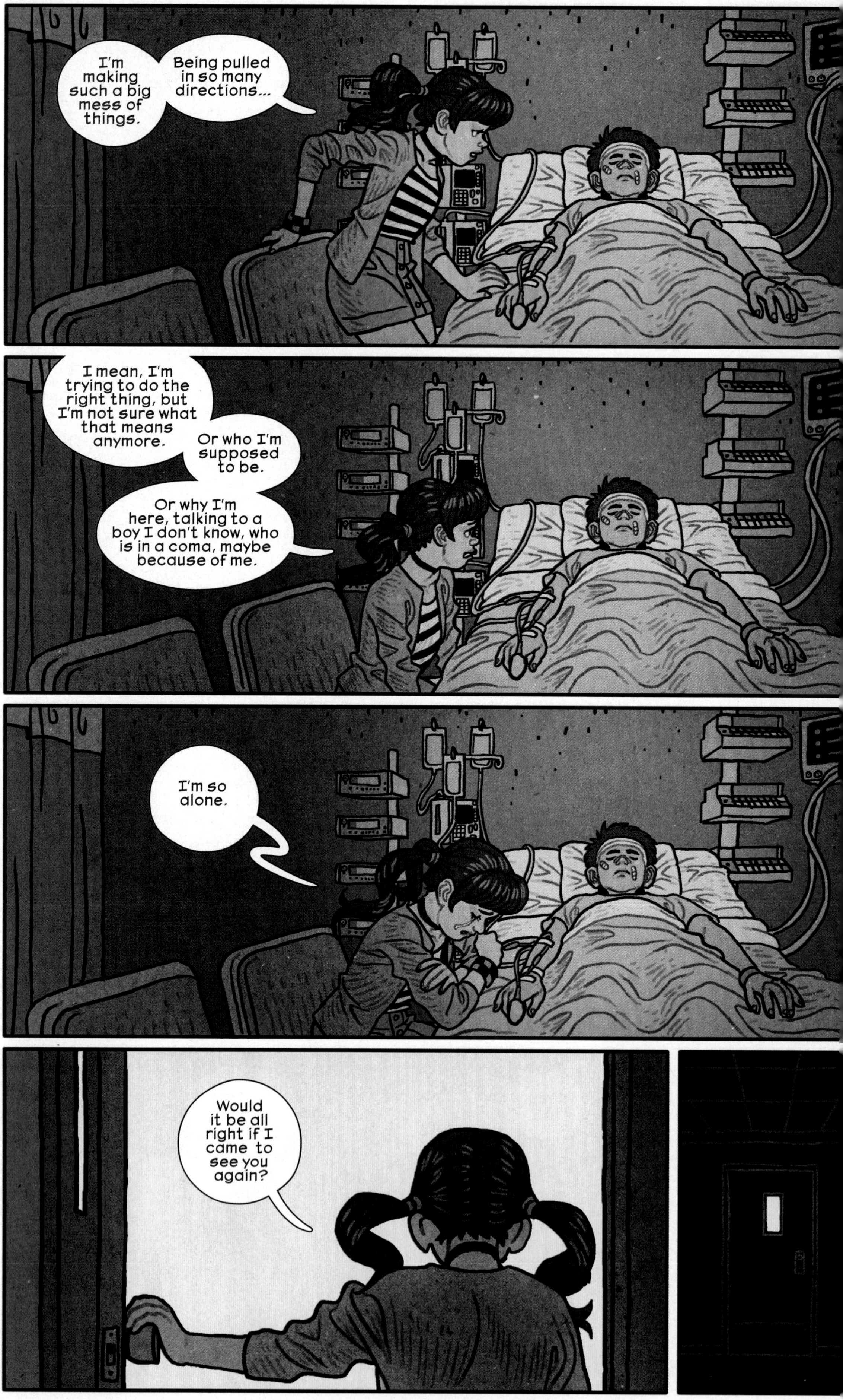
I'm making such a big mess of things.
Being pulled in so many directions...
I mean, I'm trying to do the right thing, but I'm not sure what that means anymore.
Or who I'm supposed to be.
Or why I'm here, talking to a boy I don't know, who is in a coma, maybe because of me.
I'm so alone.
Would it be all right if I came to see you again?

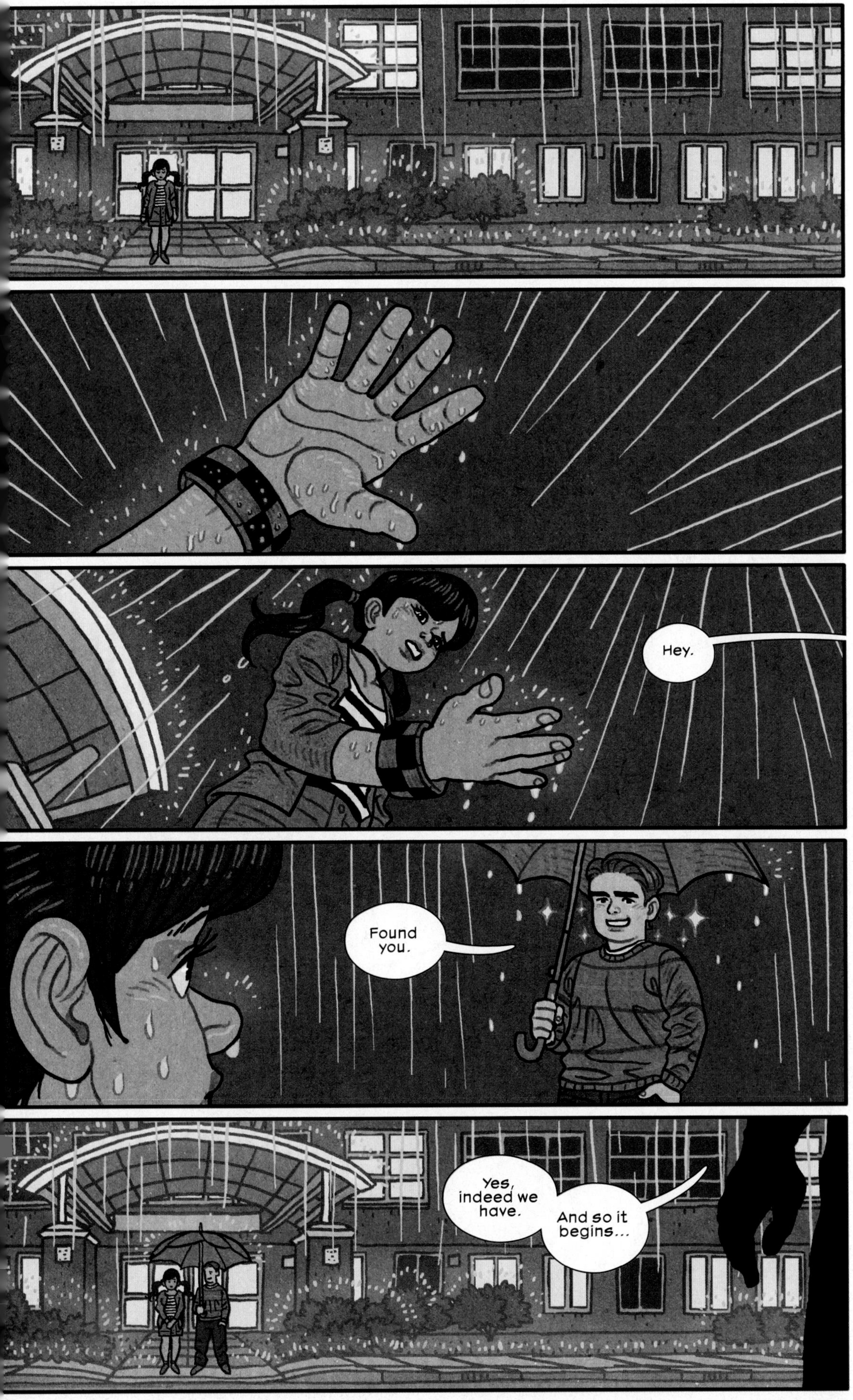
Hey.
Found you.
Yes, indeed we have.
And so it begins...

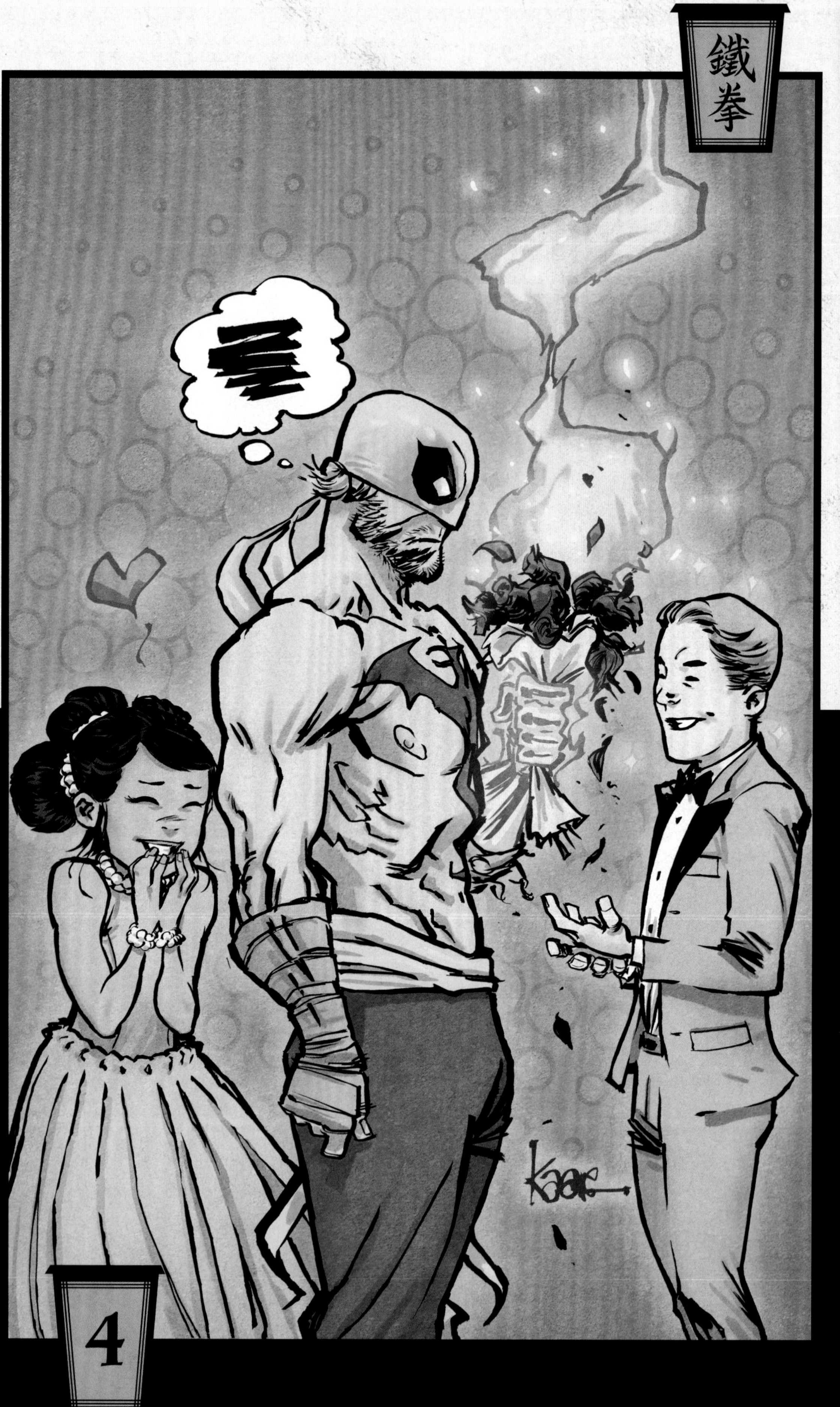
鐵拳
4

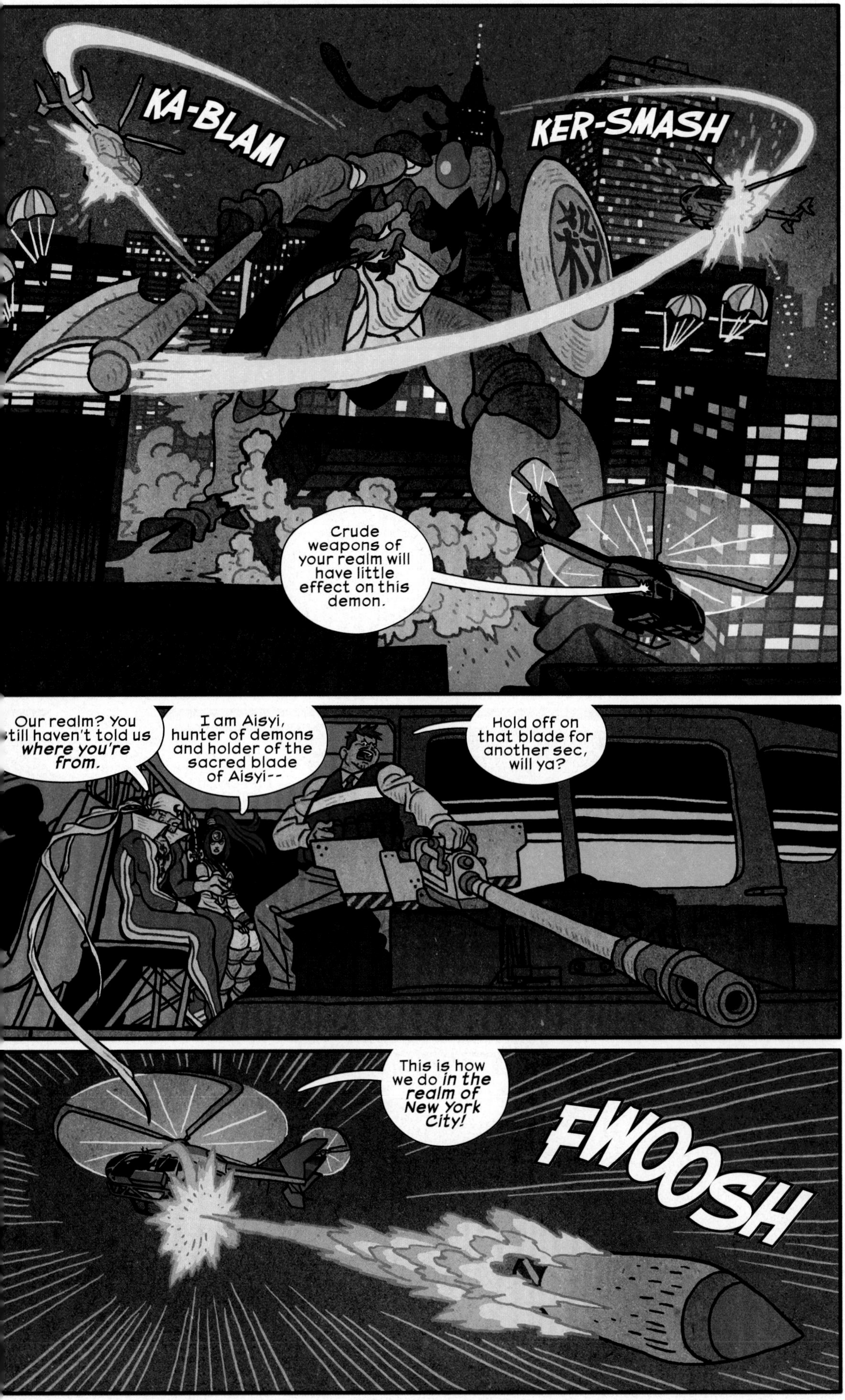
KA-BLAM
KER-SMASH
Crude weapons of your realm will have little effect on this demon.
Our realm? You still haven't told us *where you're from.*
I am Aisyi, hunter of demons and holder of the sacred blade of Aisyi--
Hold off on that blade for another sec, will ya?
This is how we do *in the realm of New York City!*
FWOOSH

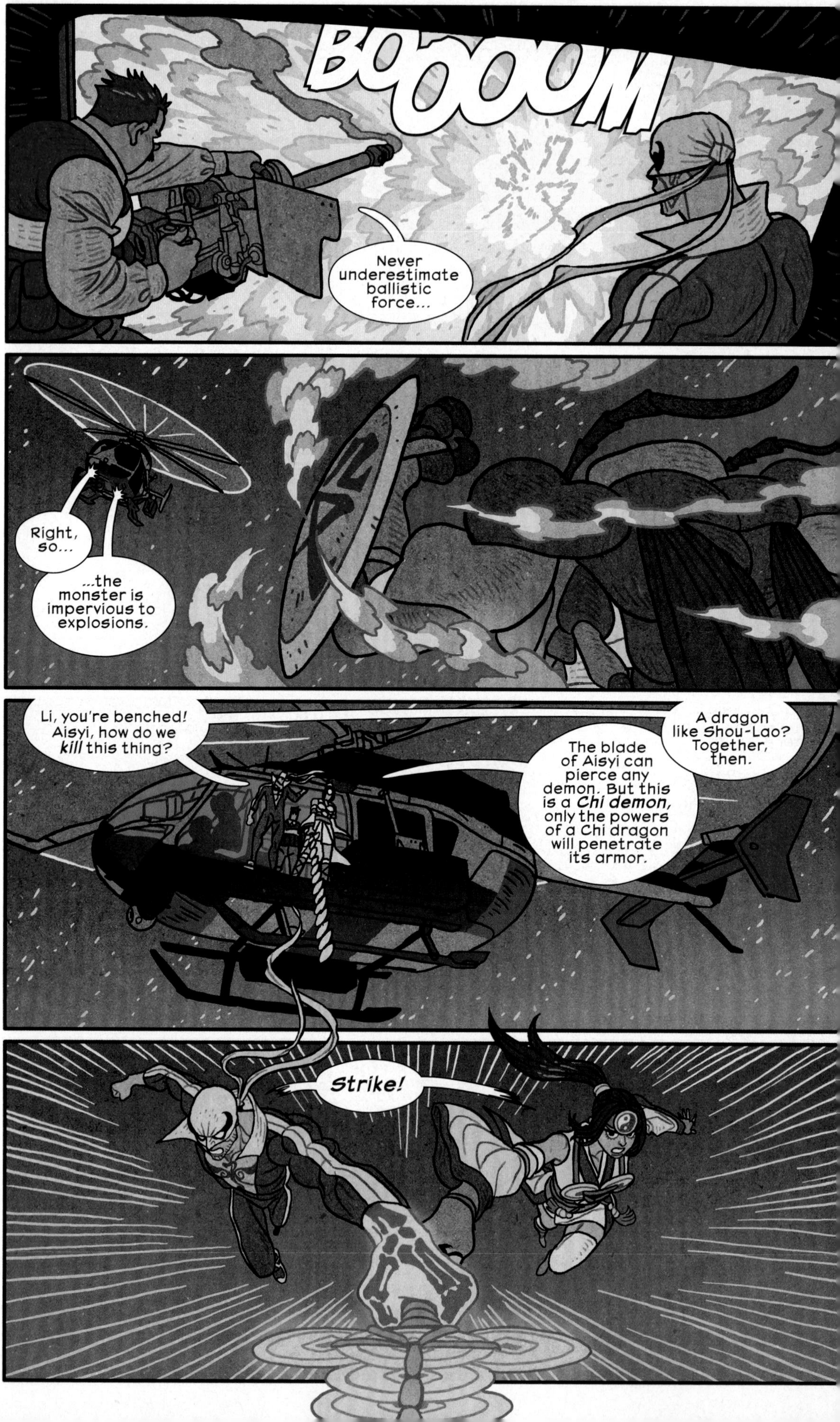
BOOOOOM
Never underestimate ballistic force...
Right, so...
...the monster is impervious to explosions.
Li, you're benched! Aisyi, how do we *kill* this thing?
The blade of Aisyi can pierce any demon. But this is a *Chi demon,* only the powers of a Chi dragon will penetrate its armor.
A dragon like Shou-Lao? Together, then.
Strike!

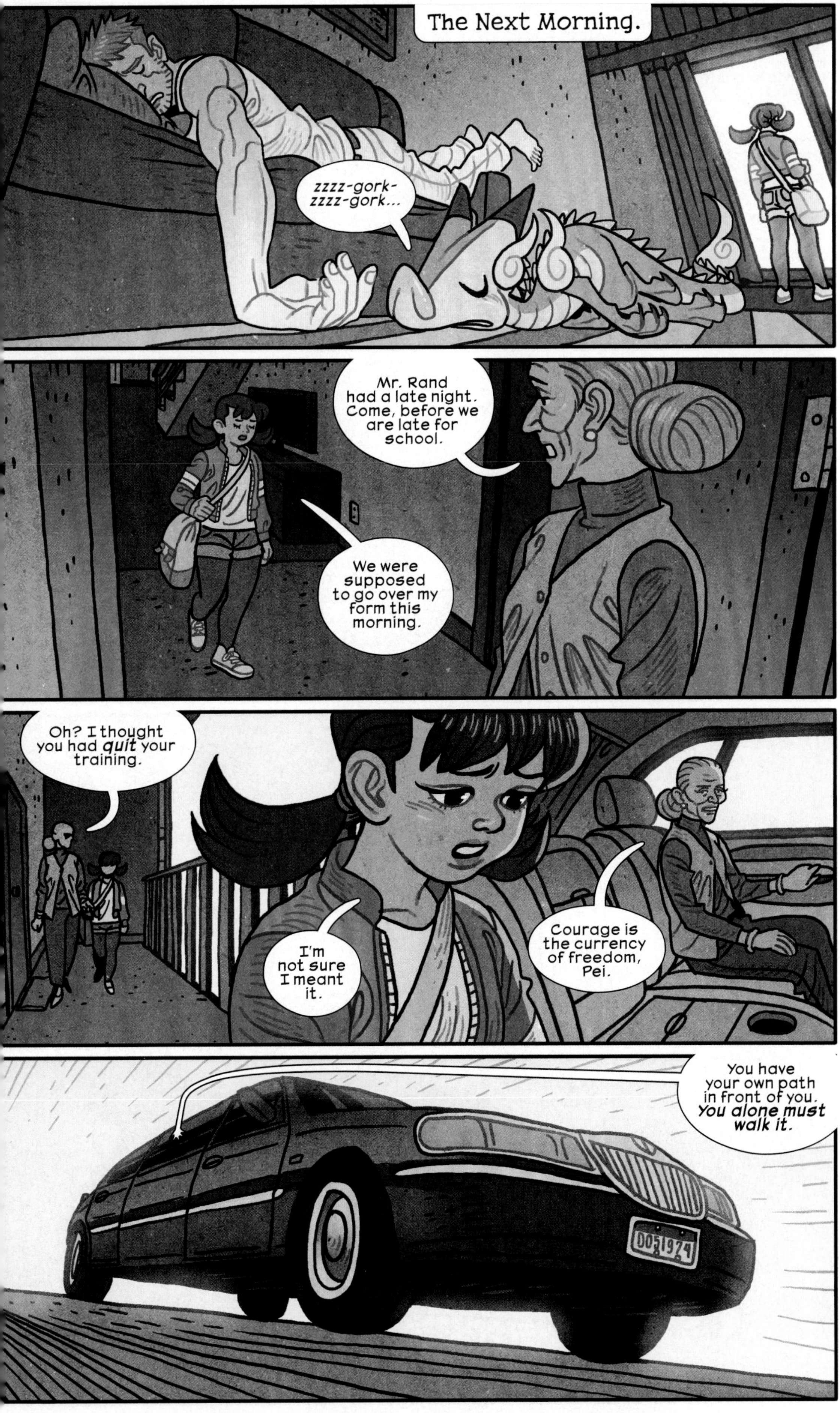

The Next Morning.
zzzz-gork-
zzzz-gork...
Mr. Rand had a late night. Come, before we are late for school.
We were supposed to go over my form this morning.
Oh? I thought you had *quit* your training.
I'm not sure I meant it.
Courage is the currency of freedom, Pei.
You have your own path in front of you. ***You alone must walk it.***
DO51924

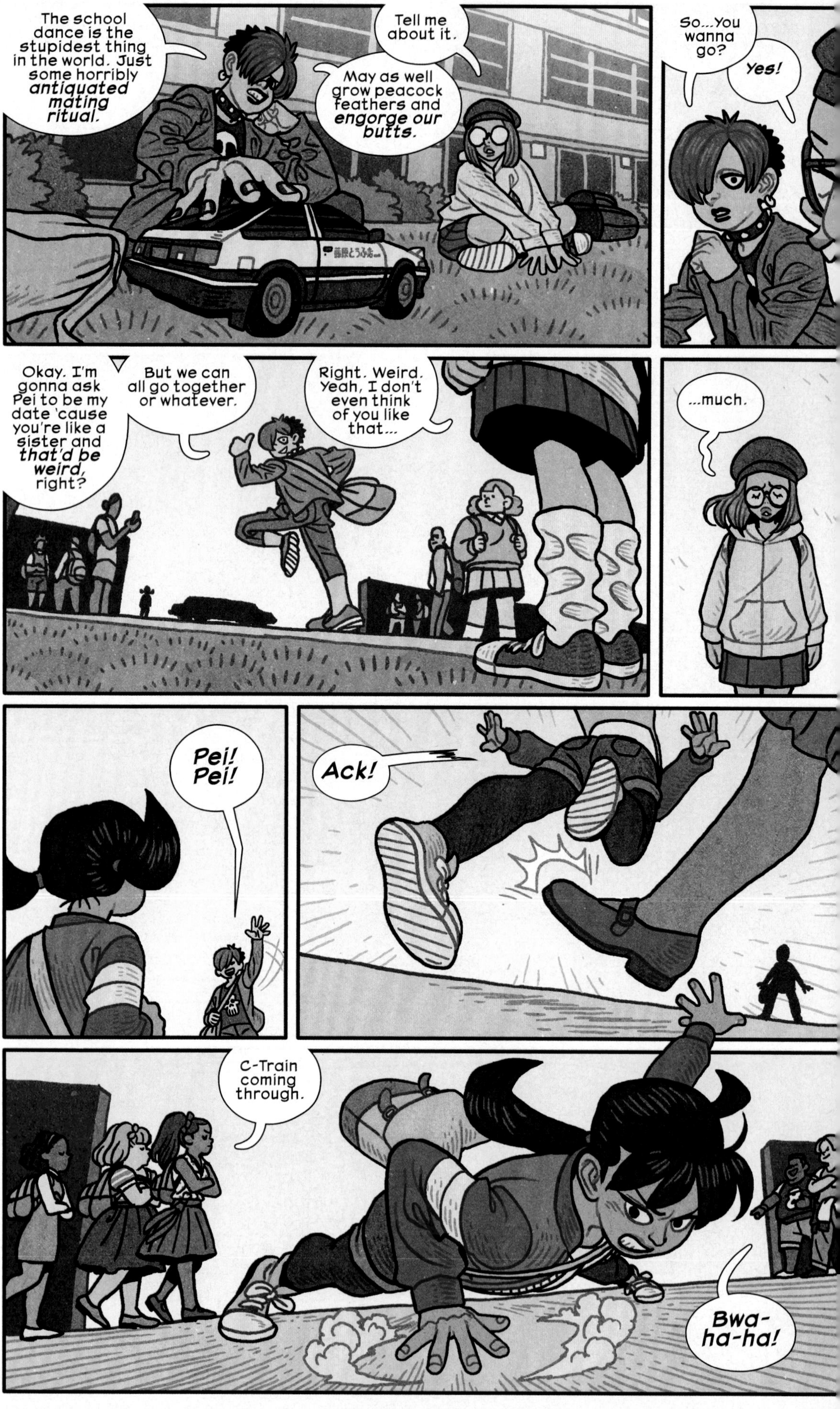

The school dance is the stupidest thing in the world. Just some horribly *antiquated mating ritual.*
Tell me about it.
May as well grow peacock feathers and *engorge our butts.*
So...You wanna go?
Yes!
Okay. I'm gonna ask Pei to be my date 'cause you're like a sister and *that'd be weird,* right?
But we can all go together or whatever.
Right. Weird. Yeah, I don't even think of you like that...
...much.
Pei! Pei!
Ack!
C-Train coming through.
Bwa-ha-ha!

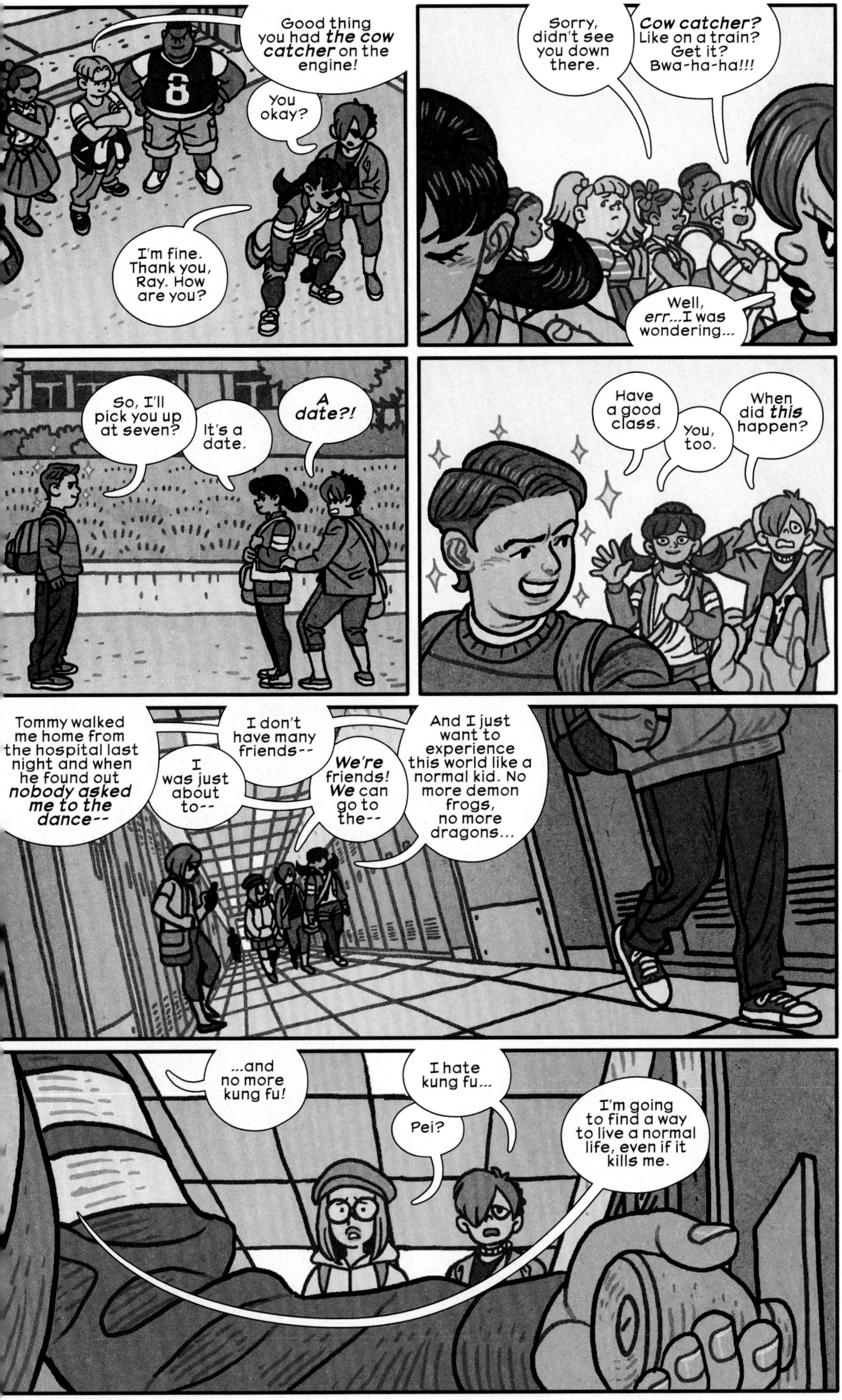

Good thing you had *the cow catcher* on the engine!
You okay?
I'm fine. Thank you, Ray. How are you?
Sorry, didn't see you down there.
Cow catcher? Like on a train? Get it? Bwa-ha-ha!!!
Well, *err*...I was wondering...
So, I'll pick you up at seven?
It's a date.
A date?!
Have a good class.
You, too.
When did *this* happen?
Tommy walked me home from the hospital last night and when he found out *nobody asked me to the dance*--
I was just about to--
I don't have many friends--
We're friends! *We* can go to the--
And I just want to experience this world like a normal kid. No more demon frogs, no more dragons...
...and no more kung fu!
I hate kung fu...
Pei?
I'm going to find a way to live a normal life, even if it kills me.

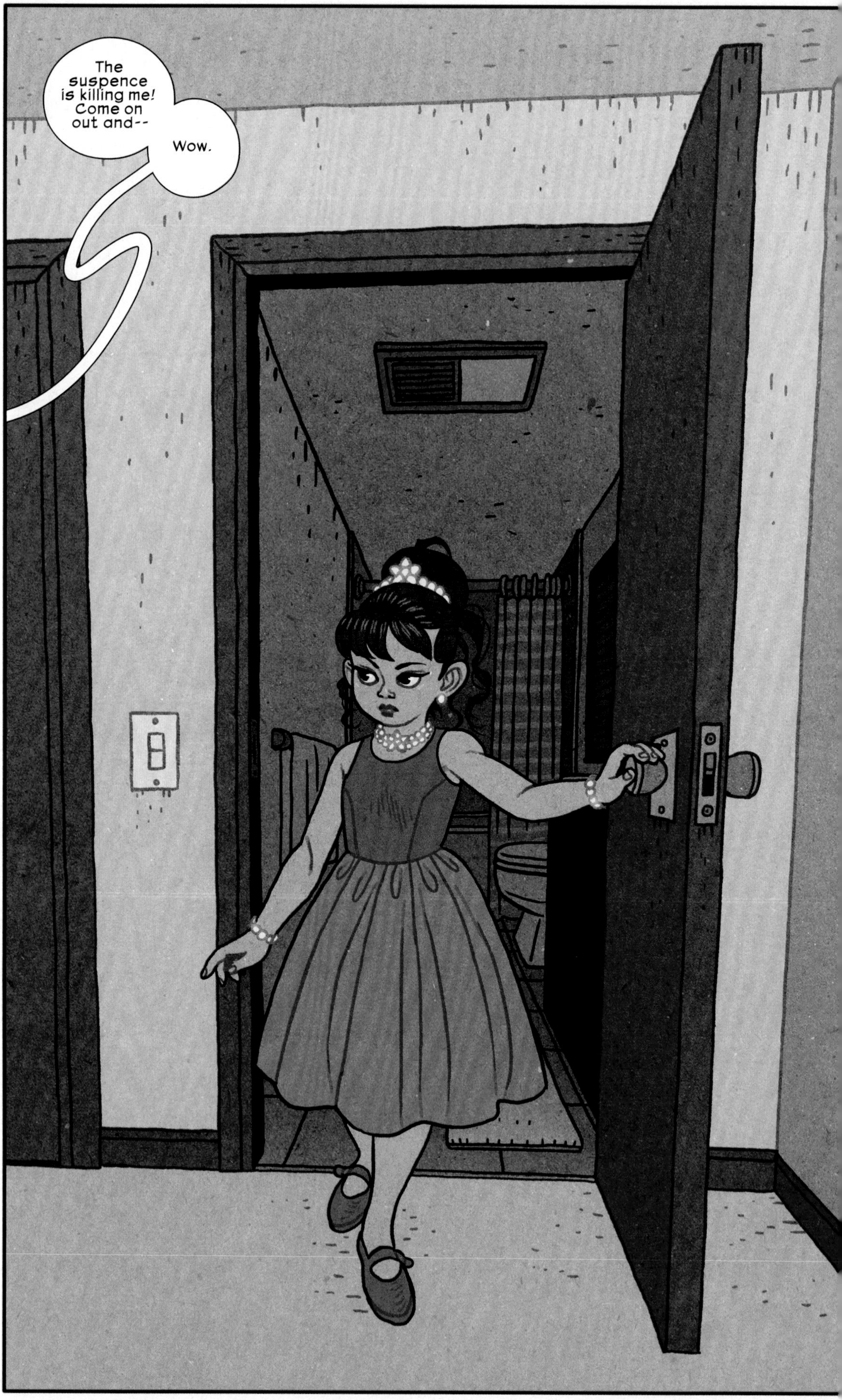
The suspence is killing me! Come on out and--
Wow.

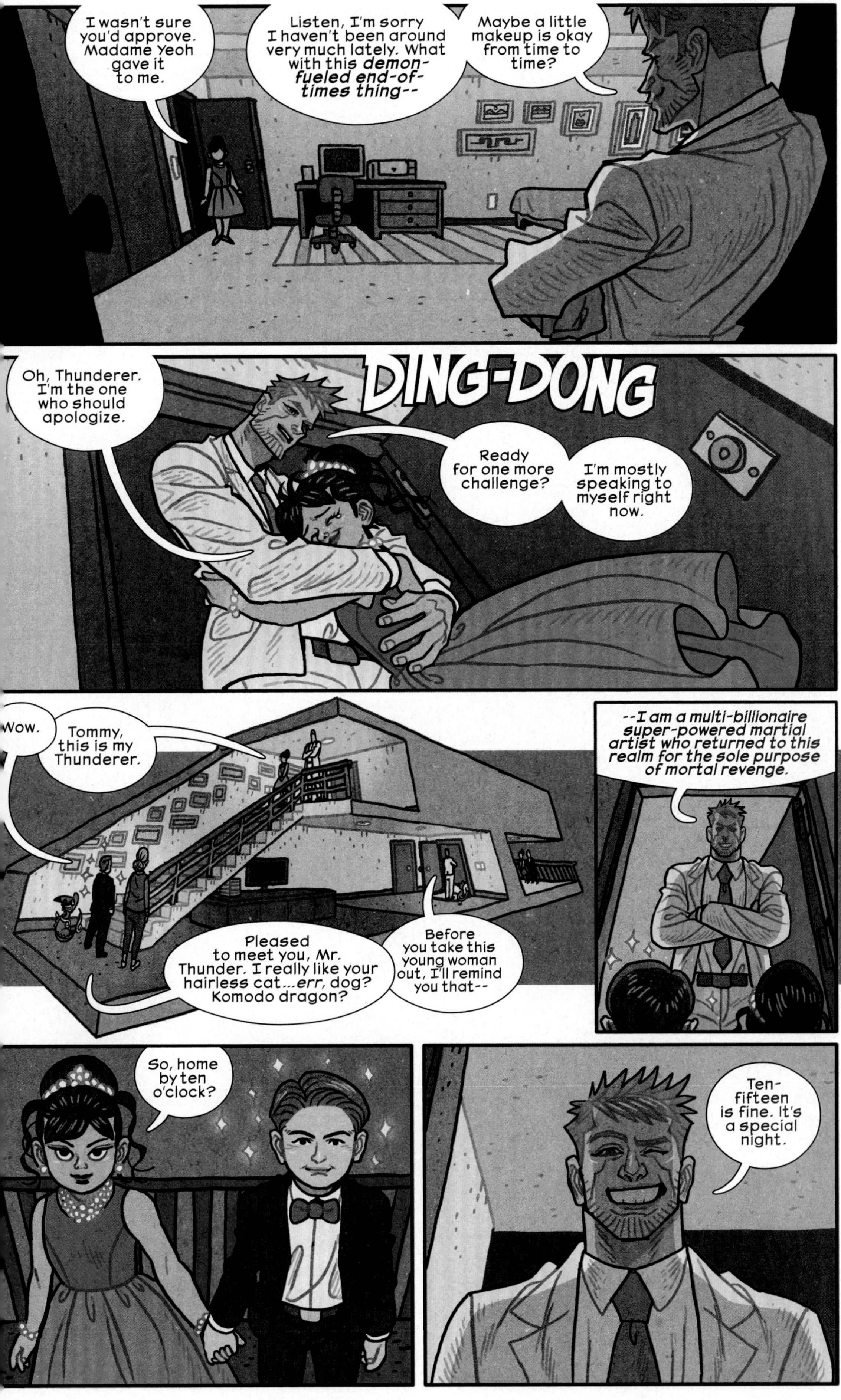
I wasn't sure you'd approve. Madame Yeoh gave it to me.
Listen, I'm sorry I haven't been around very much lately. What with this *demon-fueled end-of-times thing--*
Maybe a little makeup is okay from time to time?
Oh, Thunderer. I'm the one who should apologize.
DING-DONG
Ready for one more challenge?
I'm mostly speaking to myself right now.
Wow.
Tommy, this is my Thunderer.
Pleased to meet you, Mr. Thunder. I really like your hairless cat*...err,* dog? Komodo dragon?
Before you take this young woman out, I'll remind you that--
--I am a multi-billionaire super-powered martial artist who returned to this realm for the sole purpose of mortal revenge.
So, home by ten o'clock?
Ten-fifteen is fine. It's a special night.

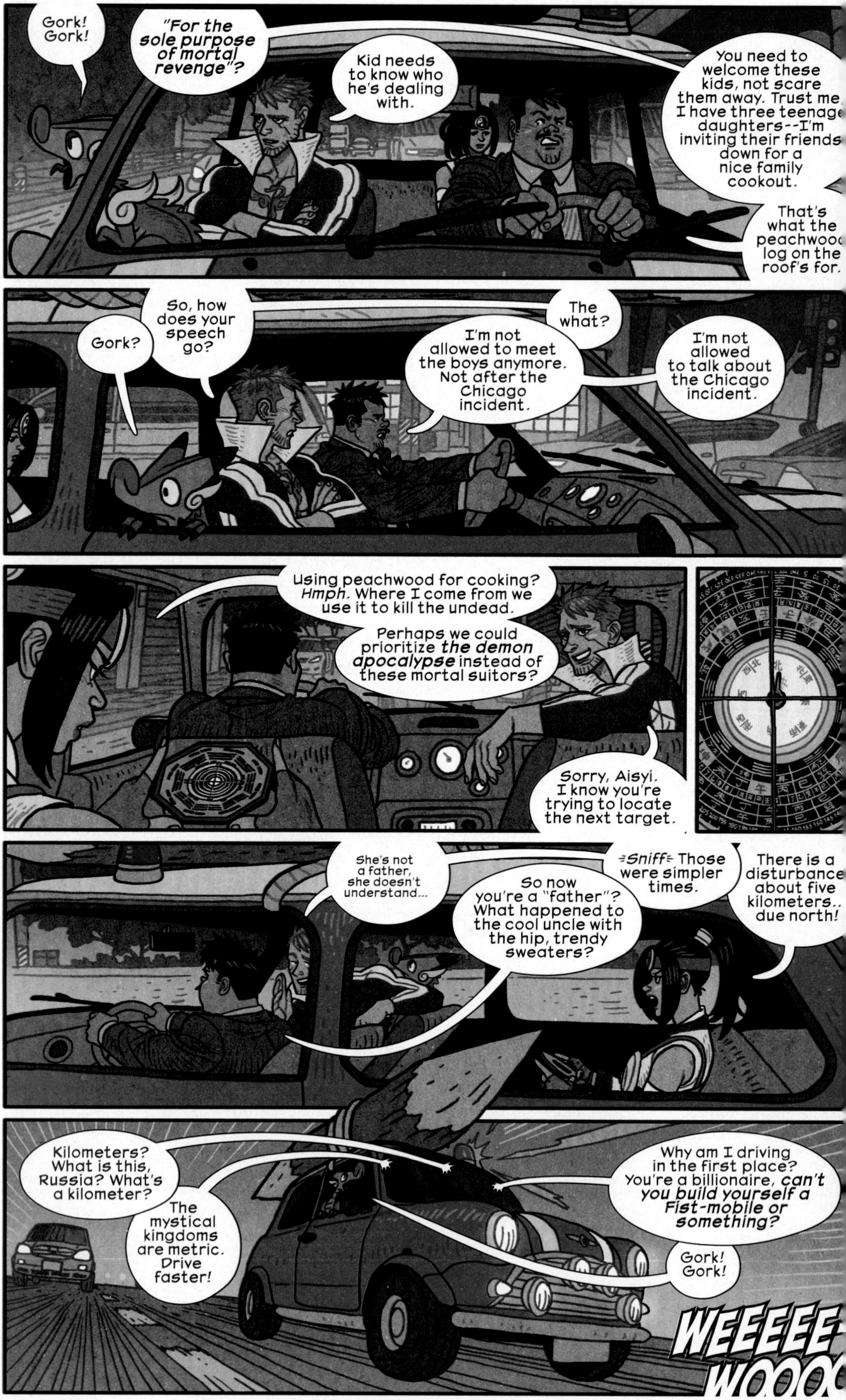
Gork! Gork!
"For the sole purpose of mortal revenge"?
Kid needs to know who he's dealing with.
You need to welcome these kids, not scare them away. Trust me, I have three teenage daughters--I'm inviting their friends down for a nice family cookout.
That's what the peachwoo log on the roof's for.
Gork?
So, how does your speech go?
The what?
I'm not allowed to meet the boys anymore. Not after the Chicago incident.
I'm not allowed to talk about the Chicago incident.
Using peachwood for cooking? Hmph. Where I come from we use it to kill the undead.
Perhaps we could prioritize the demon apocalypse instead of these mortal suitors?
Sorry, Aisyi. I know you're trying to locate the next target.
She's not a father, she doesn't understand...
So now you're a "father"? What happened to the cool uncle with the hip, trendy sweaters?
=Sniff= Those were simpler times.
There is a disturbance about five kilometers... due north!
Kilometers? What is this, Russia? What's a kilometer?
The mystical kingdoms are metric. Drive faster!
Why am I driving in the first place? You're a billionaire, can't you build yourself a Fist-mobile or something?
Gork! Gork!
WEEEEE WOOO

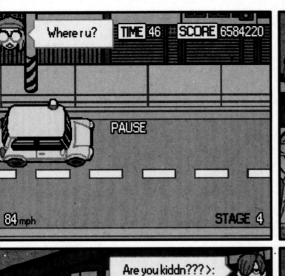

Where r u? TIME 46 SCORE 6584220

PAUSE

84 mph

STAGE 4

At home. Laughing at the sheep...

Thought you forgot about me and went 2 dance with Pei.

Are you kiddn??? >:

FALL BALL

Refuse 2 be herded into a society empowered by autocratic fascism.

Tell me about it.

So you wanna go?

Iz?

While I agree with everything you just stated, I've got my dancing shoes on and they're fairly non-partisan about such matters.

They just wanna dance.

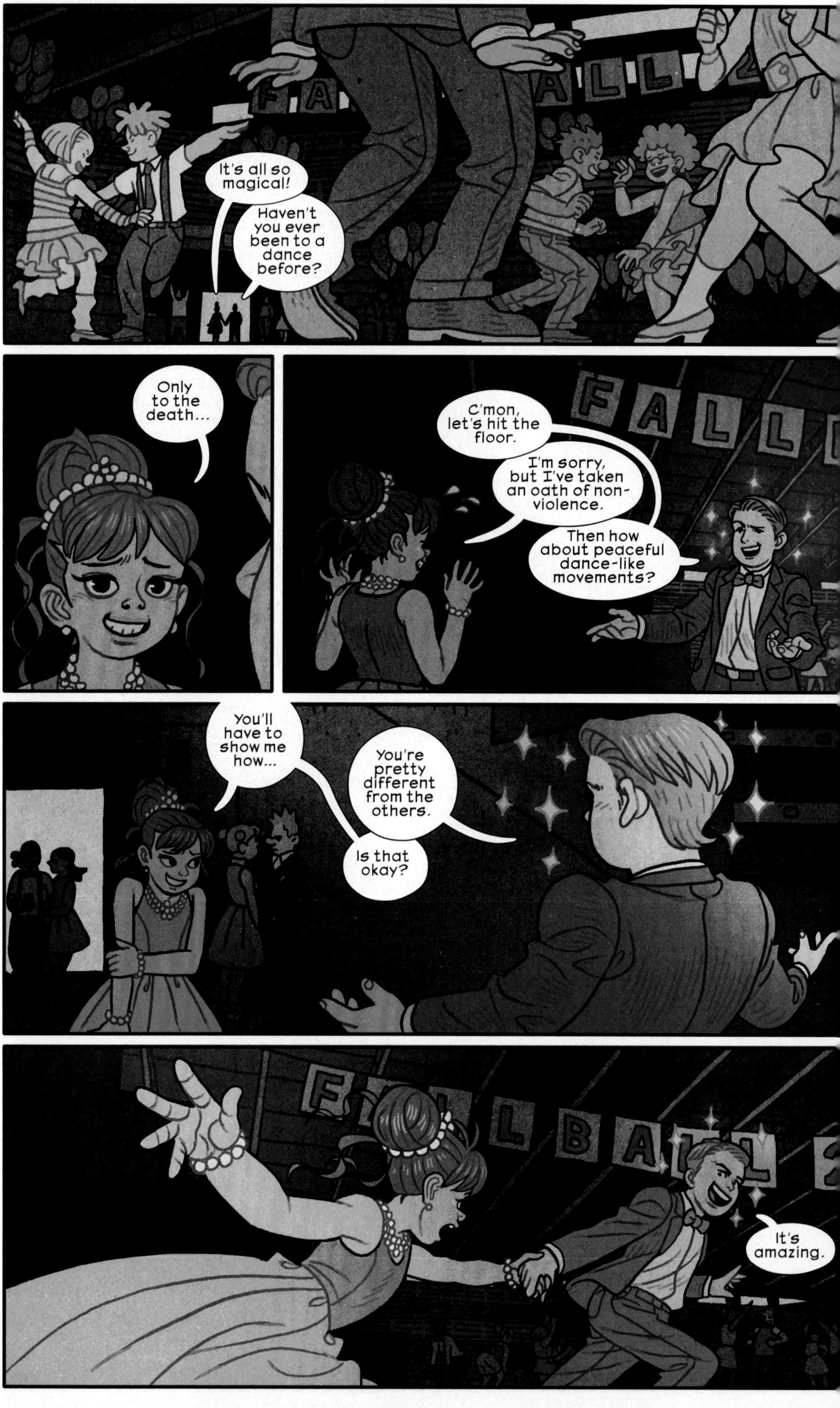

It's all so magical!
Haven't you ever been to a dance before?
Only to the death...
C'mon, let's hit the floor.
I'm sorry, but I've taken an oath of non-violence.
Then how about peaceful dance-like movements?
You'll have to show me how...
You're pretty different from the others.
Is that okay?
It's amazing.
FALL BALL

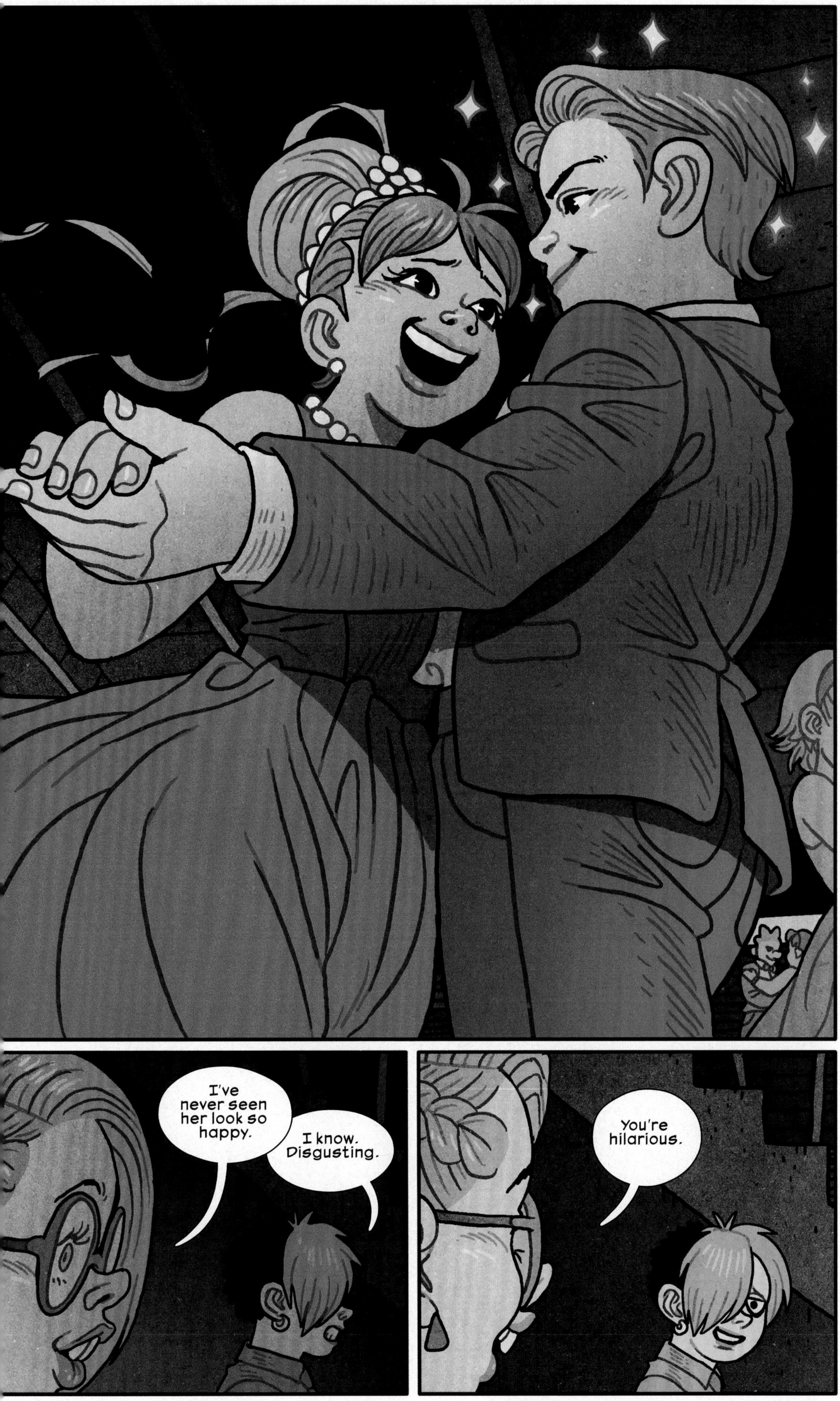
I've never seen her look so happy.
I know. Disgusting.
You're hilarious.

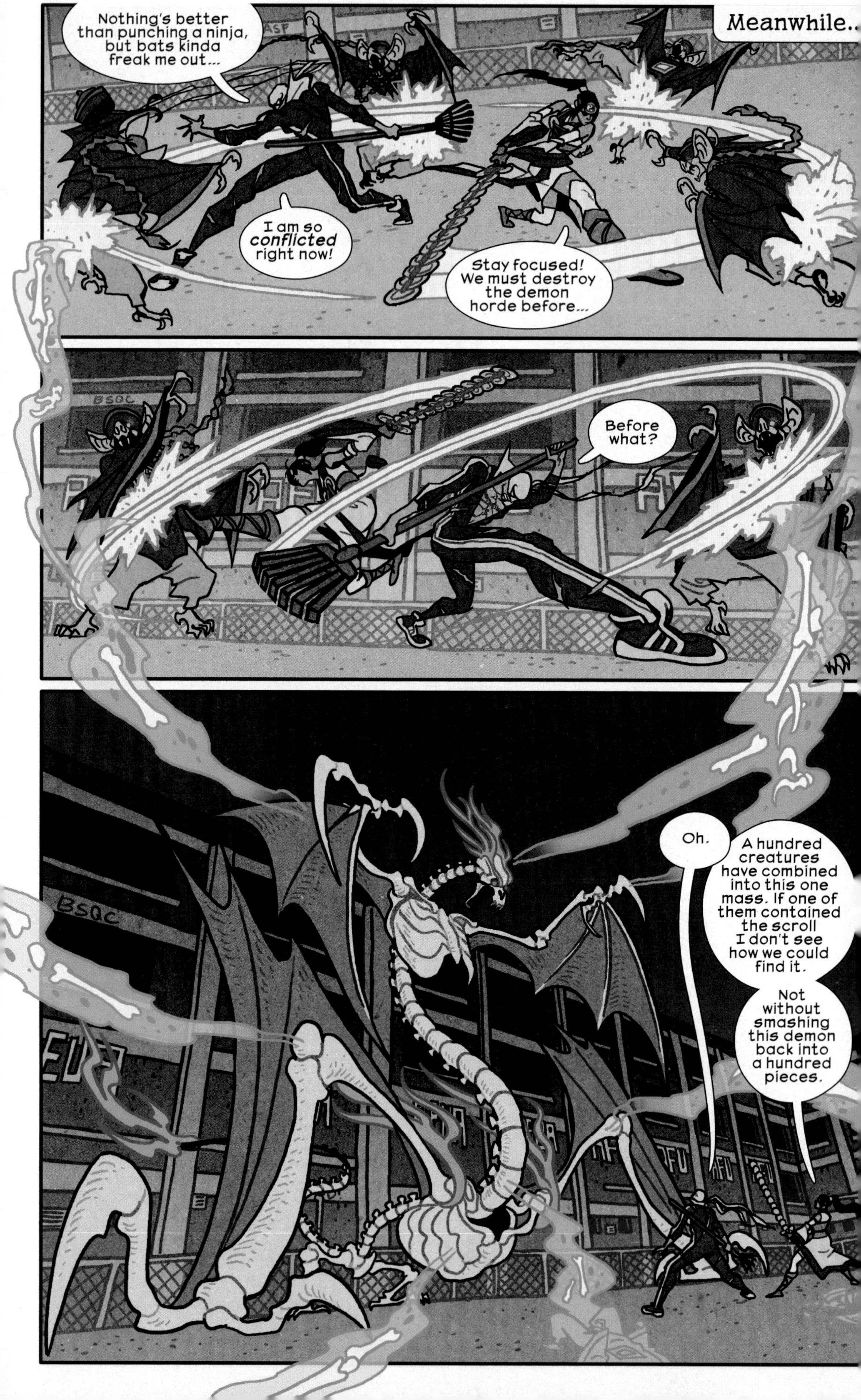
Meanwhile..
Nothing's better than punching a ninja, but bats kinda freak me out...
I am so conflicted right now!
Stay focused! We must destroy the demon horde before...
Before what?
Oh.
A hundred creatures have combined into this one mass. If one of them contained the scroll I don't see how we could find it.
Not without smashing this demon back into a hundred pieces.

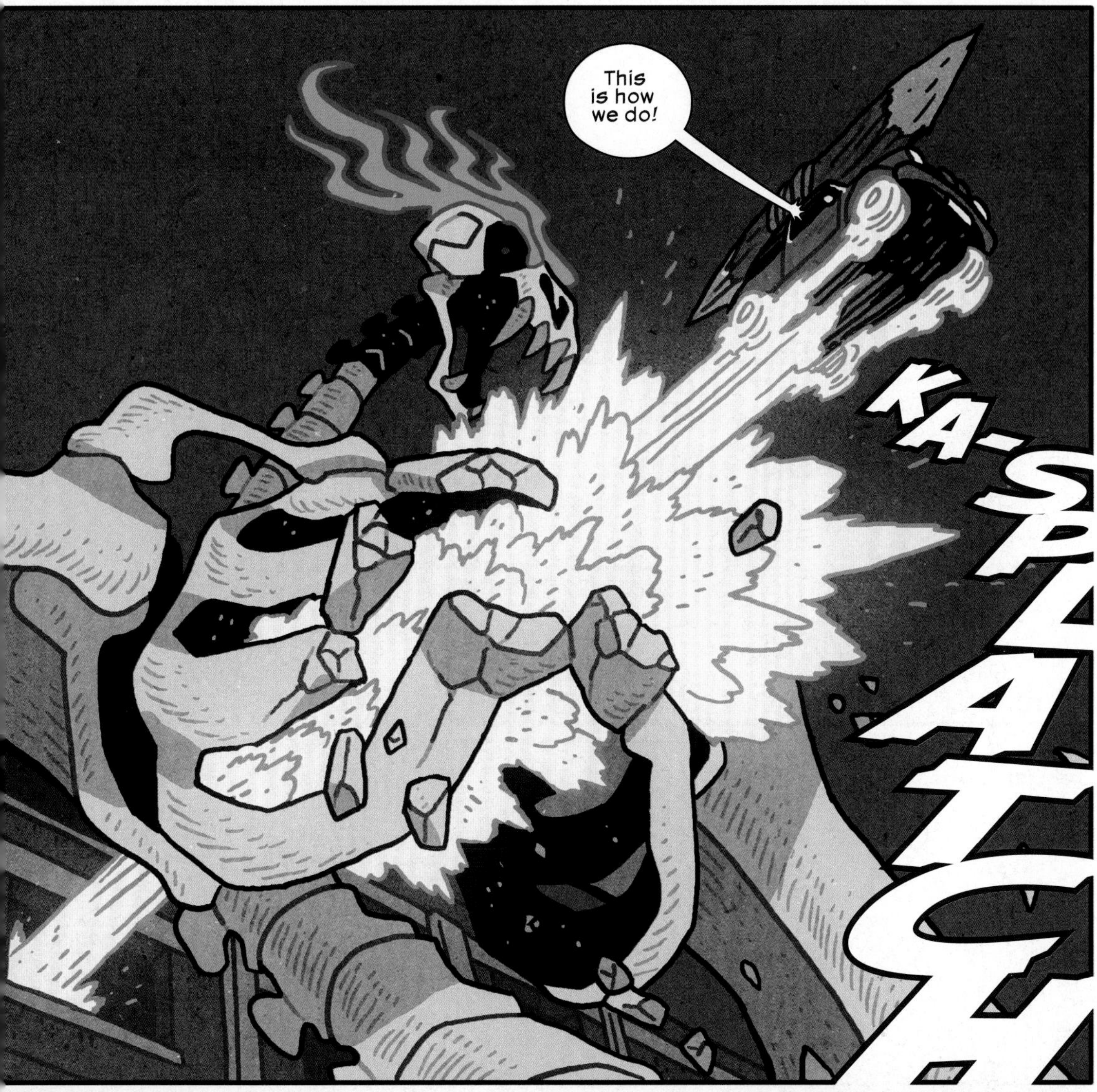
This is how we do!
KA-SPLATCH!

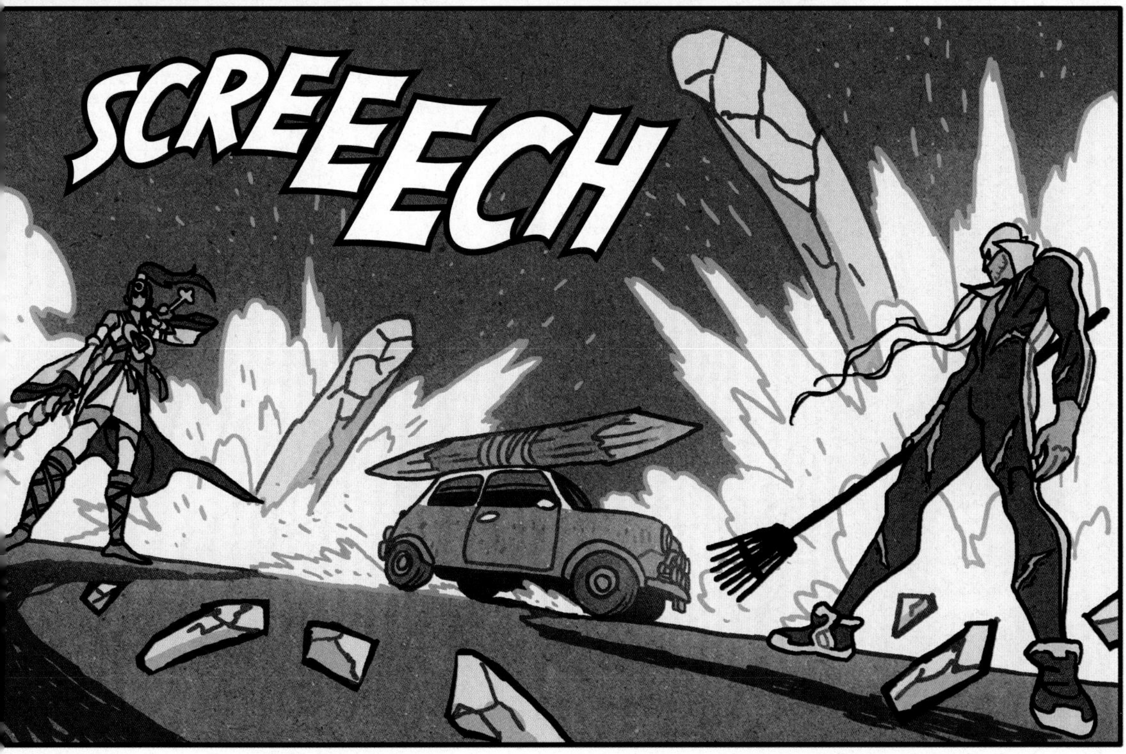
SCREEECH

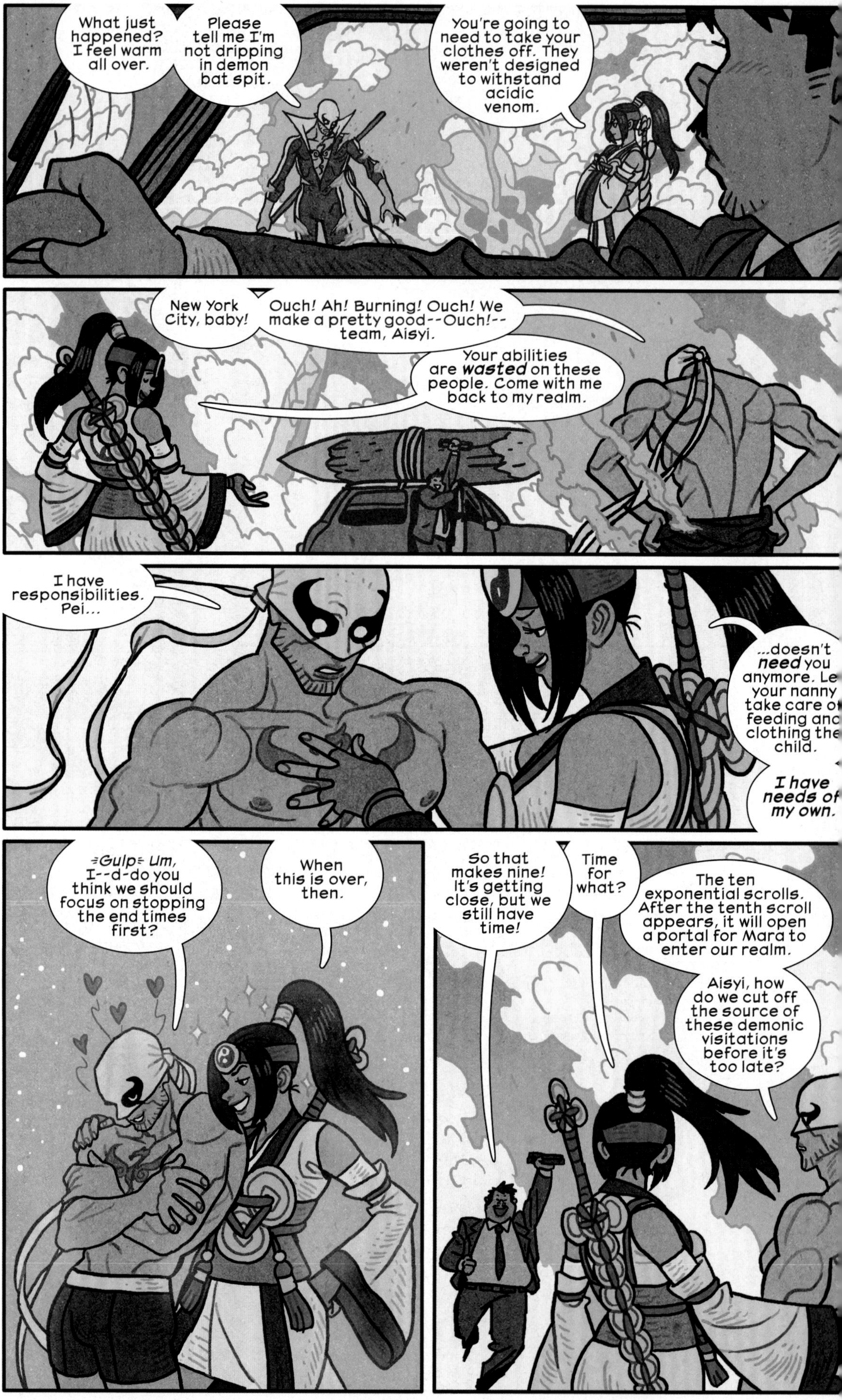
What just happened? I feel warm all over.
Please tell me I'm not dripping in demon bat spit.
You're going to need to take your clothes off. They weren't designed to withstand acidic venom.
New York City, baby!
Ouch! Ah! Burning! Ouch! We make a pretty good--Ouch!--team, Aisyi.
Your abilities are *wasted* on these people. Come with me back to my realm.
I have responsibilities. Pei...
...doesn't *need* you anymore. Le your nanny take care o feeding anc clothing the child.
I have needs of my own.
=Gulp= Um, I--d-do you think we should focus on stopping the end times first?
When this is over, then.
So that makes nine! It's getting close, but we still have time!
Time for what?
The ten exponential scrolls. After the tenth scroll appears, it will open a portal for Mara to enter our realm.
Aisyi, how do we cut off the source of these demonic visitations before it's too late?

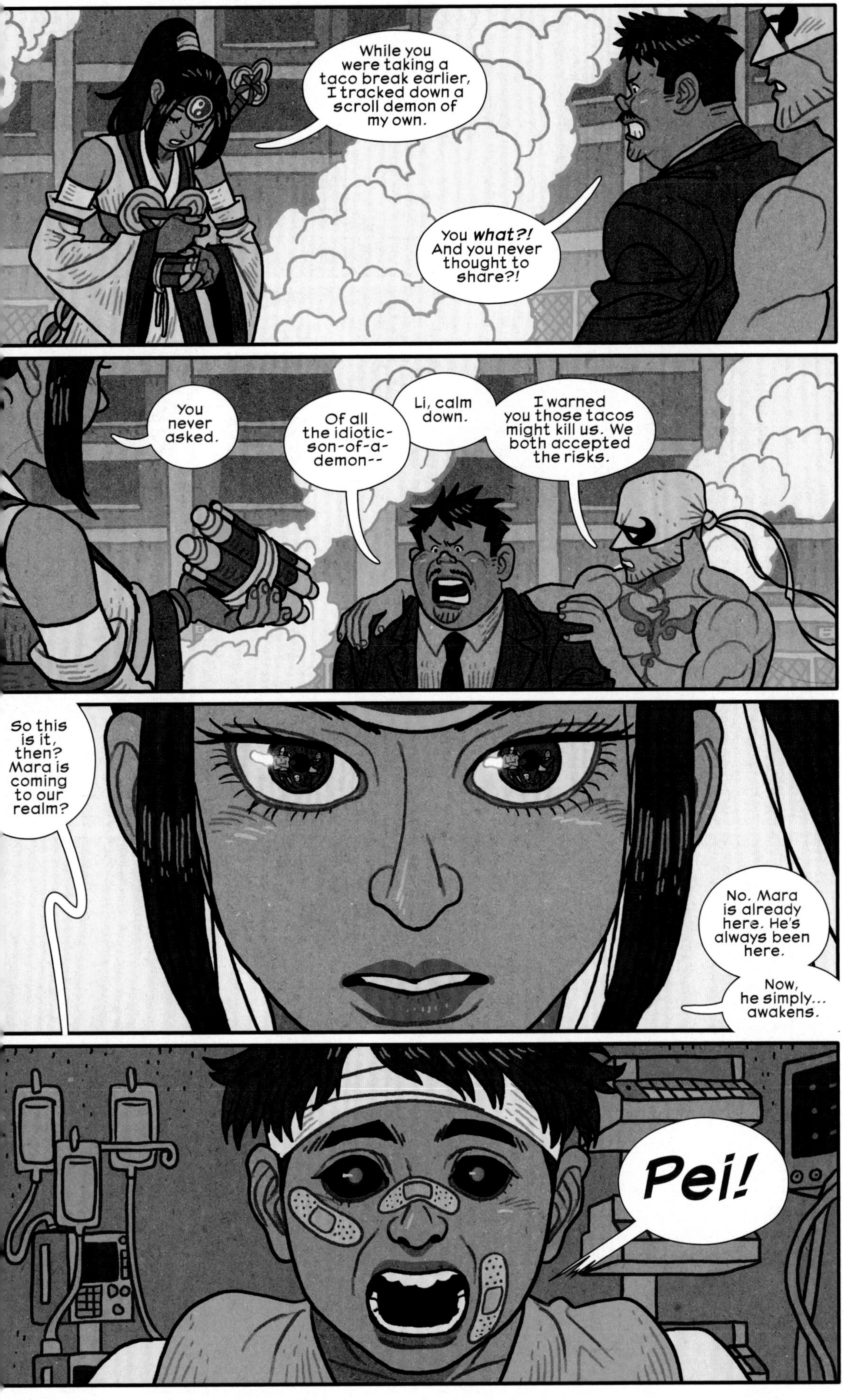

While you were taking a taco break earlier, I tracked down a scroll demon of my own.
You *what?!* And you never thought to share?!
You never asked.
Of all the idiotic-son-of-a-demon--
Li, calm down.
I warned you those tacos might kill us. We both accepted the risks.
So this is it, then? Mara is coming to our realm?
No. Mara is already here. He's always been here.
Now, he simply... awakens.
Pei!

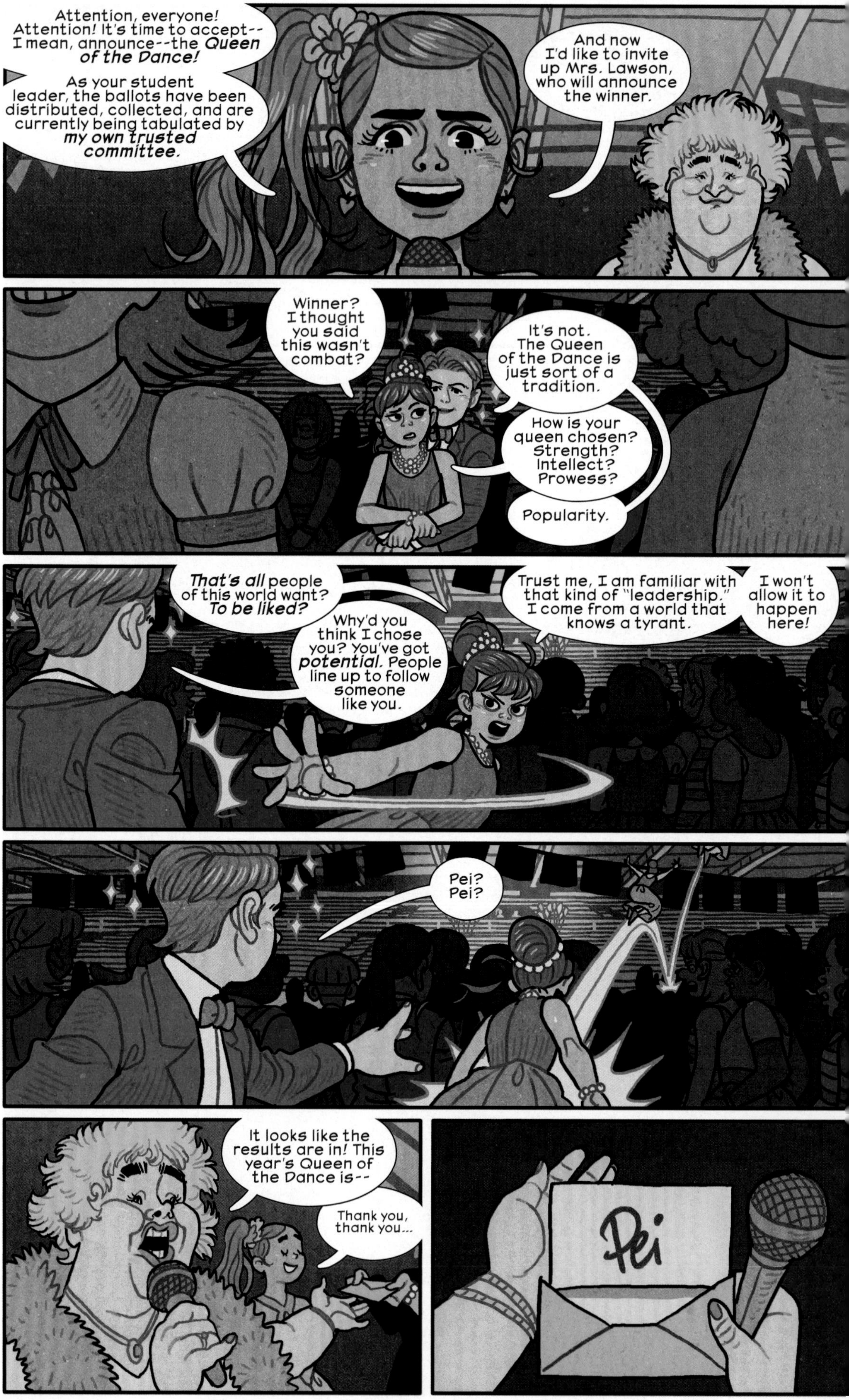

Attention, everyone! Attention! It's time to accept-- I mean, announce--the *Queen of the Dance!*
As your student leader, the ballots have been distributed, collected, and are currently being tabulated by **my own trusted committee.**
And now I'd like to invite up Mrs. Lawson, who will announce the winner.
Winner? I thought you said this wasn't combat?
It's not. The Queen of the Dance is just sort of a tradition.
How is your queen chosen? Strength? Intellect? Prowess?
Popularity.
That's all people of this world want? *To be liked?*
Why'd you think I chose you? You've got **potential.** People line up to follow someone like you.
Trust me, I am familiar with that kind of "leadership." I come from a world that knows a tyrant.
I won't allow it to happen here!
Pei? Pei?
It looks like the results are in! This year's Queen of the Dance is--
Thank you, thank you...
Pei

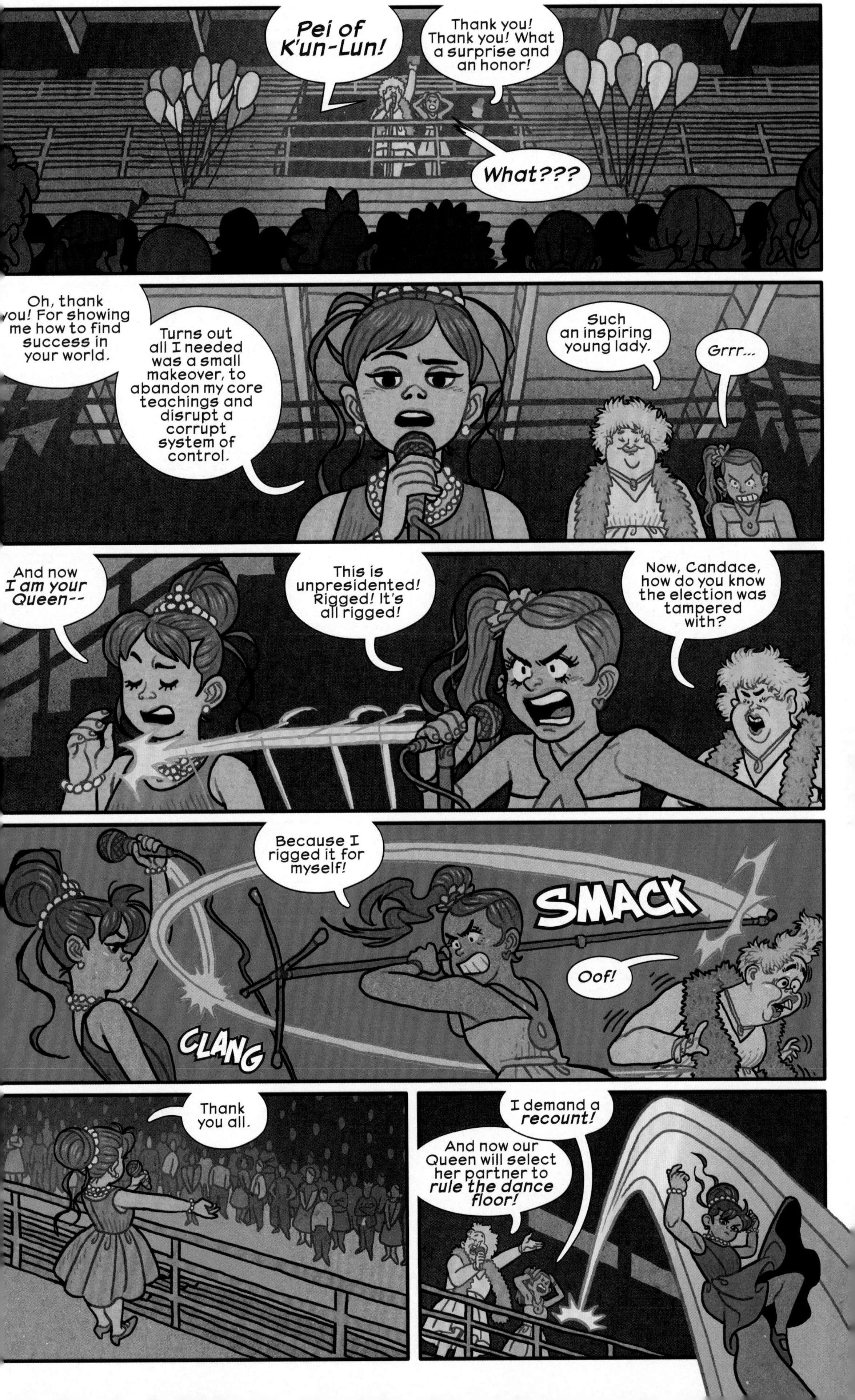
Pei of K'un-Lun!
Thank you! Thank you! What a surprise and an honor!
What???
Oh, thank you! For showing me how to find success in your world.
Turns out all I needed was a small makeover, to abandon my core teachings and disrupt a corrupt system of control.
Such an inspiring young lady.
Grrr...
And now I am your Queen--
This is unpresidented! Rigged! It's all rigged!
Now, Candace, how do you know the election was tampered with?
Because I rigged it for myself!
SMACK
Oof!
CLANG
Thank you all.
I demand a recount!
And now our Queen will select her partner to rule the dance floor!

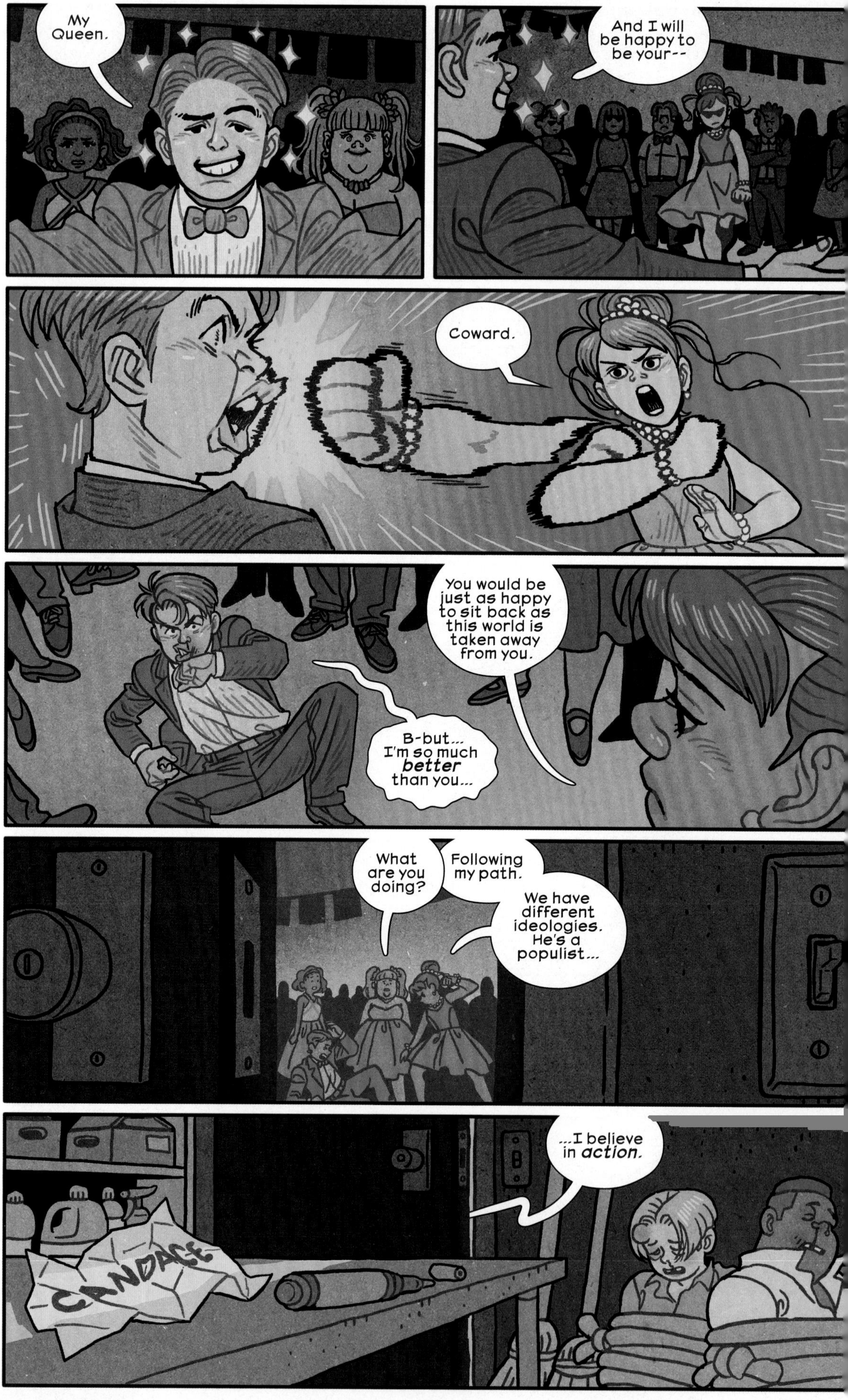
My Queen.
And I will be happy to be your--
Coward.
You would be just as happy to sit back as this world is taken away from you.
B-but... I'm so much *better* than you...
What are you doing?
Following my path.
We have different ideologies. He's a populist...
...I believe in *action.*
CANDACE

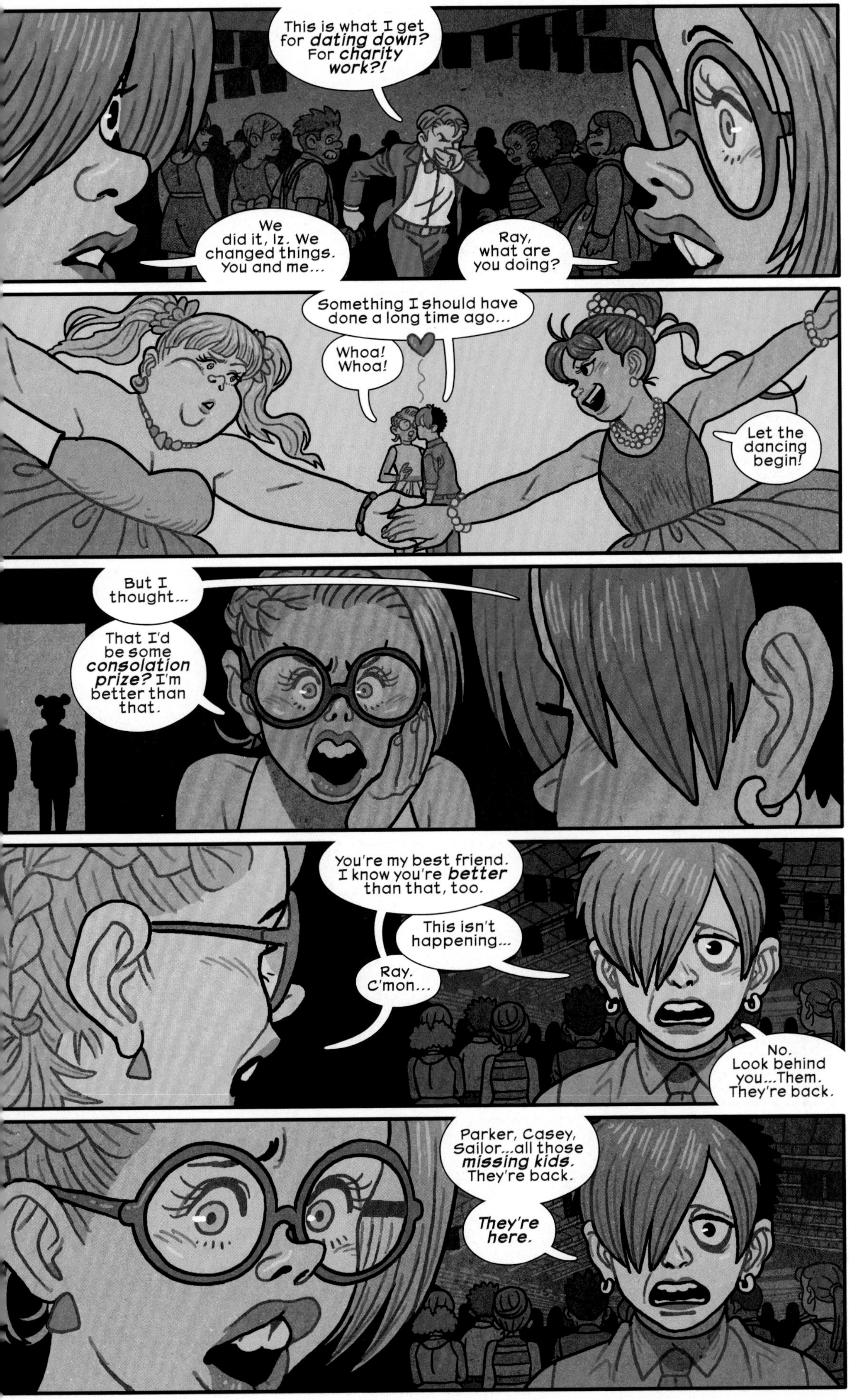
This is what I get for *dating down?* For *charity work?!*
We did it, Iz. We changed things. You and me...
Ray, what are you doing?
Something I should have done a long time ago...
Whoa! Whoa!
Let the dancing begin!
But I thought...
That I'd be some *consolation prize?* I'm better than that.
You're my best friend. I know you're *better* than that, too.
This isn't happening...
Ray. C'mon...
No. Look behind you...Them. They're back.
Parker, Casey, Sailor...all those *missing kids.* They're back.
They're here.

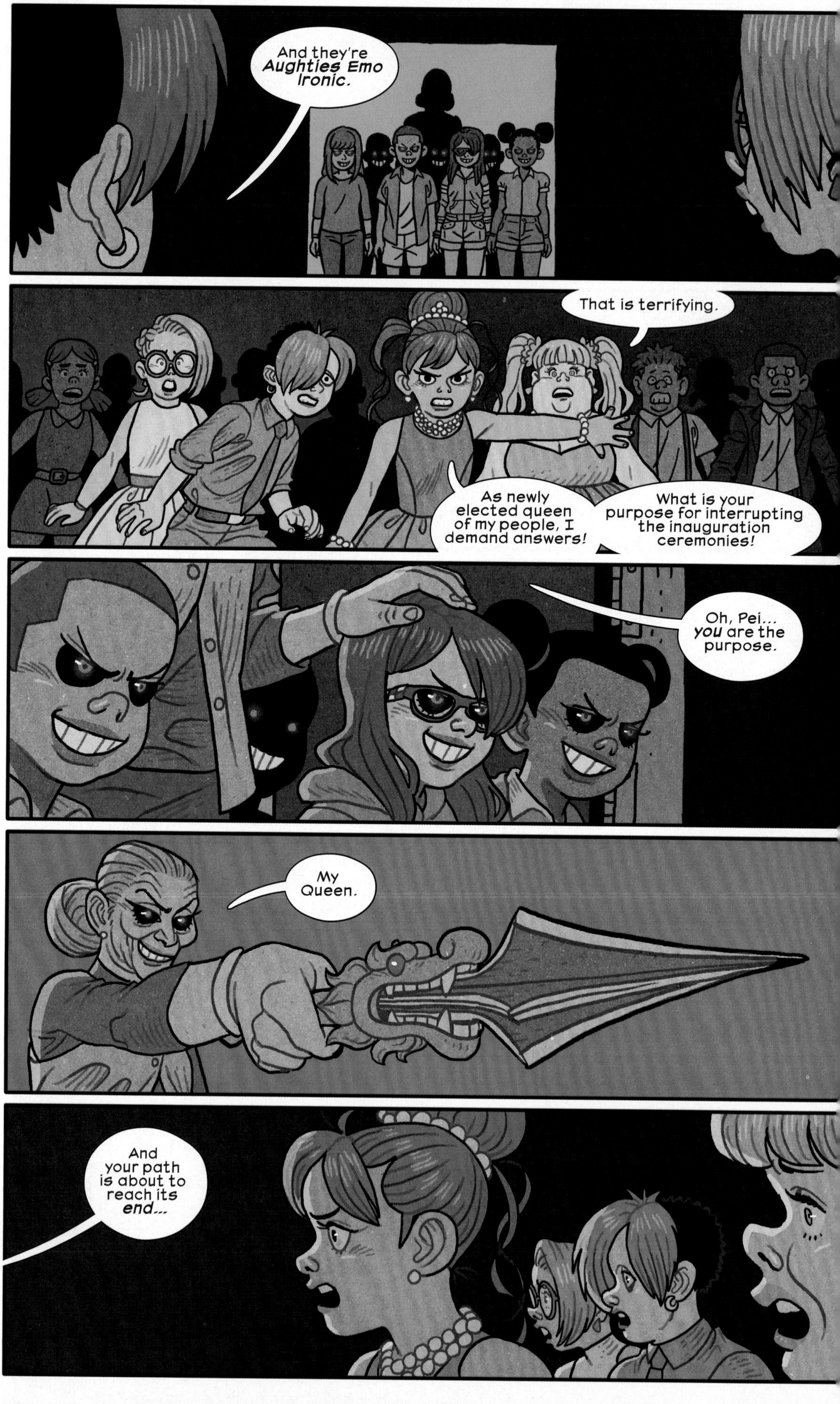

And they're *Aughties Emo Ironic.*
That is terrifying.
As newly elected queen of my people, I demand answers!
What is your purpose for interrupting the inauguration ceremonies!
Oh, Pei... *you* are the purpose.
My Queen.
And your path is about to reach its *end...*

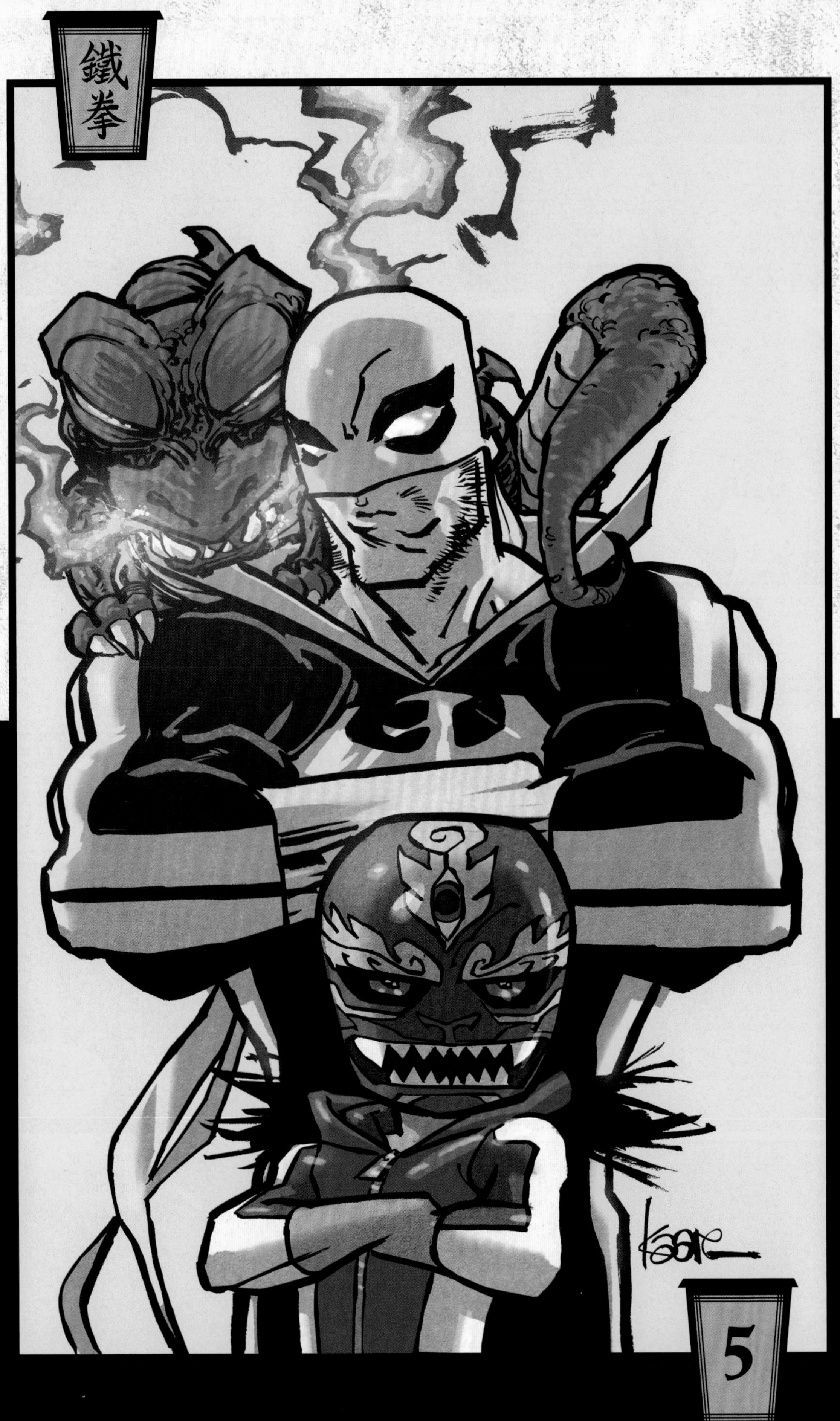
鐵拳
5

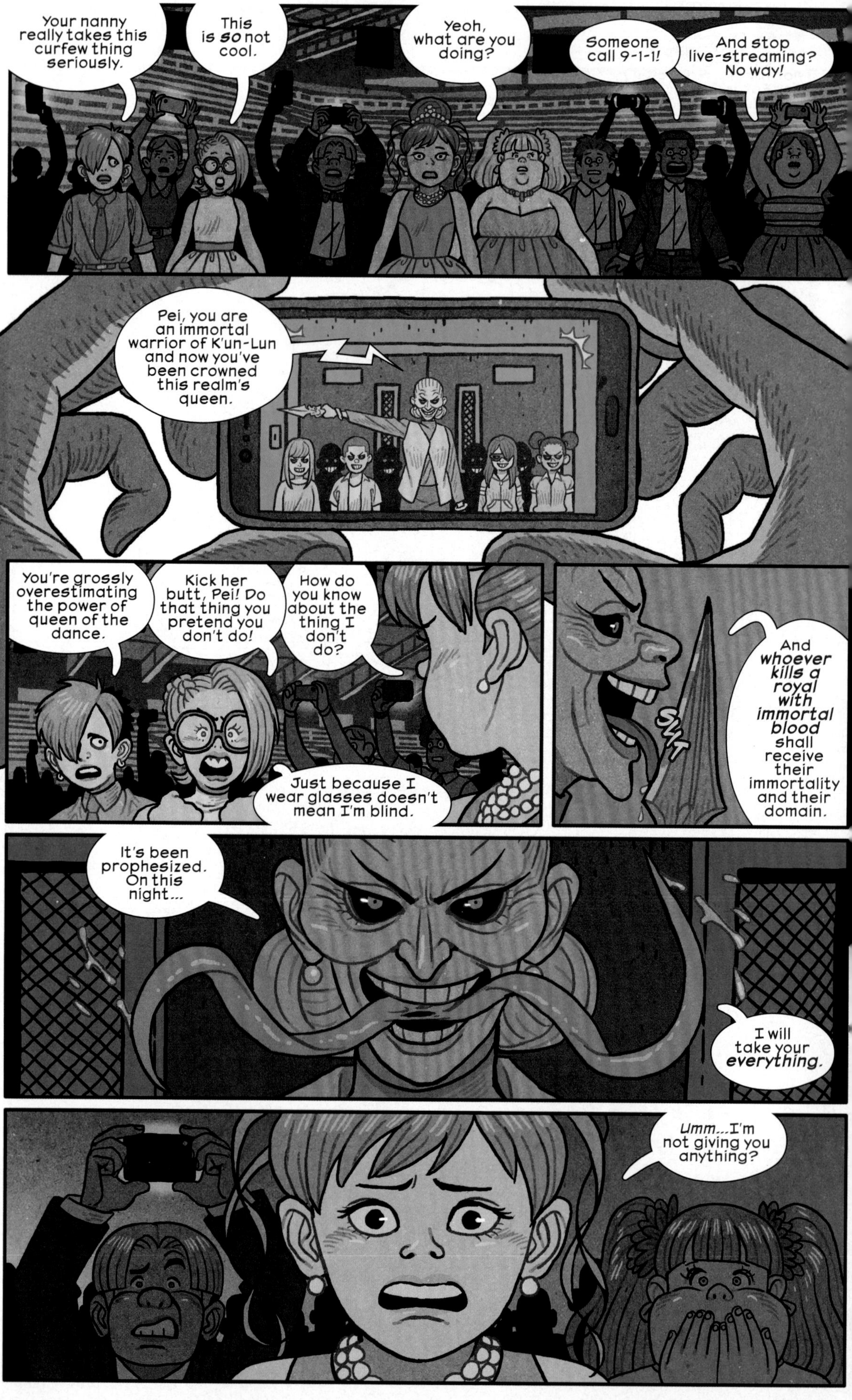
Your nanny really takes this curfew thing seriously.
This is *so* not cool.
Yeoh, what are you doing?
Someone call 9-1-1!
And stop live-streaming? No way!
Pei, you are an immortal warrior of K'un-Lun and now you've been crowned this realm's queen.
You're grossly overestimating the power of queen of the dance.
Kick her butt, Pei! Do that thing you pretend you don't do!
How do you know about the thing I don't do?
Just because I wear glasses doesn't mean I'm blind.
And *whoever kills a royal with immortal blood* shall receive their immortality and their domain.
SLIT
It's been prophesized. On this night...
I will take your *everything.*
Umm... I'm not giving you anything?

Oh, it's not for me. It's for Father. He intends to visit your world for a very long time.

I am a daughter of Mara. And he hungers for this world. He just needs a ticket.

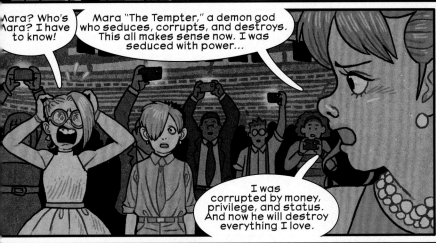

Mara? Who's Mara? I have to know!

Mara "The Tempter," a demon god who seduces, corrupts, and destroys. This all makes sense now. I was seduced with power...

I was corrupted by money, privilege, and status. And now he will destroy everything I love.

You *had* to know.

I could give a bubbling *shui gui* about your friends.

I'm just going to destroy *you.*

Whew! We're safe! Oh, but Pei isn't! Oh no! I'm so conflicted right now.

Don't worry. After Mara destroys me, she'll enslave *the world!*

You *had* to know.

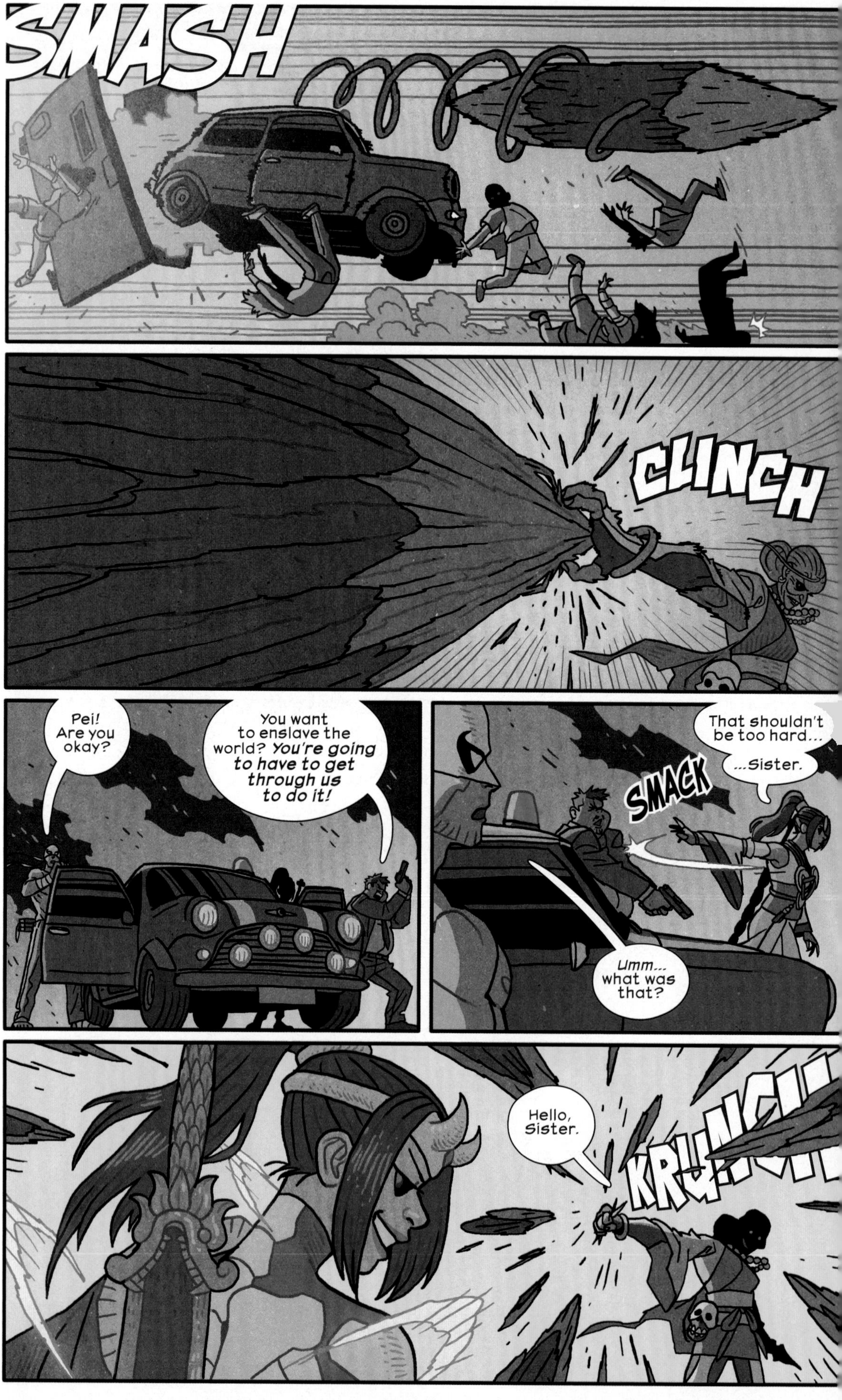
SMASH
CLINCH
Pei! Are you okay?
You want to enslave the world? *You're going to have to get through us to do it!*
That shouldn't be too hard...
SMACK
...Sister.
Umm... what was that?
Hello, Sister.
KRUNCH

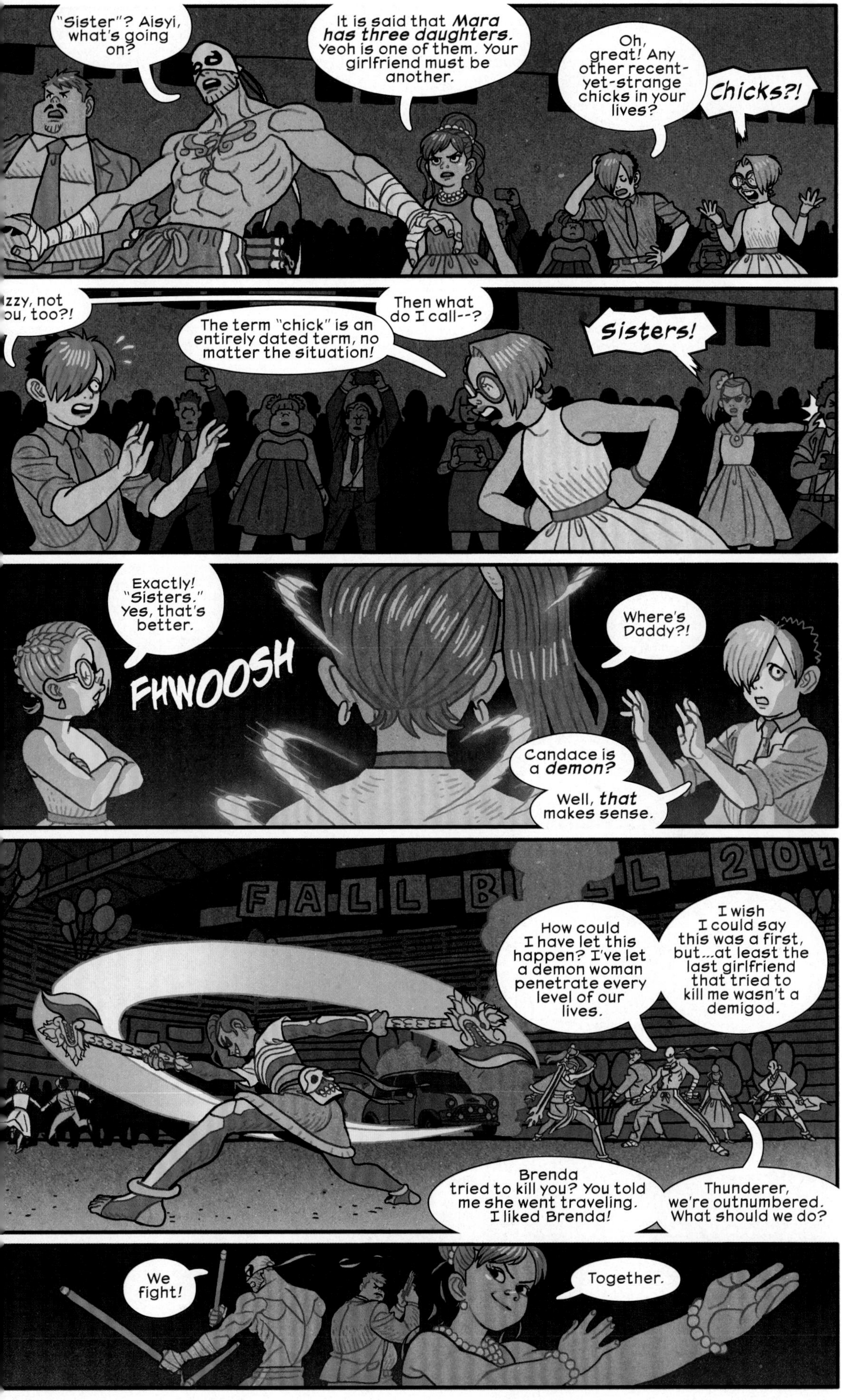
"Sister"? Aisyi, what's going on?
It is said that *Mara* ***has three daughters.*** Yeoh is one of them. Your girlfriend must be another.
Oh, great! Any other recent-yet-strange chicks in your lives?
Chicks?!
zzy, not ou, too?!
The term "chick" is an entirely dated term, no matter the situation!
Then what do I call--?
Sisters!
Exactly! "Sisters." Yes, that's better.
FHWOOSH
Where's Daddy?!
Candace is a *demon?*
Well, ***that*** makes *sense.*
FALL B LL 201
How could I have let this happen? I've let a demon woman penetrate every level of our lives.
I wish I could say this was a first, but...at least the last girlfriend that tried to kill me wasn't a *demigod.*
Brenda tried to kill you? You told me she went traveling. I liked Brenda!
Thunderer, we're outnumbered. What should we do?
We fight!
Together.

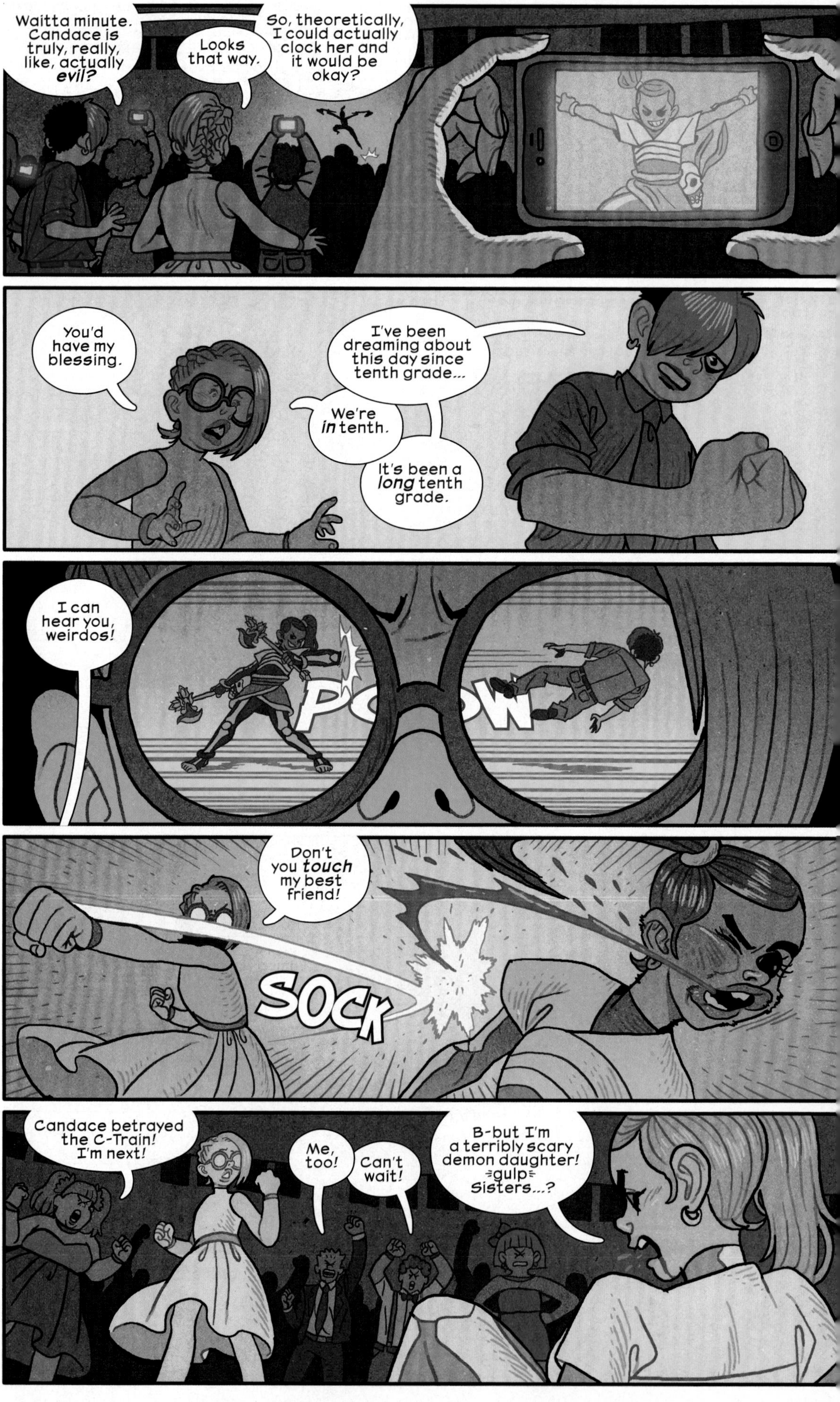
Waitta minute. Candace is truly, really, like, actually evil?
Looks that way.
So, theoretically, I could actually clock her and it would be okay?
You'd have my blessing.
I've been dreaming about this day since tenth grade...
We're in tenth.
It's been a long tenth grade.
I can hear you, weirdos!
POW
Don't you touch my best friend!
SOCK
Candace betrayed the C-Train! I'm next!
Me, too!
Can't wait!
B-but I'm a terribly scary demon daughter! gulp Sisters...?

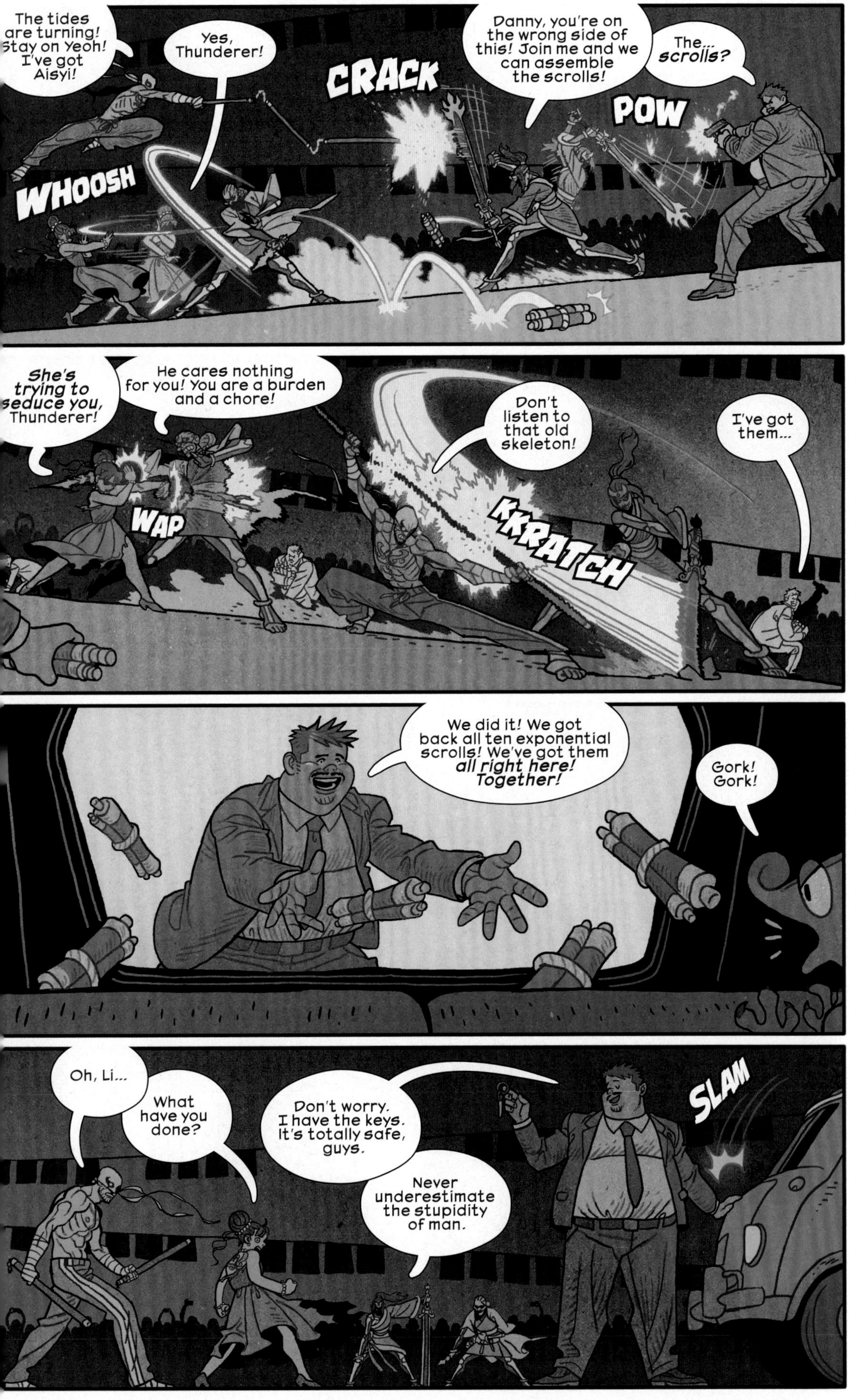
The tides are turning! Stay on Yeoh! I've got Aisyi!
Yes, Thunderer!
CRACK
Danny, you're on the wrong side of this! Join me and we can assemble the scrolls!
The... scrolls?
POW
WHOOSH
She's trying to seduce you, Thunderer!
He cares nothing for you! You are a burden and a chore!
Don't listen to that old skeleton!
I've got them...
WAP
KKRATCH
We did it! We got back all ten exponential scrolls! We've got them all right here! Together!
Gork! Gork!
Oh, Li...
What have you done?
Don't worry. I have the keys. It's totally safe, guys.
Never underestimate the stupidity of man.
SLAM

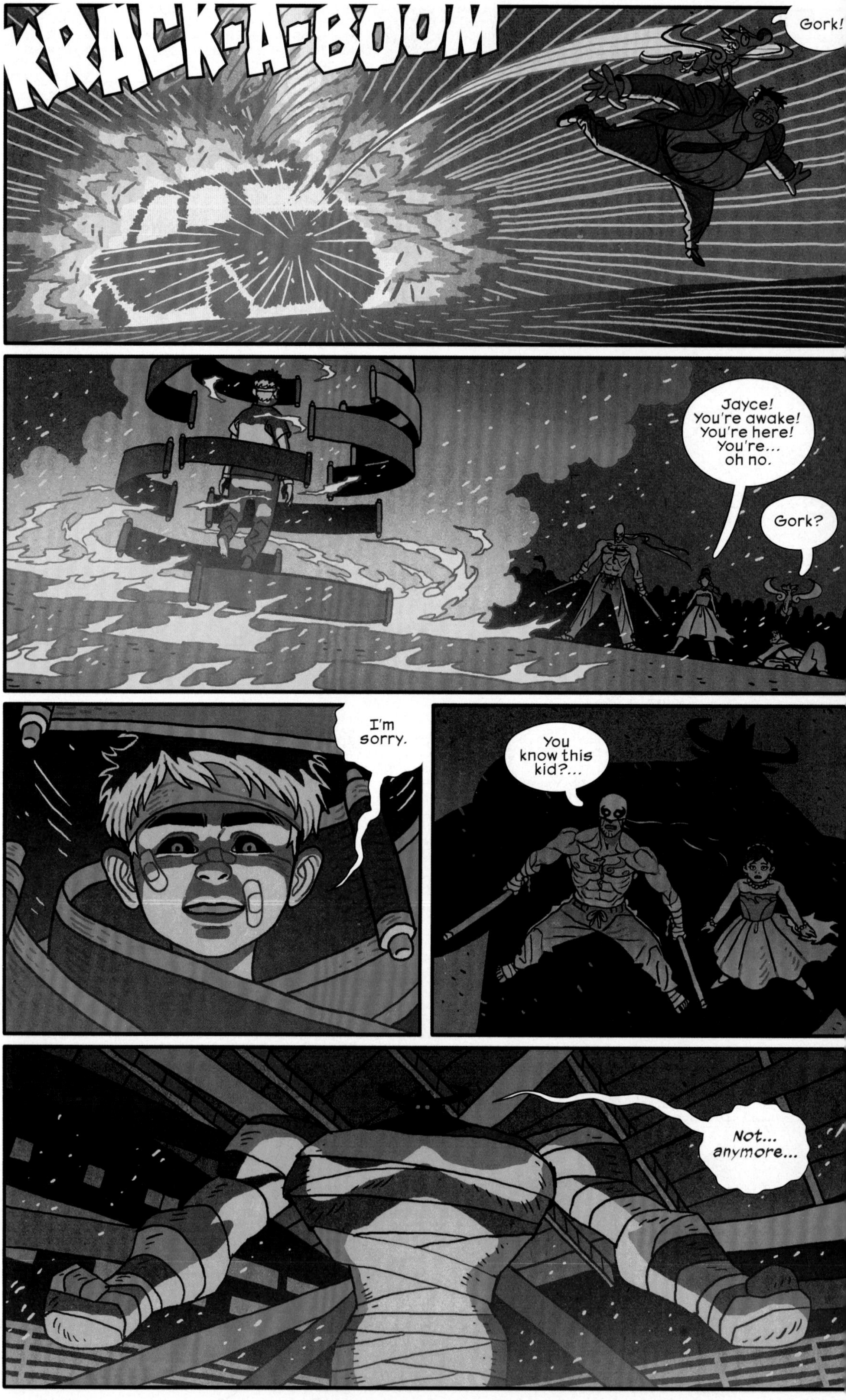
KRACK-A-BOOM
Gork!
Jayce! You're awake! You're here! You're... oh no.
Gork?
I'm sorry.
You know this kid?...
Not... anymore...

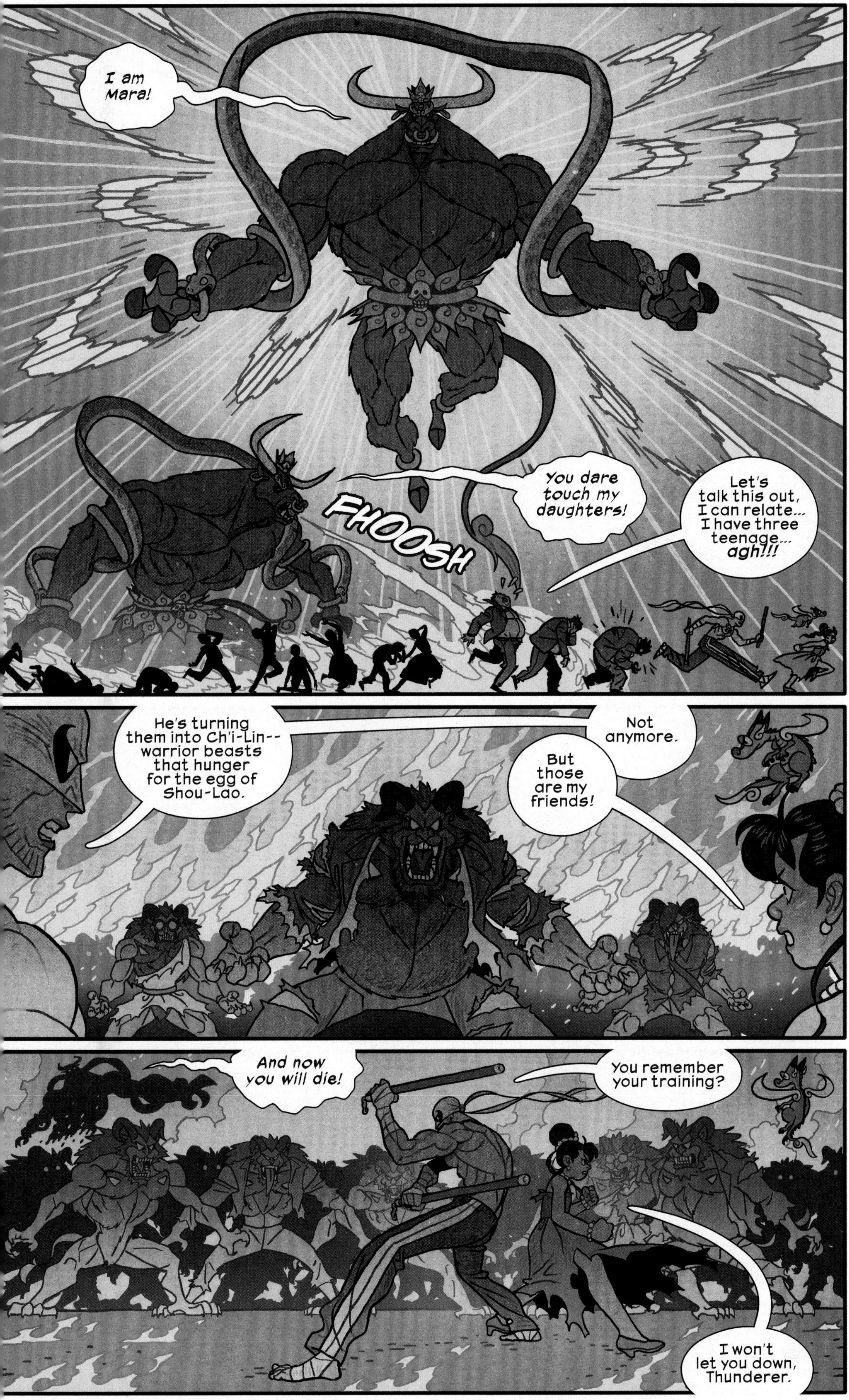
I am Mara!
FHOOSH
You dare touch my daughters!
Let's talk this out, I can relate... I have three teenage... agh!!!
He's turning them into Ch'i-Lin--warrior beasts that hunger for the egg of Shou-Lao.
Not anymore.
But those are my friends!
And now you will die!
You remember your training?
I won't let you down, Thunderer.

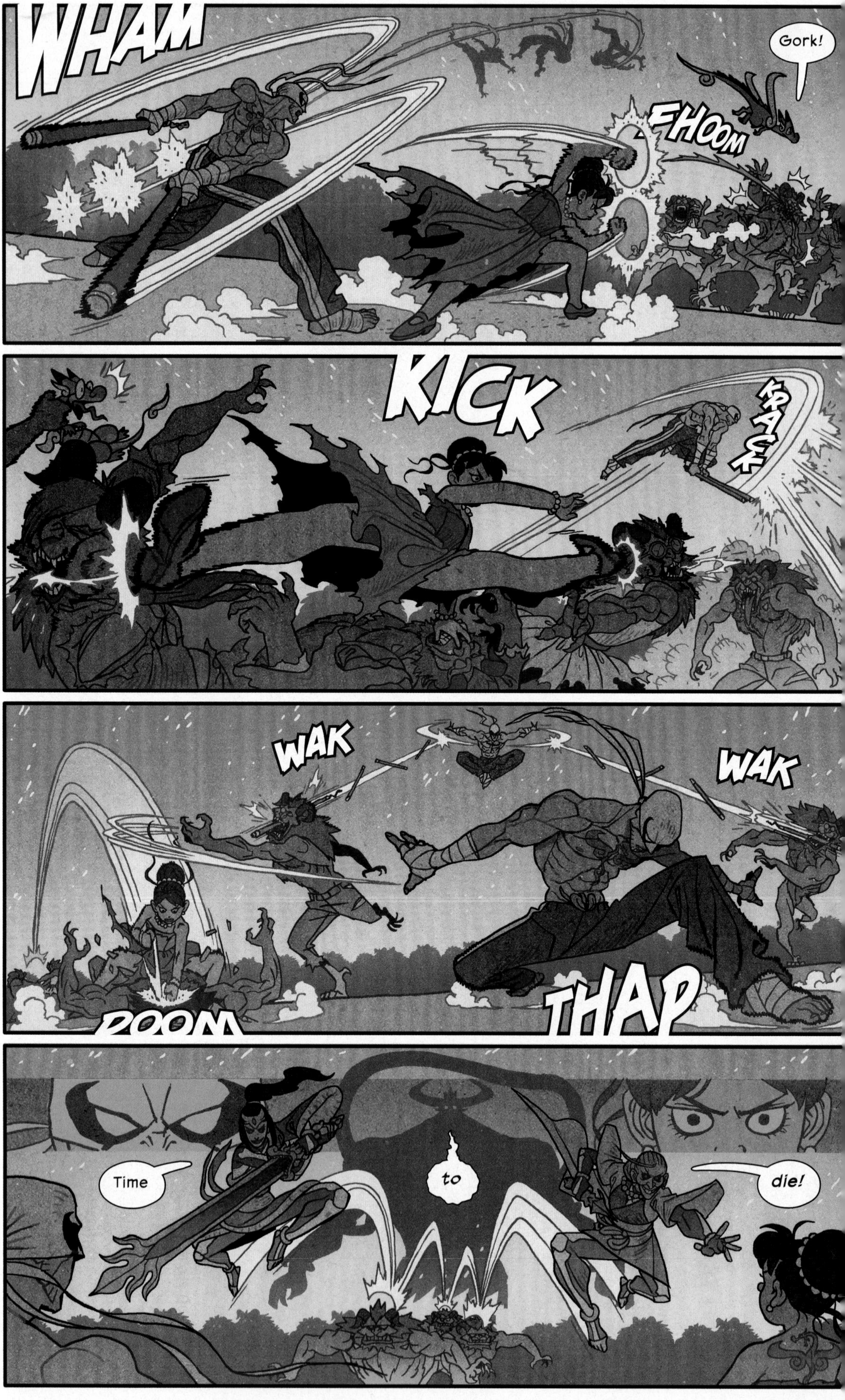
WHAM
Gork!
FHOOM
KICK
KRACK
WAK
WAK
THAP
Time
to
die!

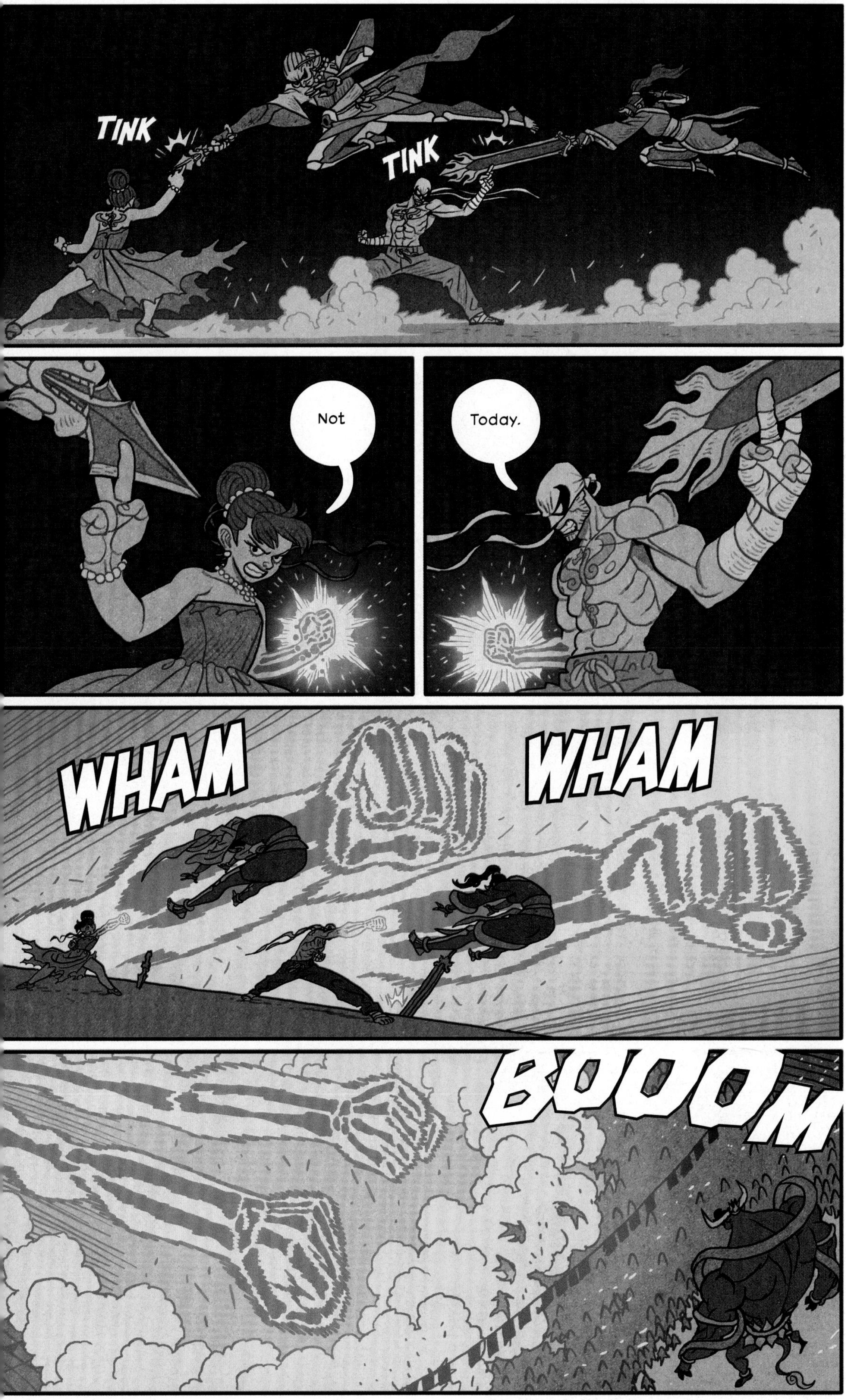
TINK
TINK
Not
Today.
WHAM
WHAM
BOOOM

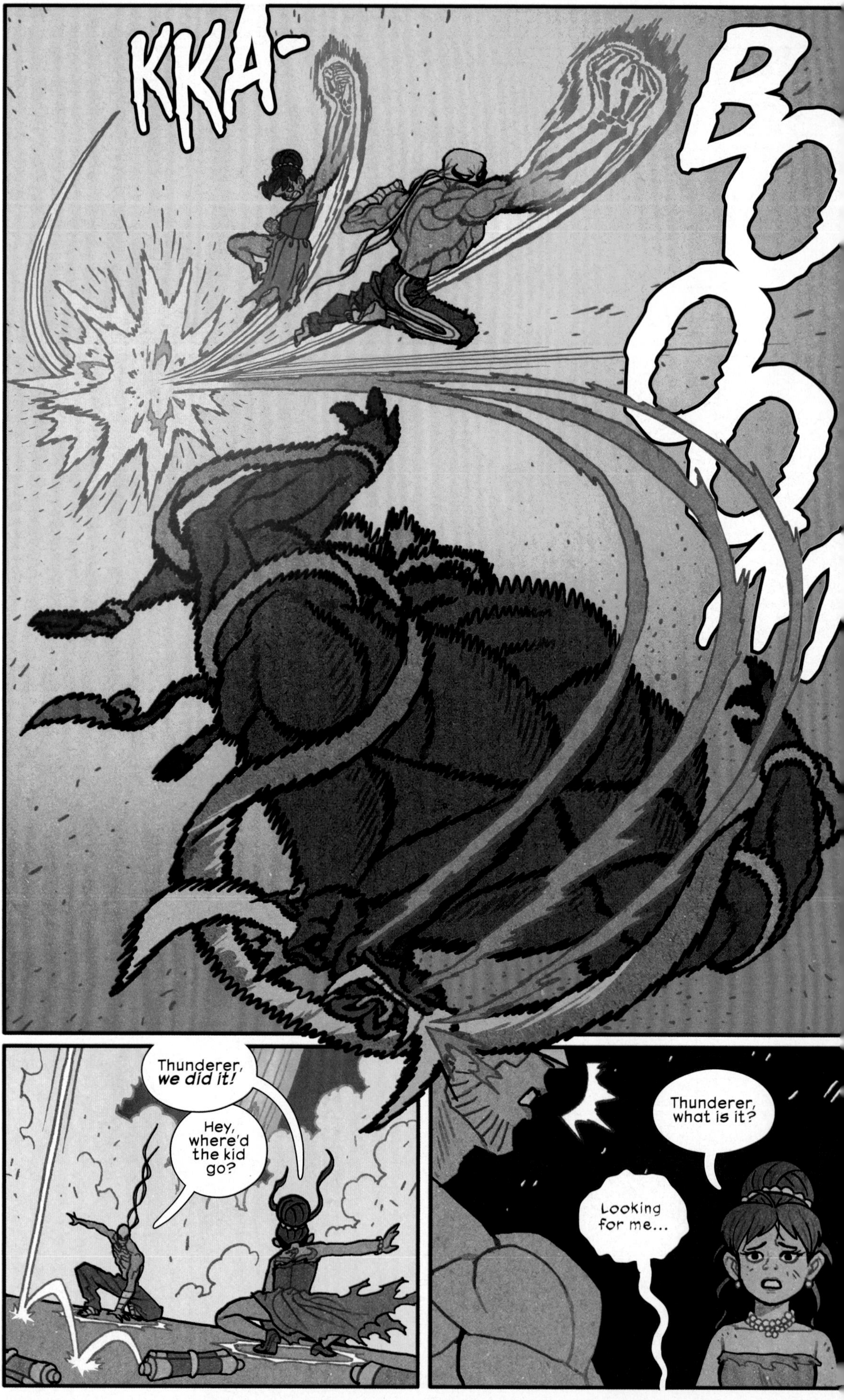
KKA-
BOOOM
Thunderer, we did it!
Hey, where'd the kid go?
Thunderer, what is it?
Looking for me...

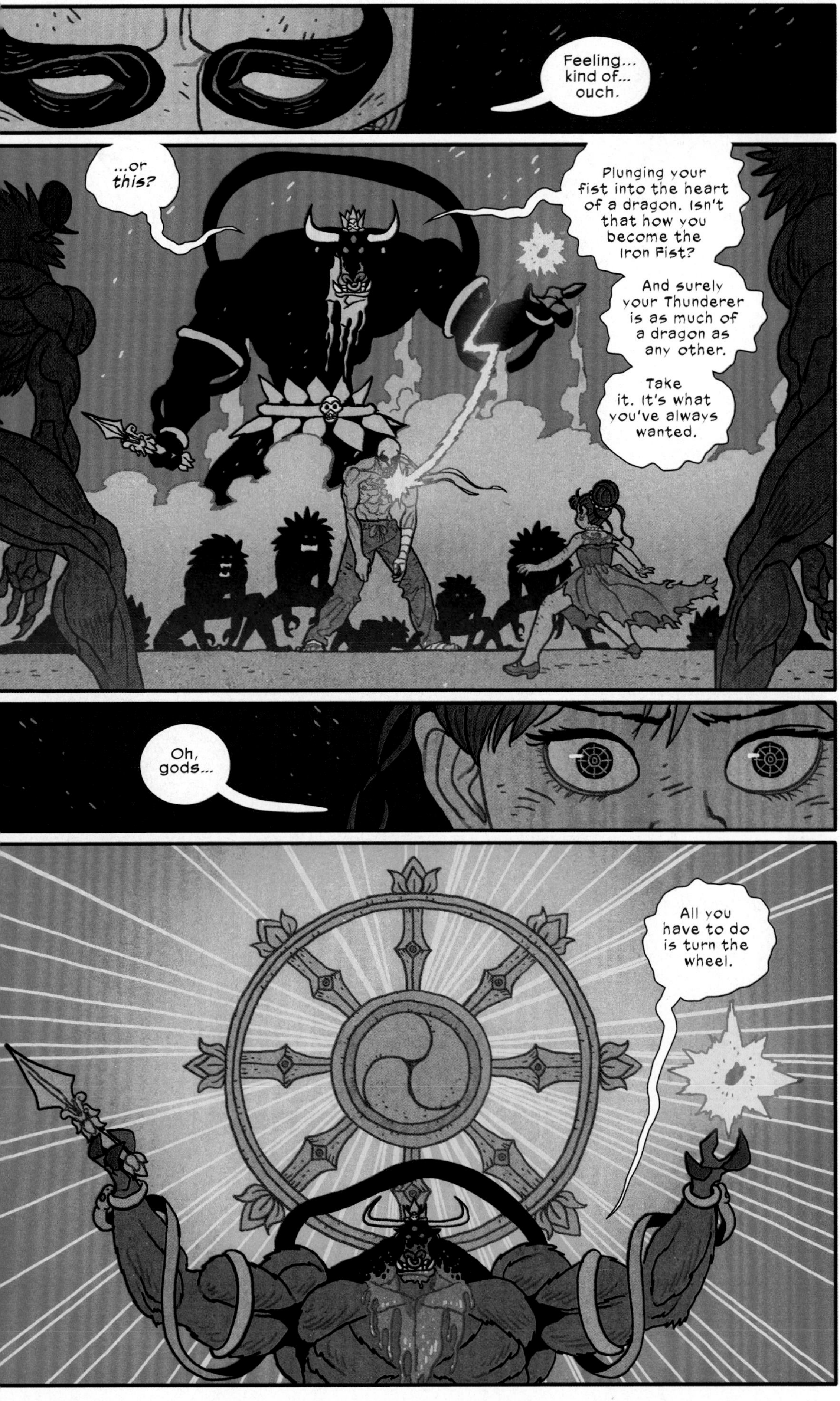
Feeling... kind of... ouch.
...or *this?*
Plunging your fist into the heart of a dragon. Isn't that how you become the Iron Fist?
And surely your Thunderer is as much of a dragon as any other.
Take it. It's what you've always wanted.
Oh, gods...
All you have to do is turn the wheel.

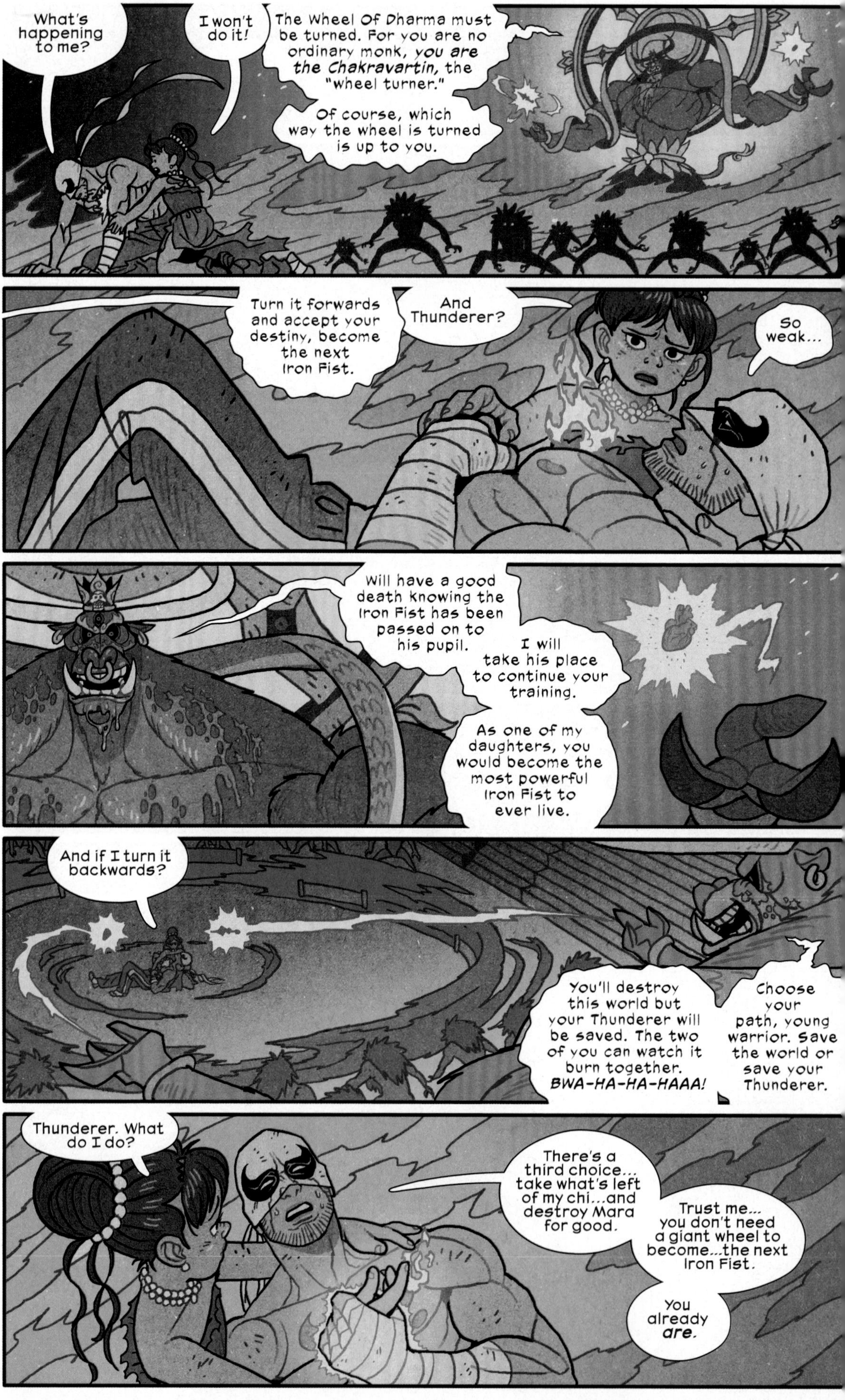
What's happening to me?
I won't do it!
The Wheel Of Dharma must be turned. For you are no ordinary monk, *you are the Chakravartin,* the "wheel turner."
Of course, which way the wheel is turned is up to you.
Turn it forwards and accept your destiny, become the next Iron Fist.
And Thunderer?
So weak...
Will have a good death knowing the Iron Fist has been passed on to his pupil.
I will take his place to continue your training.
As one of my daughters, you would become the most powerful Iron Fist to ever live.
And if I turn it backwards?
You'll destroy this world but your Thunderer will be saved. The two of you can watch it burn together. *BWA-HA-HA-HAAA!*
Choose your path, young warrior. Save the world or save your Thunderer.
Thunderer. What do I do?
There's a third choice... take what's left of my chi...and destroy Mara for good.
Trust me... you don't need a giant wheel to become...the next Iron Fist.
You already *are.*

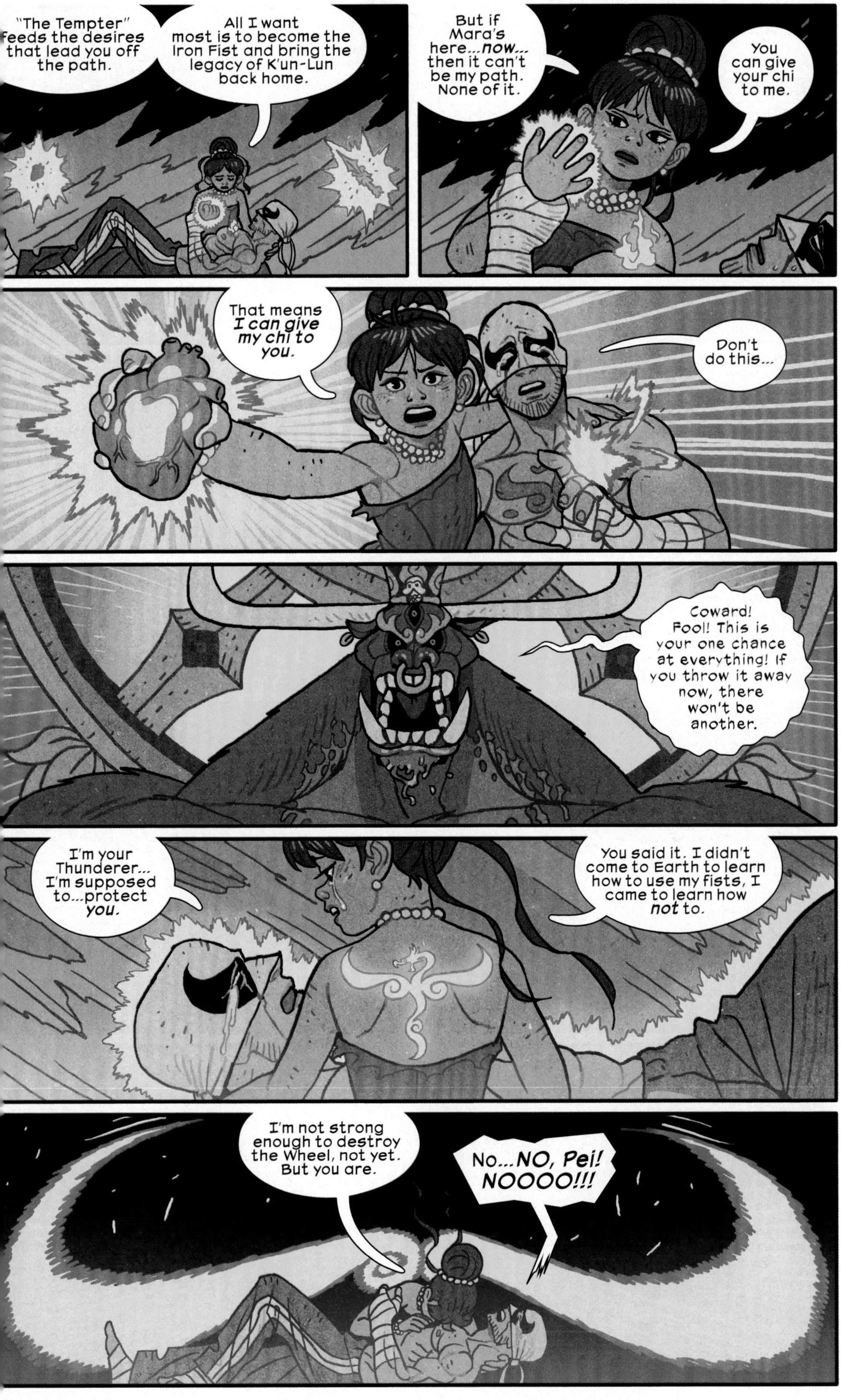
"The Tempter" feeds the desires that lead you off the path.
All I want most is to become the Iron Fist and bring the legacy of K'un-Lun back home.
But if Mara's here...*now*... then it can't be my path. None of it.
You can give your chi to me.
That means *I can give my chi to you.*
Don't do this...
Coward! Fool! This is your one chance at everything! If you throw it away now, there won't be another.
I'm your Thunderer... I'm supposed to...protect *you.*
You said it. I didn't come to Earth to learn how to use my fists, I came to learn how *not* to.
I'm not strong enough to destroy the Wheel, not yet. But you are.
No...*NO, Pei! NOOOO!!!*

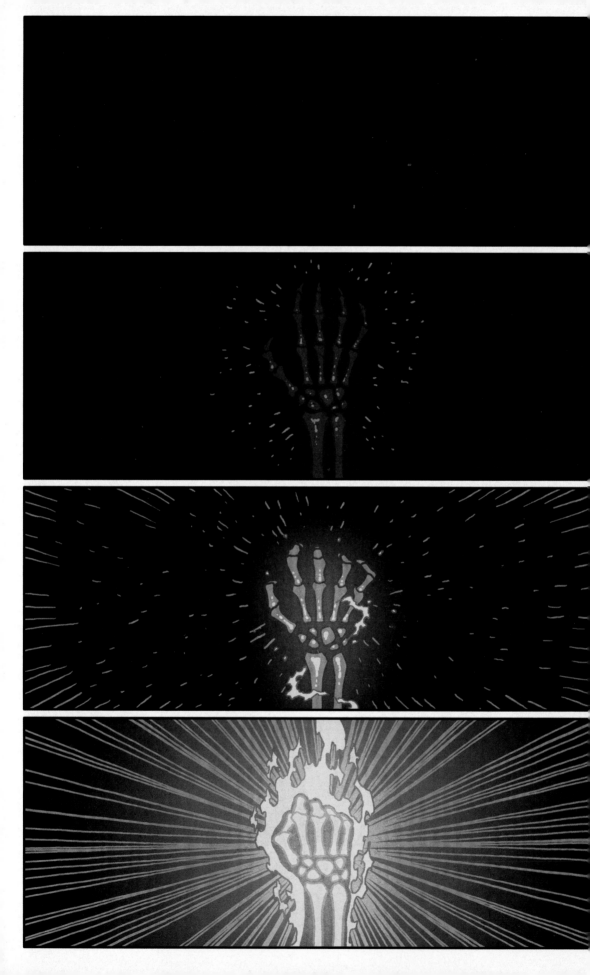

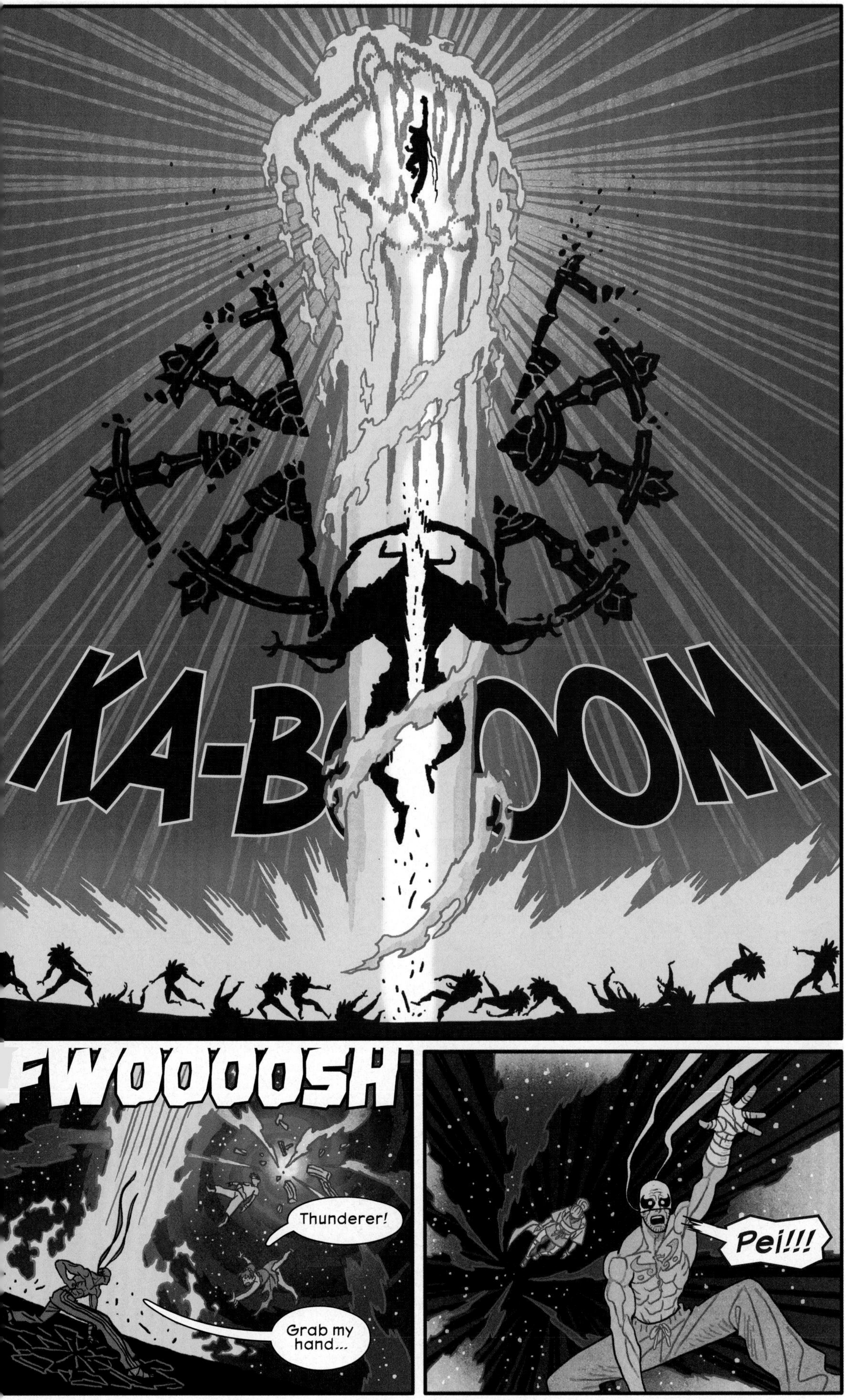
KA-B OOM
FWOOOOSH
Thunderer!
Grab my hand...
Pei!!!

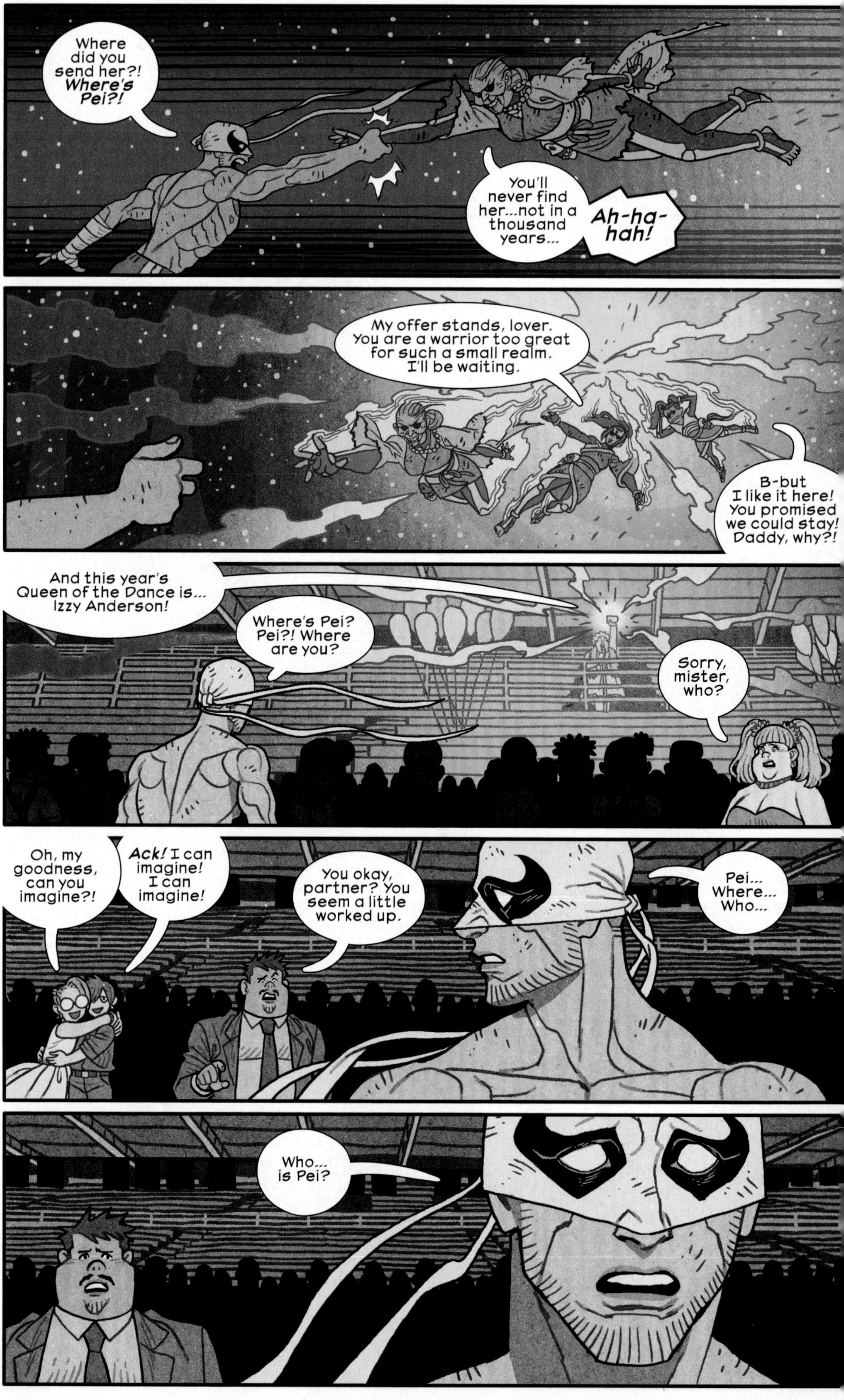

Where did you send her?! Where's Pei?!
You'll never find her...not in a thousand years...
Ah-ha-hah!
My offer stands, lover. You are a warrior too great for such a small realm. I'll be waiting.
B-but I like it here! You promised we could stay! Daddy, why?!
And this year's Queen of the Dance is... Izzy Anderson!
Where's Pei? Pei?! Where are you?
Sorry, mister, who?
Oh, my goodness, can you imagine?!
Ack! I can imagine! I can imagine!
You okay, partner? You seem a little worked up.
Pei... Where... Who...
Who... is Pei?

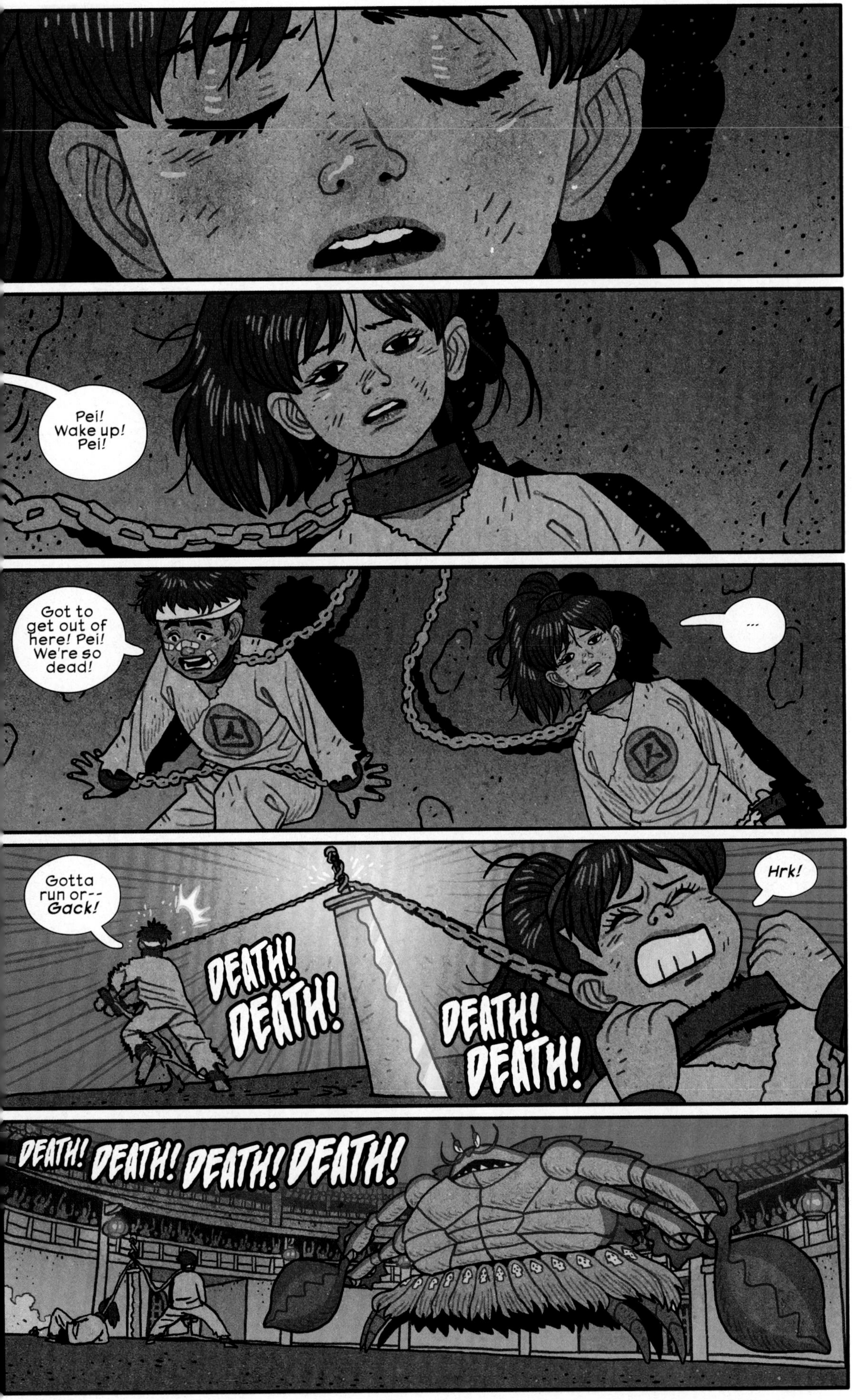
Pei! Wake up! Pei!
Got to get out of here! Pei! We're so dead!
...
Gotta run or-- Gack!
Hrk!
DEATH! DEATH!
DEATH! DEATH!
DEATH! DEATH! DEATH! DEATH!

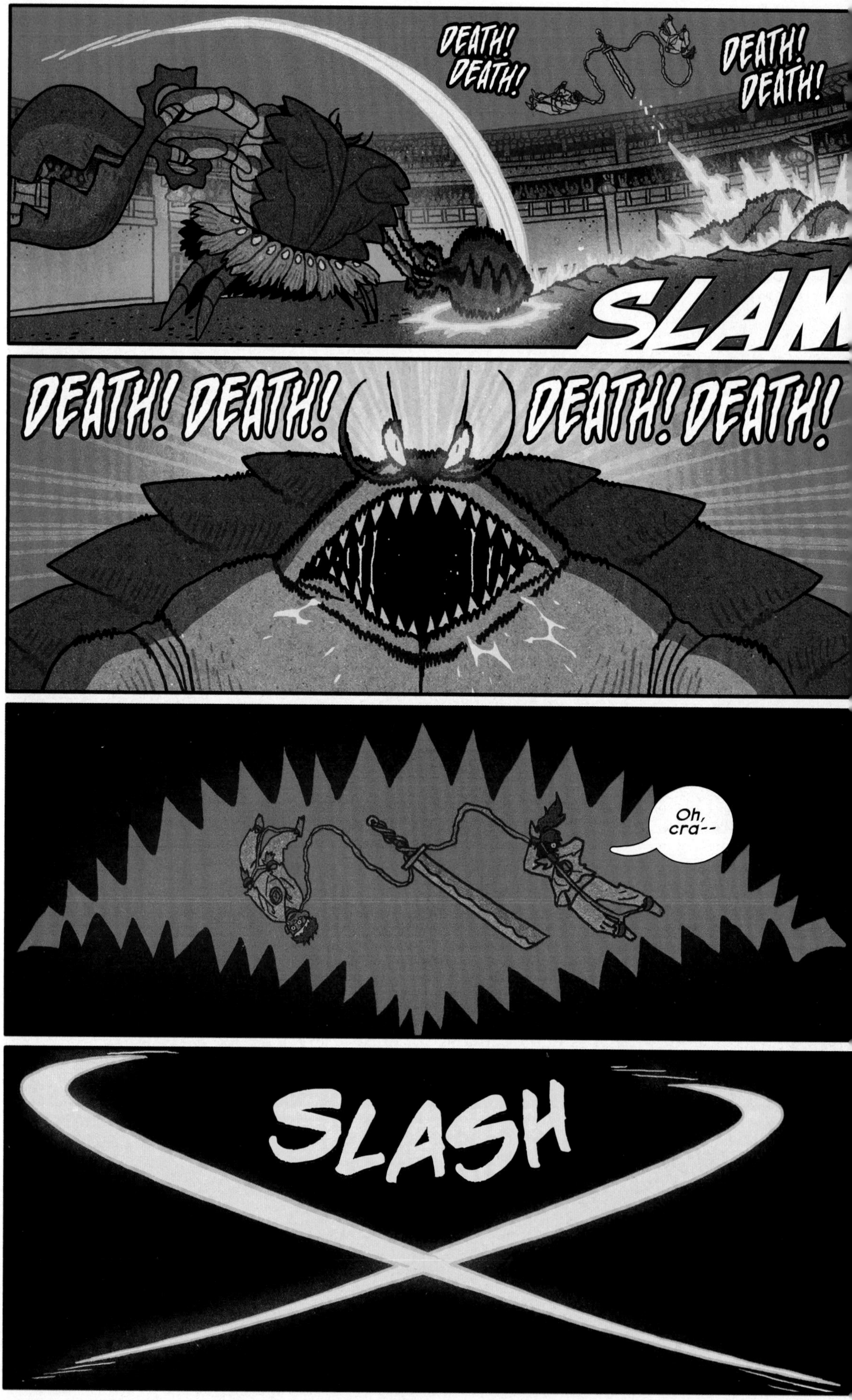
DEATH! DEATH!
DEATH! DEATH!
SLAM
DEATH! DEATH!
DEATH! DEATH!
Oh, cra--
SLASH

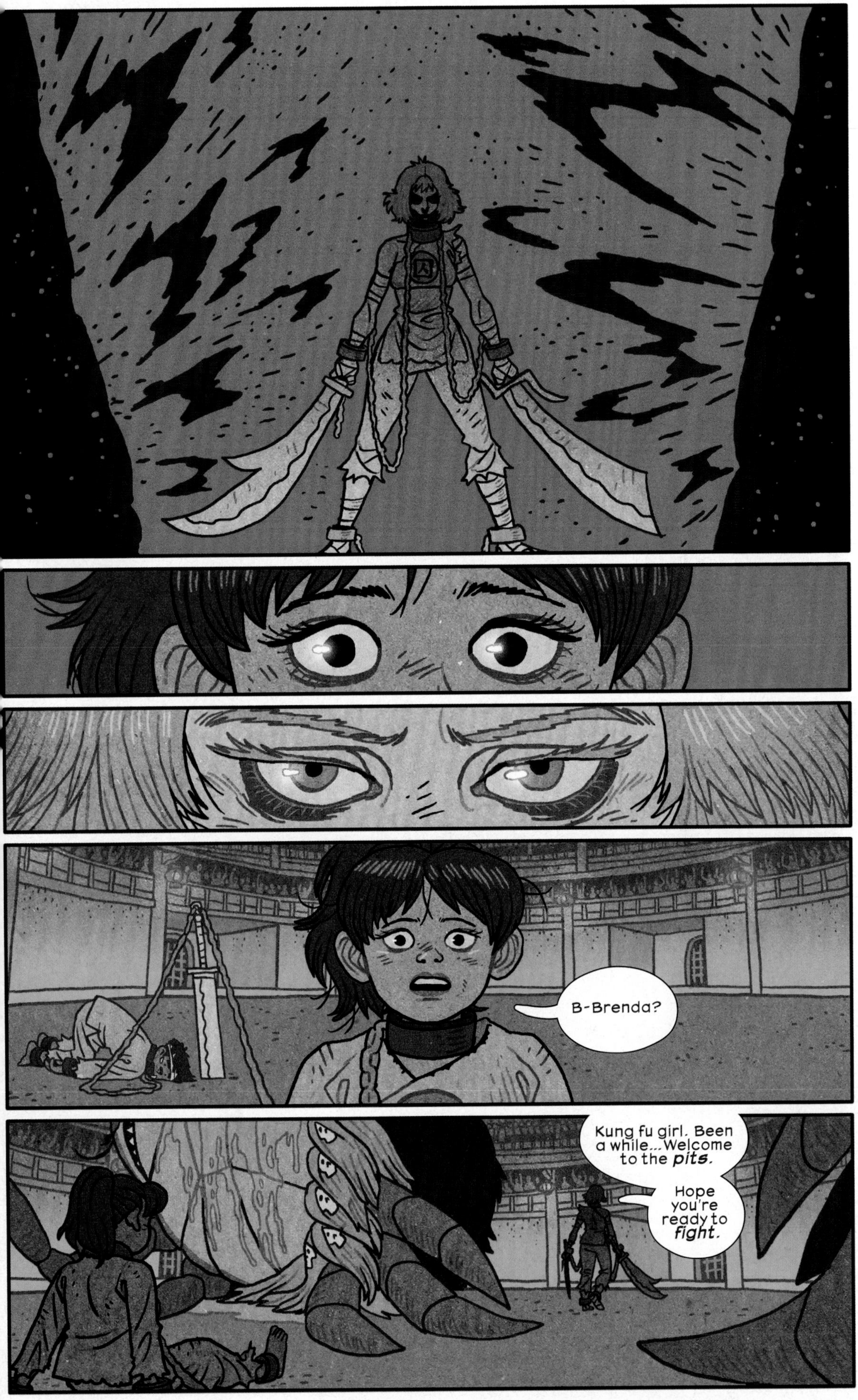
B-Brenda?
Kung fu girl. Been a while... Welcome to the *pits.*
Hope you're ready to *fight.*

鐵拳

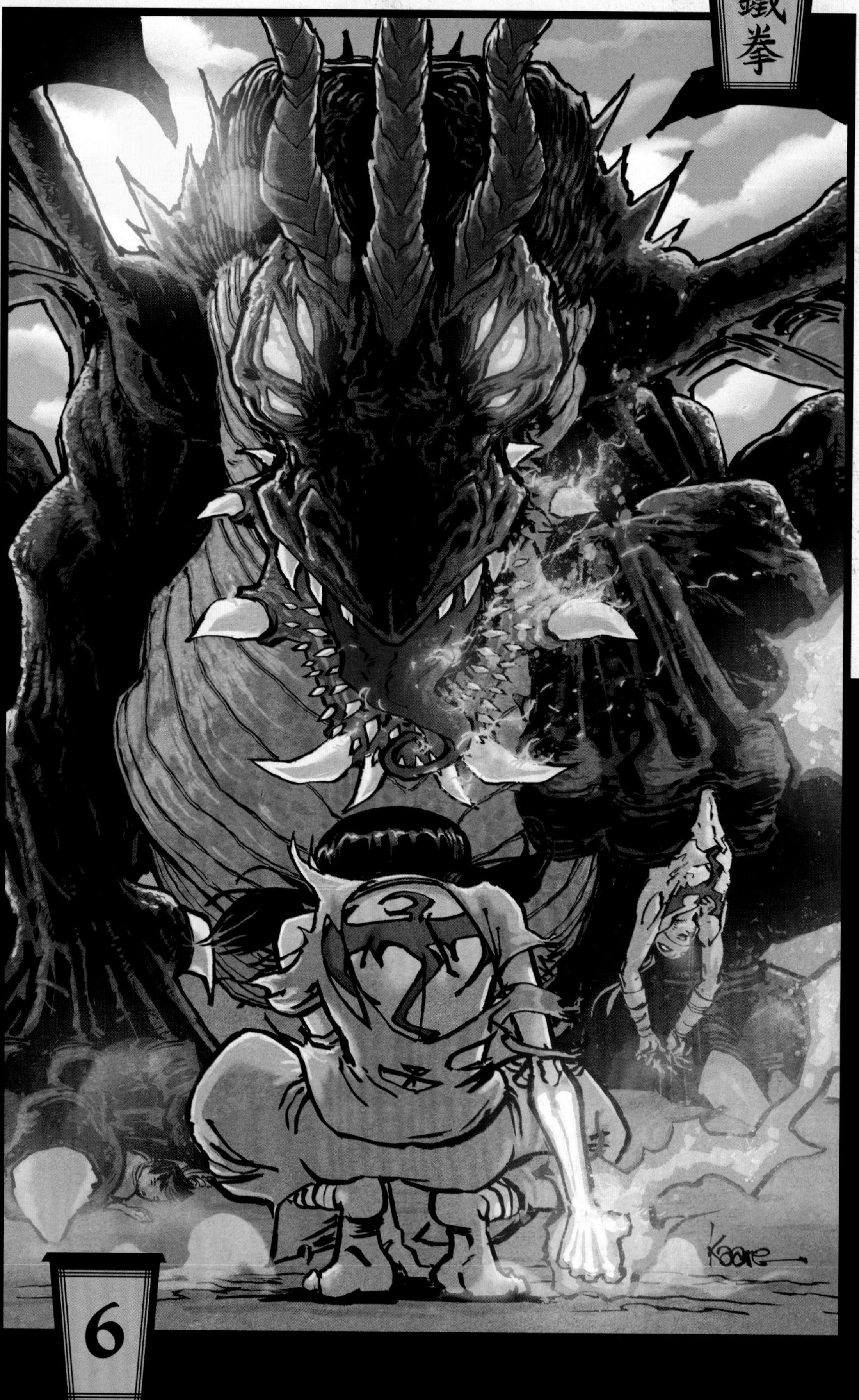

6

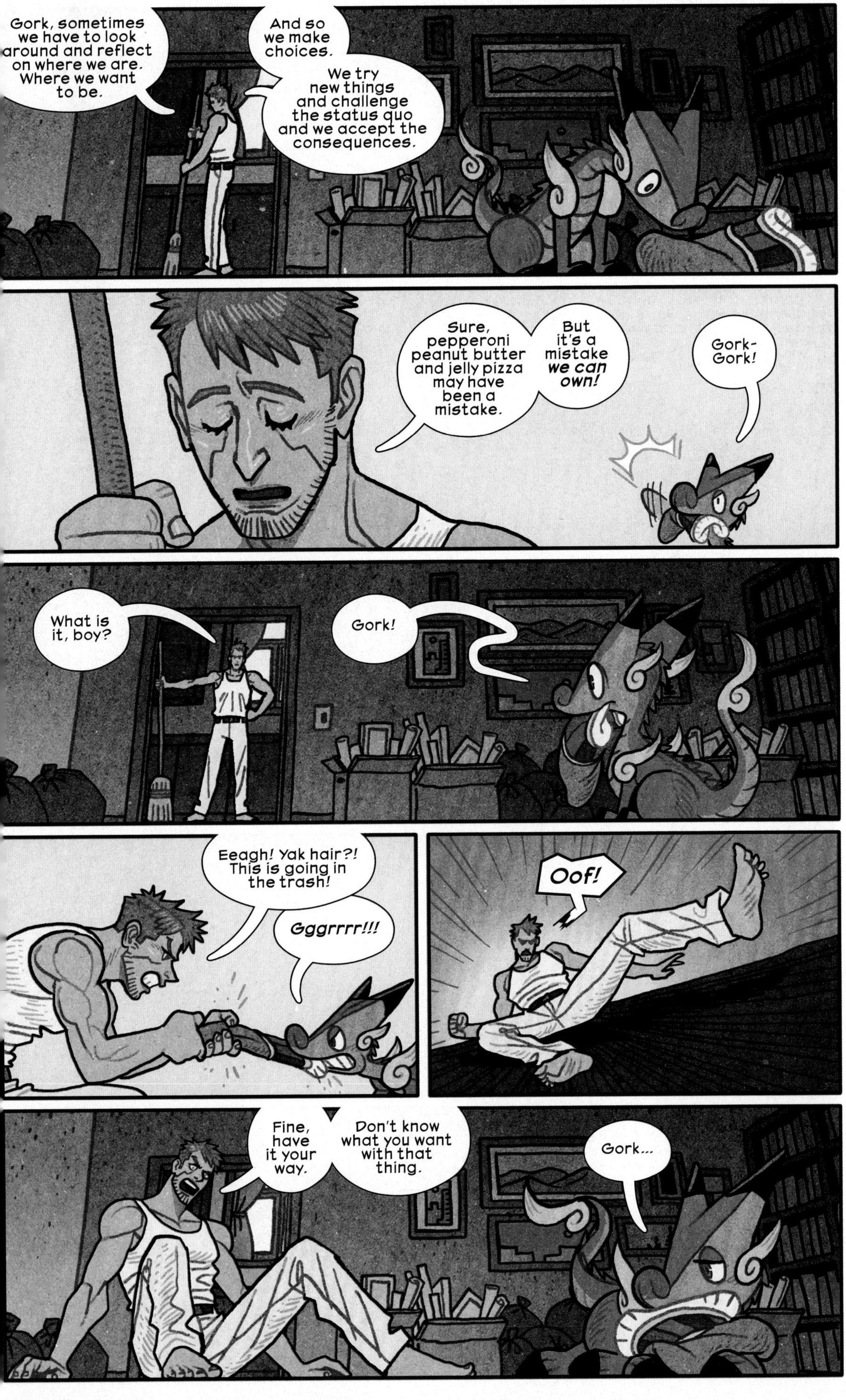

Gork, sometimes we have to look around and reflect on where we are. Where we want to be.
And so we make choices.
We try new things and challenge the status quo and we accept the consequences.
Sure, pepperoni peanut butter and jelly pizza may have been a mistake.
But it's a mistake *we can own!*
Gork-Gork!
What is it, boy?
Gork!
Eeagh! Yak hair?! This is going in the trash!
Gggrrrr!!!
Oof!
Fine, have it your way.
Don't know what you want with that thing.
Gork...

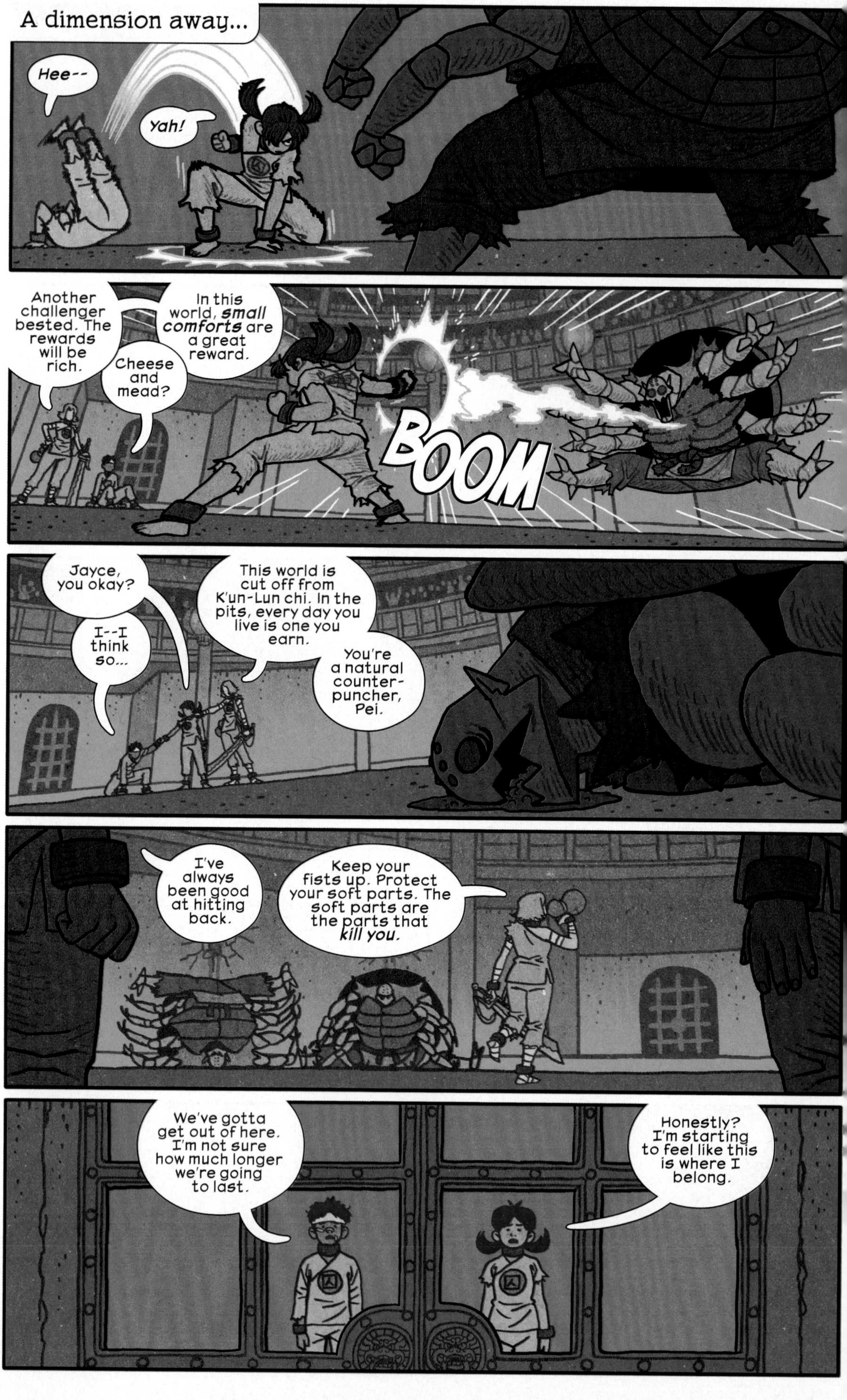
A dimension away...
Hee--
Yah!
Another challenger bested. The rewards will be rich.
In this world, *small comforts* are a great reward.
Cheese and mead?
BOOM
Jayce, you okay?
I--I think so...
This world is cut off from K'un-Lun chi. In the pits, every day you live is one you earn.
You're a natural counter-puncher, Pei.
I've always been good at hitting back.
Keep your fists up. Protect your soft parts. The soft parts are the parts that *kill you.*
We've gotta get out of here. I'm not sure how much longer we're going to last.
Honestly? I'm starting to feel like this is where I belong.

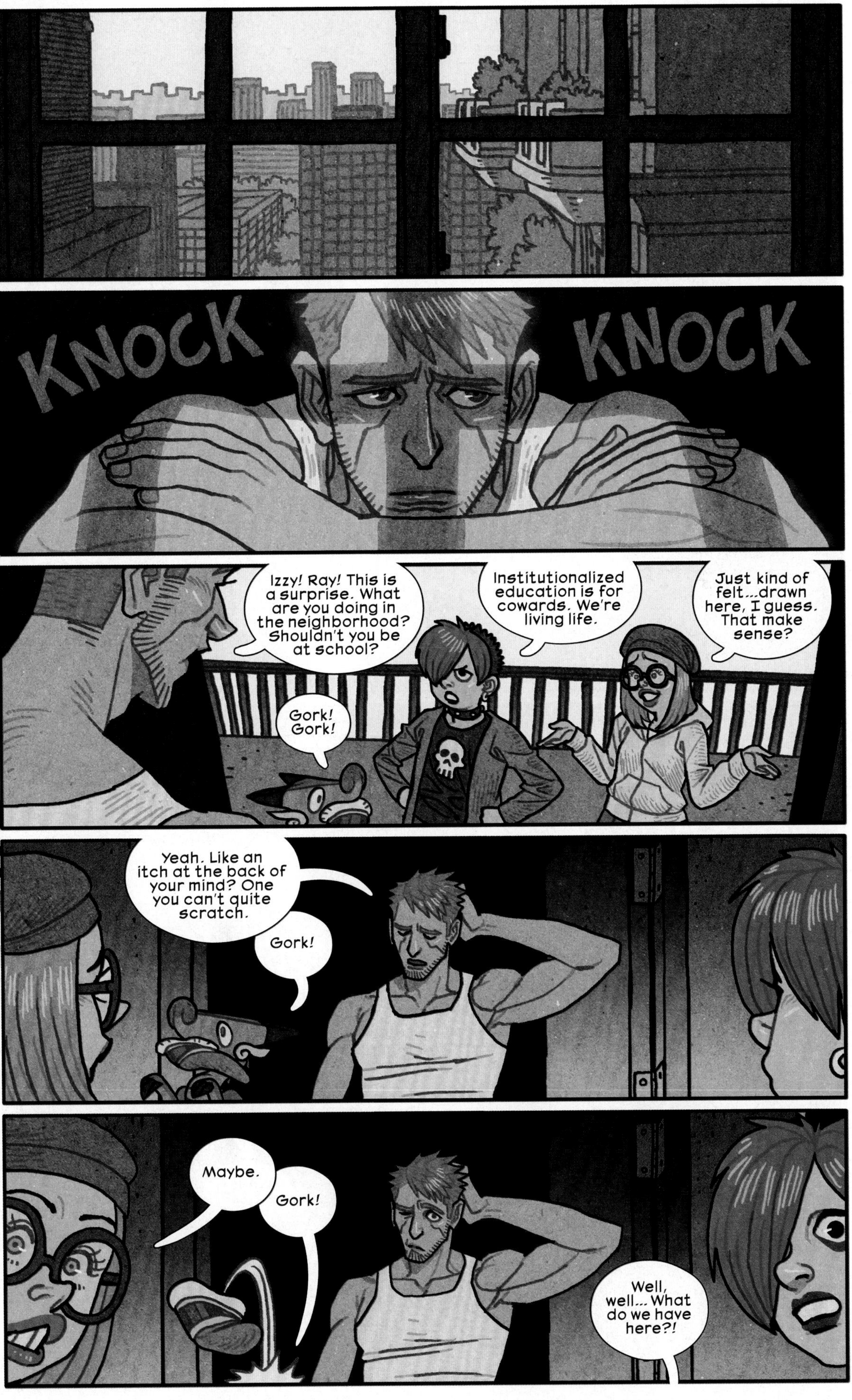
KNOCK
KNOCK
Izzy! Ray! This is a surprise. What are you doing in the neighborhood? Shouldn't you be at school?
Gork! Gork!
Institutionalized education is for cowards. We're living life.
Just kind of felt...drawn here, I guess. That make sense?
Yeah. Like an itch at the back of your mind? One you can't quite scratch.
Gork!
Maybe.
Gork!
Well, well... What do we have here?!

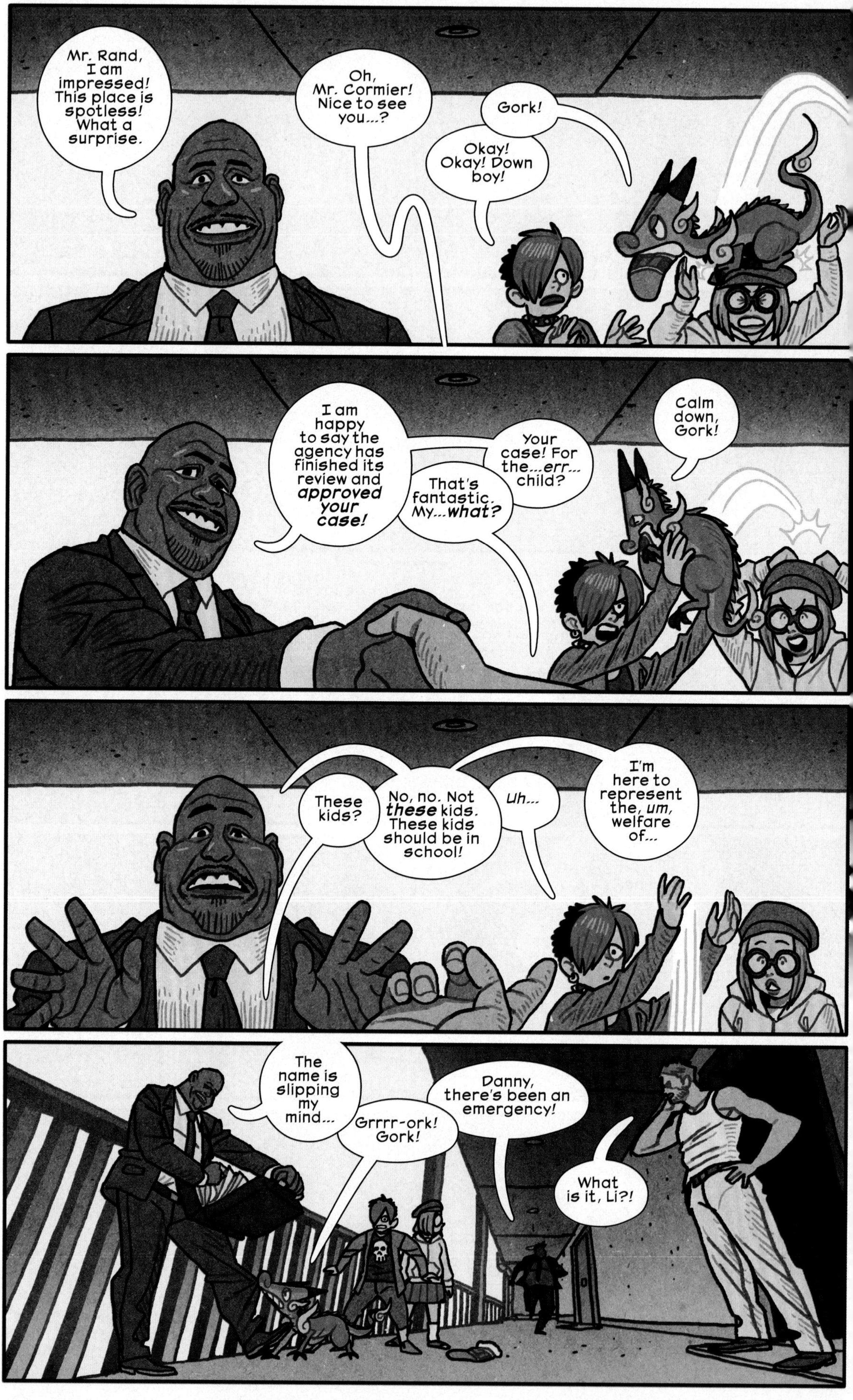
Mr. Rand, I am impressed! This place is spotless! What a surprise.
Oh, Mr. Cormier! Nice to see you...?
Gork!
Okay! Okay! Down boy!
I am happy to say the agency has finished its review and *approved your case!*
Your case! For the...*err*... child?
That's fantastic. My...*what?*
Calm down, Gork!
These kids?
No, no. Not *these* kids. These kids should be in school!
Uh...
I'm here to represent the, *um*, welfare of...
The name is slipping my mind...
Grrrr-ork! Gork!
Danny, there's been an emergency!
What is it, Li?!

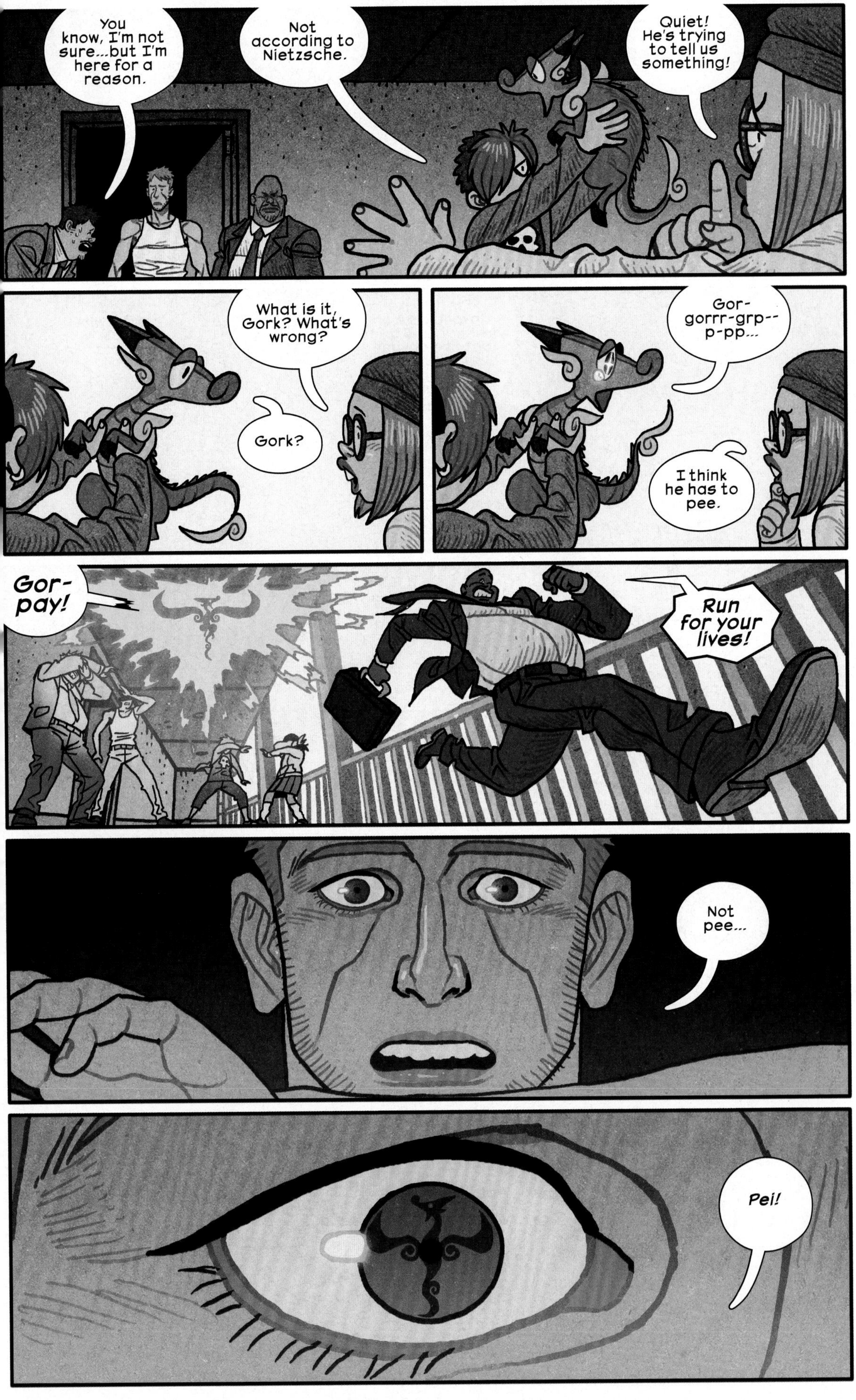
You know, I'm not sure...but I'm here for a reason.
Not according to Nietzsche.
Quiet! He's trying to tell us something!
What is it, Gork? What's wrong?
Gork?
Gor-gorrr-grp--p-pp...
I think he has to pee.
Gor-pay!
Run for your lives!
Not pee...
Pei!

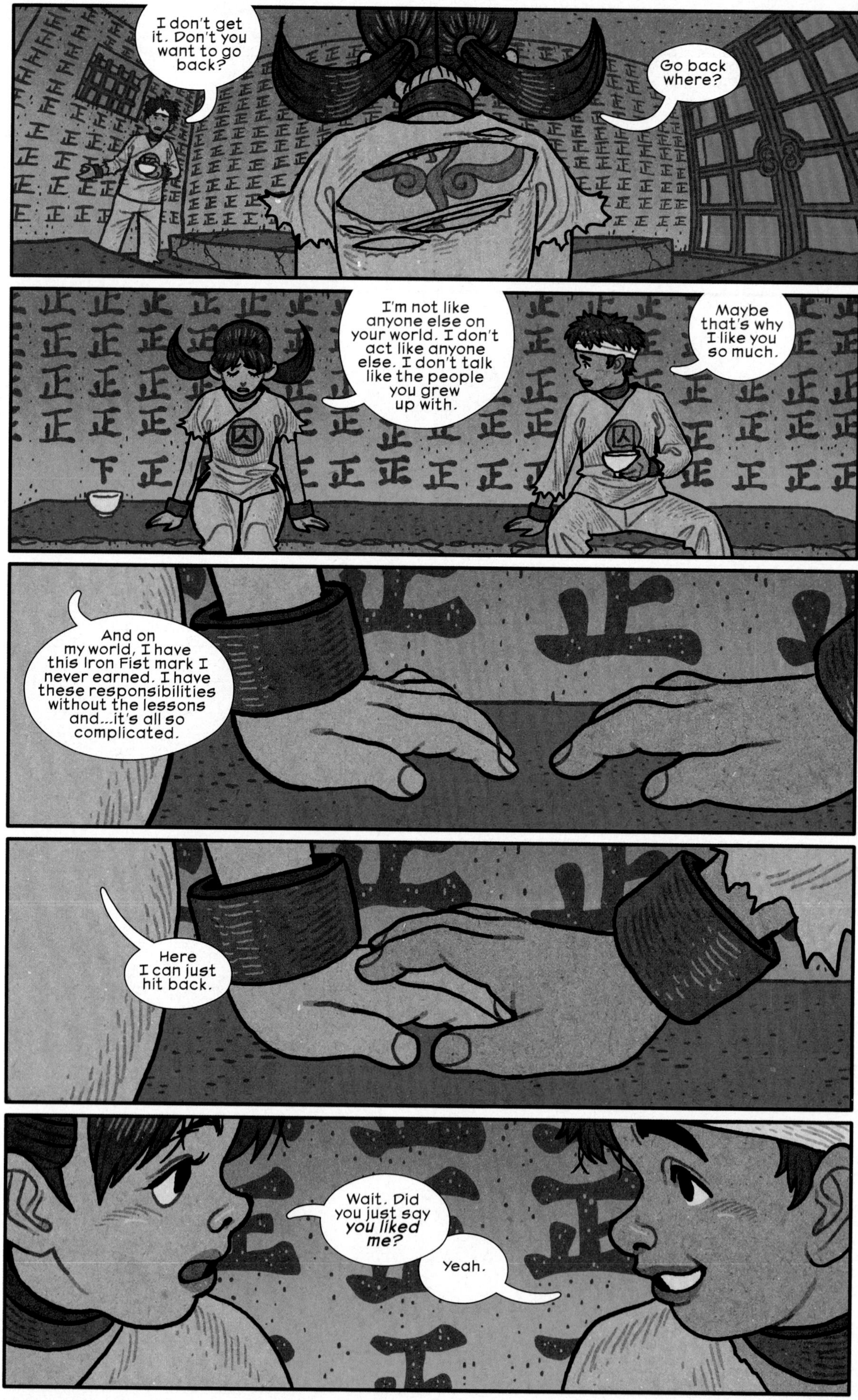

I don't get it. Don't you want to go back?
Go back where?
I'm not like anyone else on your world. I don't act like anyone else. I don't talk like the people you grew up with.
Maybe that's why I like you so much.
And on my world, I have this Iron Fist mark I never earned. I have these responsibilities without the lessons and...it's all so complicated.
Here I can just hit back.
Wait. Did you just say *you liked me?*
Yeah.

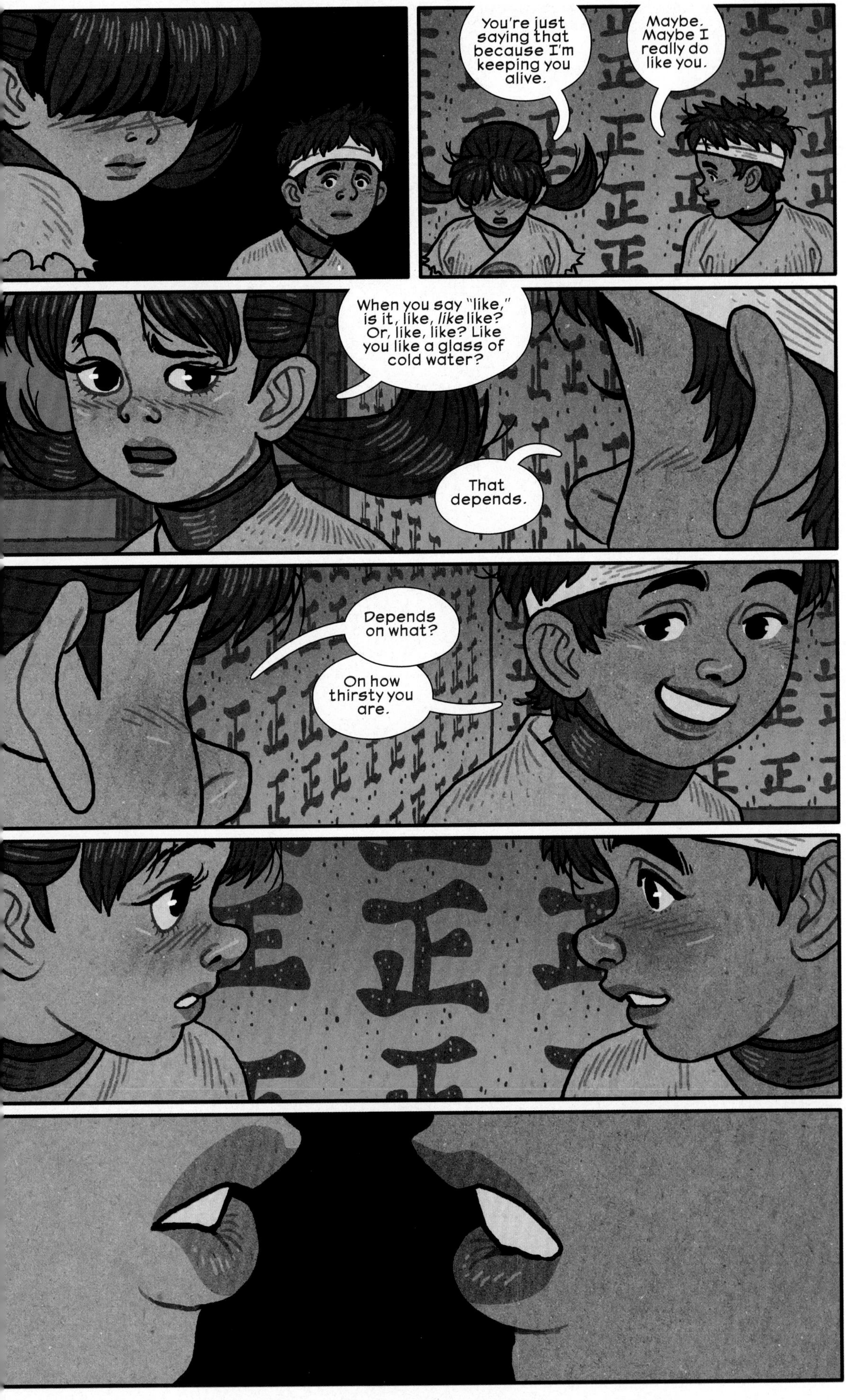
You're just saying that because I'm keeping you alive.
Maybe. Maybe I really do like you.
When you say "like," is it, like, *like* like? Or, like, like? Like you like a glass of cold water?
That depends.
Depends on what?
On how thirsty you are.

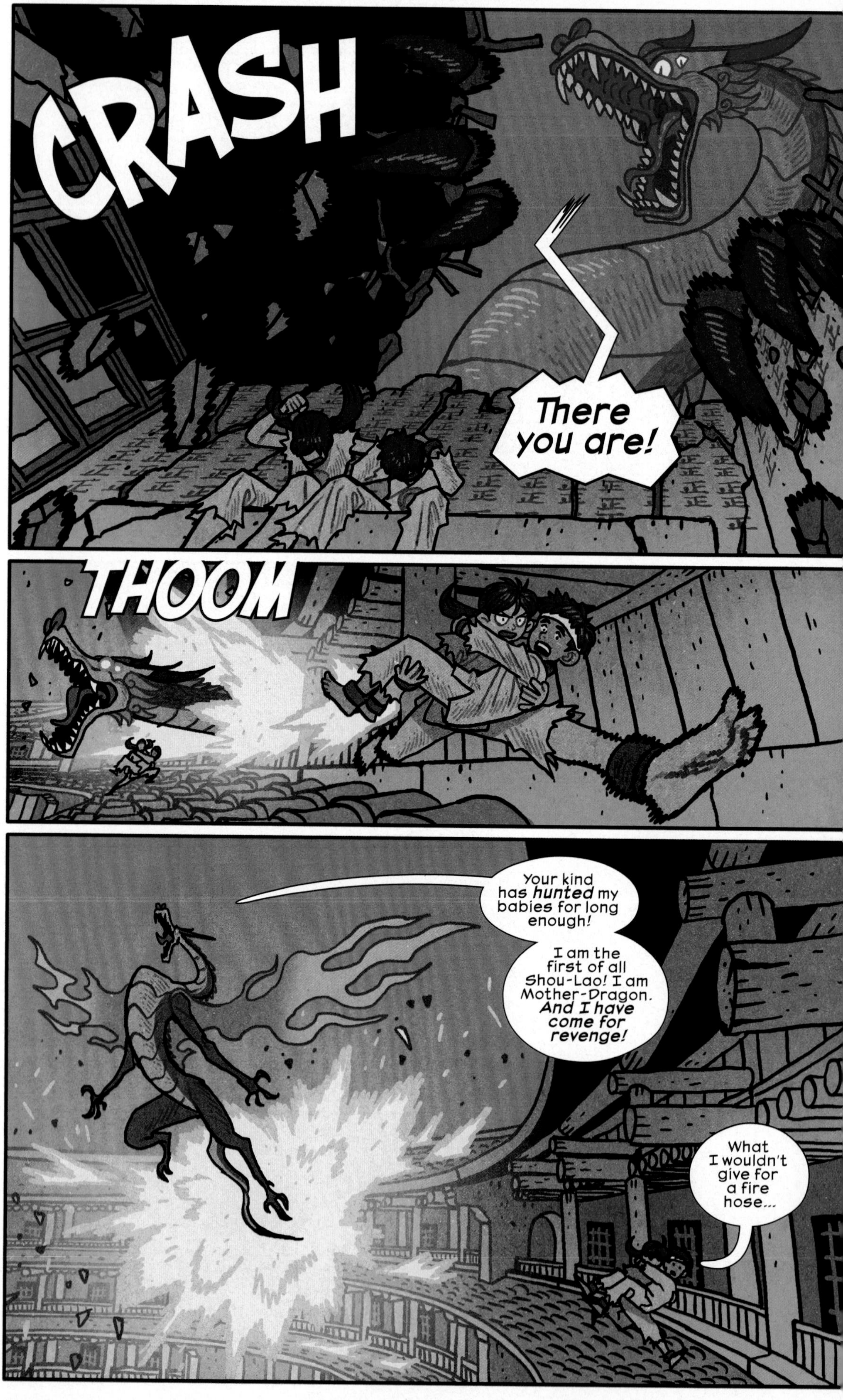
CRASH
There you are!
THOOM
Your kind has hunted my babies for long enough!
I am the first of all Shou-Lao! I am Mother-Dragon. And I have come for revenge!
What I wouldn't give for a fire hose...

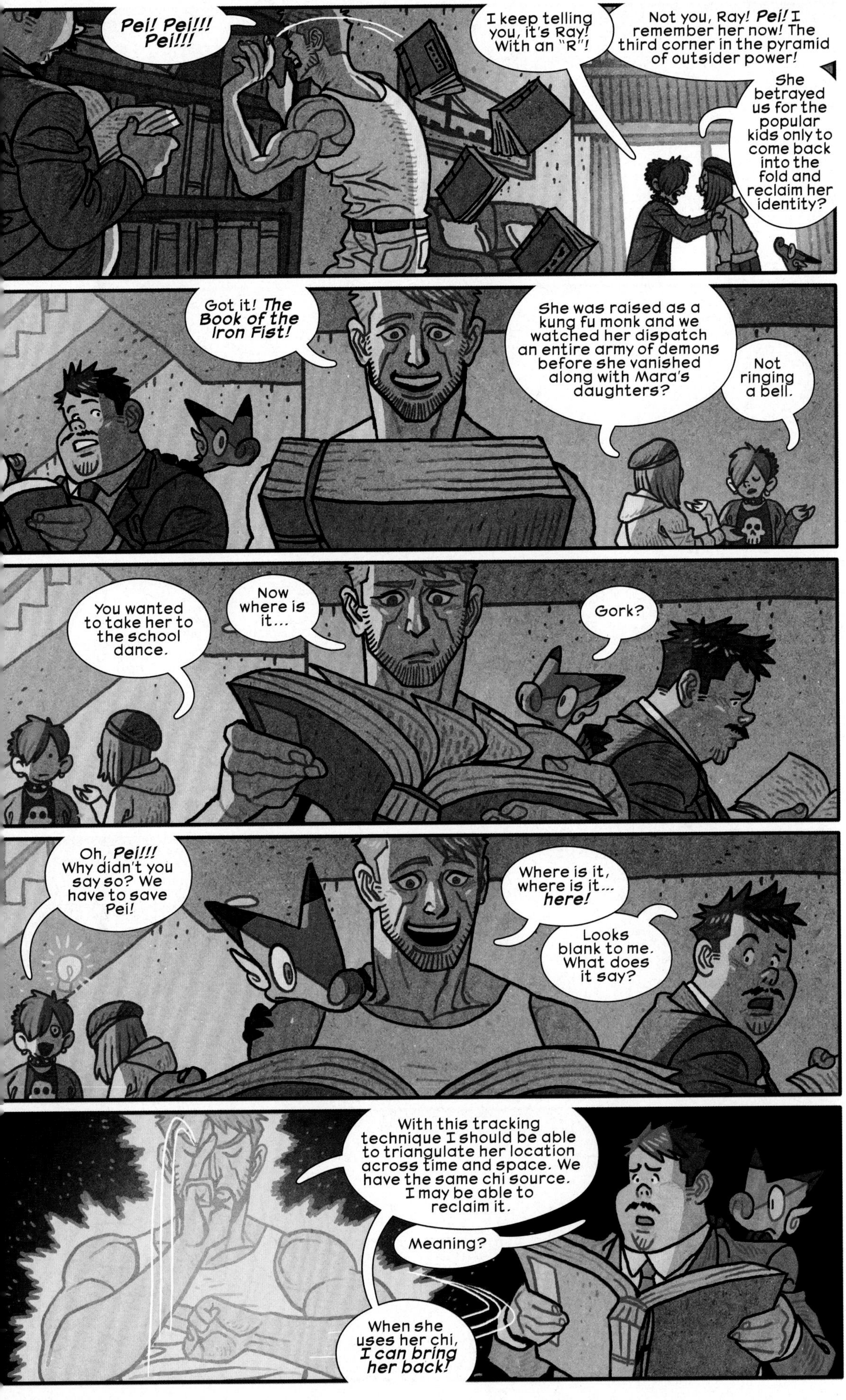
Pei! Pei!!! Pei!!!
I keep telling you, it's Ray! With an "R"!
Not you, Ray! Pei! I remember her now! The third corner in the pyramid of outsider power!
She betrayed us for the popular kids only to come back into the fold and reclaim her identity?
Got it! The Book of the Iron Fist!
She was raised as a kung fu monk and we watched her dispatch an entire army of demons before she vanished along with Mara's daughters?
Not ringing a bell.
You wanted to take her to the school dance.
Now where is it...
Gork?
Oh, Pei!!! Why didn't you say so? We have to save Pei!
Where is it, where is it... here!
Looks blank to me. What does it say?
With this tracking technique I should be able to triangulate her location across time and space. We have the same chi source. I may be able to reclaim it.
Meaning?
When she uses her chi, I can bring her back!

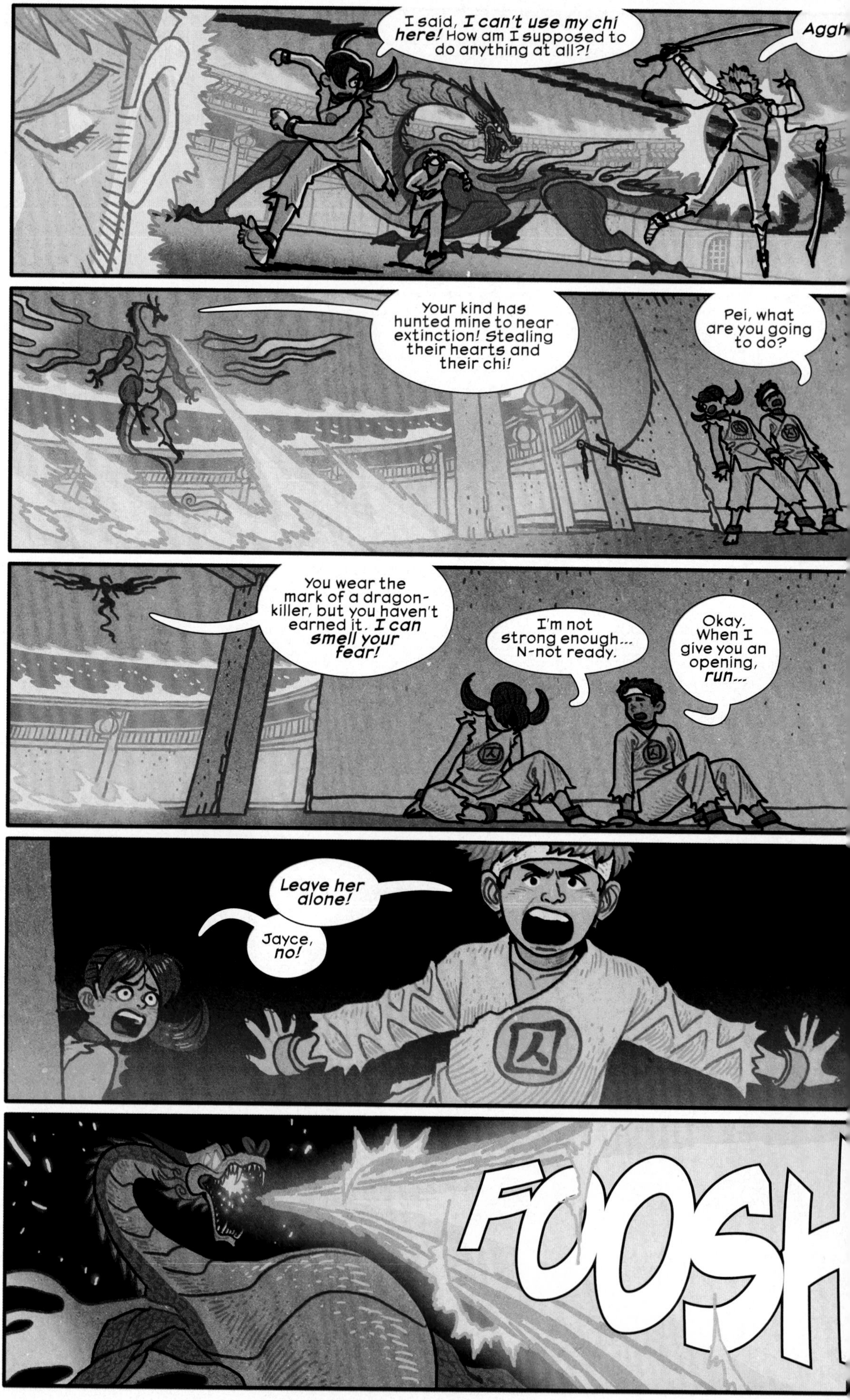
I said, I can't use my chi here! How am I supposed to do anything at all?!
Aggh
Your kind has hunted mine to near extinction! Stealing their hearts and their chi!
Pei, what are you going to do?
You wear the mark of a dragon-killer, but you haven't earned it. I can smell your fear!
I'm not strong enough... N-not ready.
Okay. When I give you an opening, run...
Leave her alone!
Jayce, no!
FOOSH

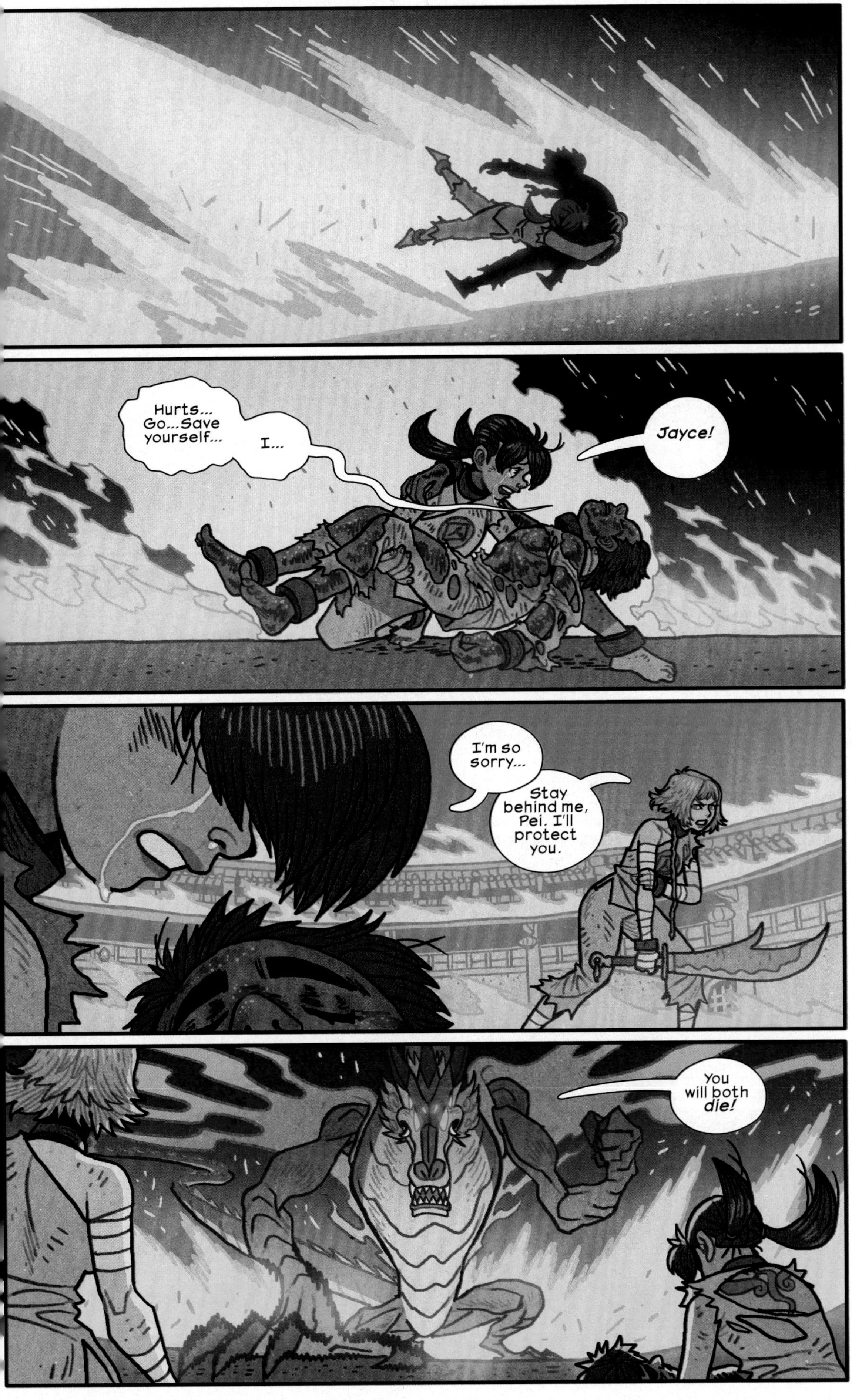
Hurts... Go...Save yourself... I...
Jayce!
I'm so sorry...
Stay behind me, Pei. I'll protect you.
You will both die!

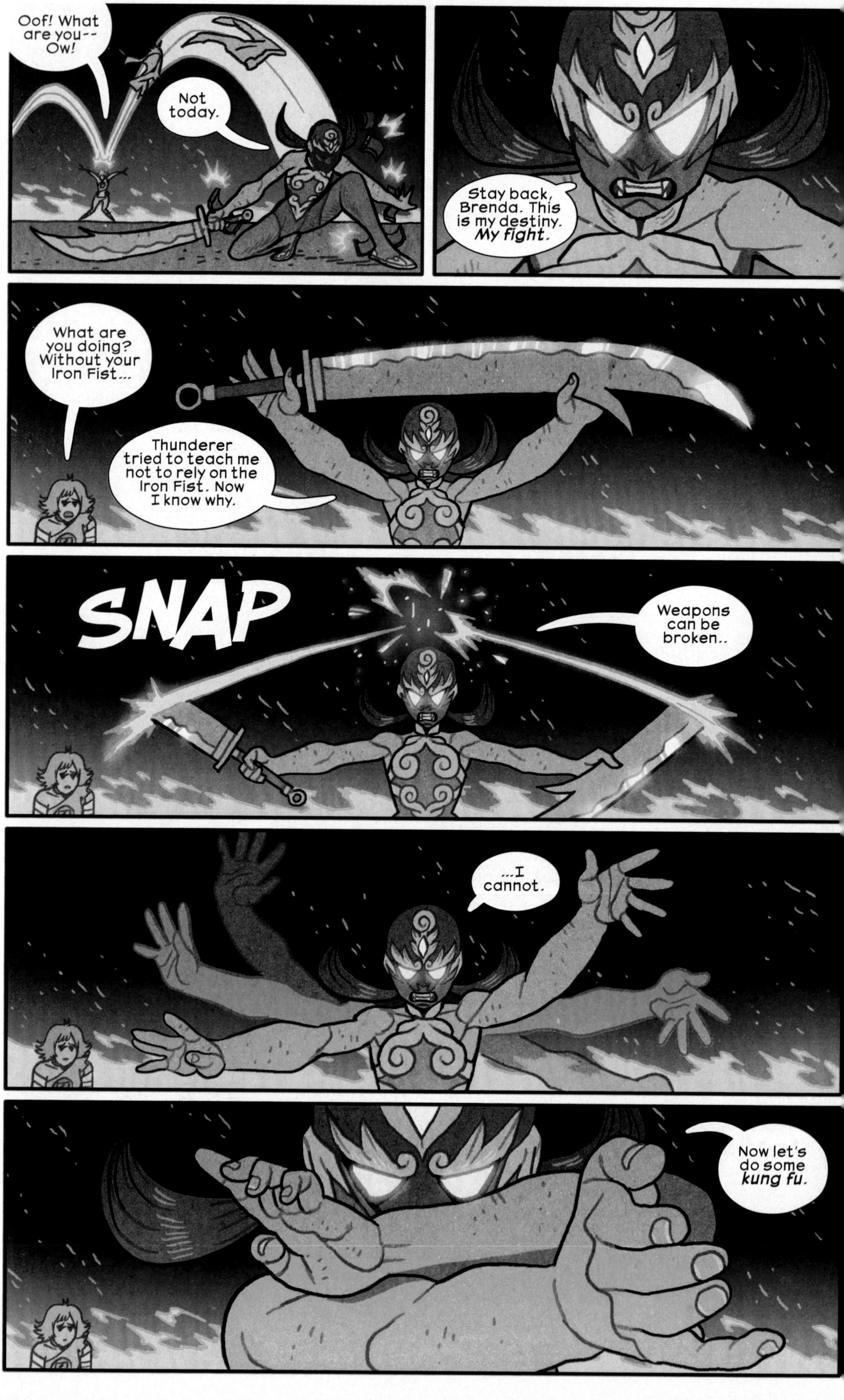
Oof! What are you-- Ow!
Not today.
Stay back, Brenda. This is my destiny. *My fight*.
What are you doing? Without your Iron Fist...
Thunderer tried to teach me not to rely on the Iron Fist. Now I know why.
SNAP
Weapons can be broken..
...I cannot.
Now let's do some *kung fu*.

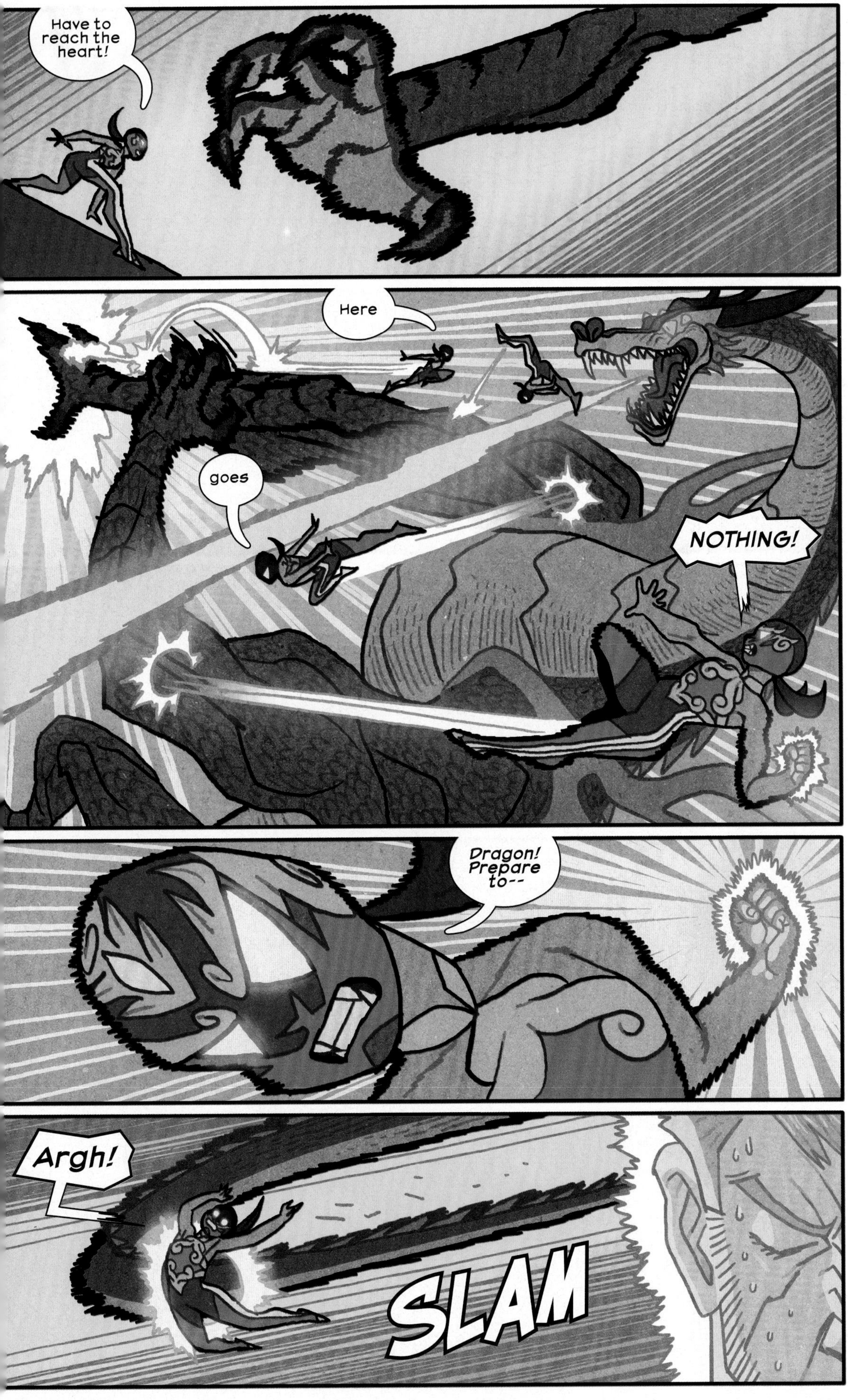

Have to reach the heart!
Here
goes
NOTHING!
Dragon! Prepare to--
Argh!
SLAM

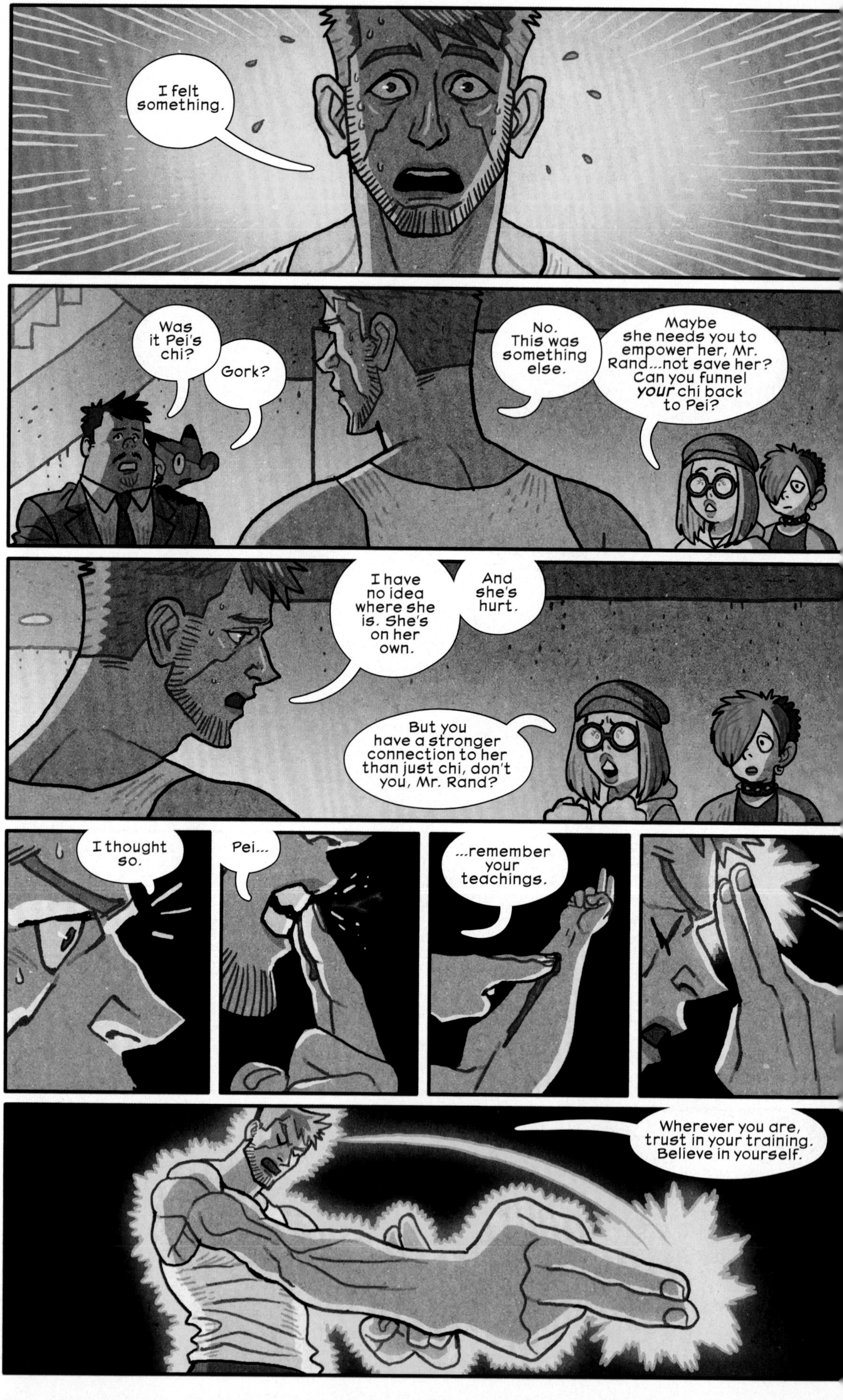

I felt something.
Was it Pei's chi?
Gork?
No. This was something else.
Maybe she needs you to empower her, Mr. Rand...not save her? Can you funnel *your* chi back to Pei?
I have no idea where she is. She's on her own.
And she's hurt.
But you have a stronger connection to her than just chi, don't you, Mr. Rand?
I thought so.
Pei...
...remember your teachings.
Wherever you are, trust in your training. Believe in yourself.

"But don't fight for yourself.

"Fight for your friends. For the ones you love.

She's hit.

KA-PWING

"I was once taught to protect the heart. That it was too soft.

"But the heart is the strongest muscle in the body.

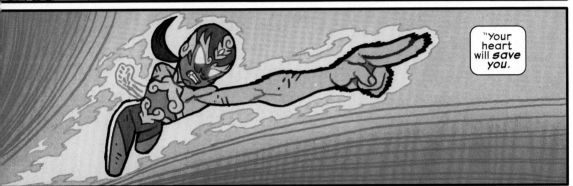

"Your heart will *save you.*

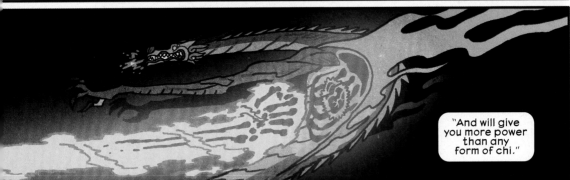

"And will give you more power than any form of chi."

PUNCH

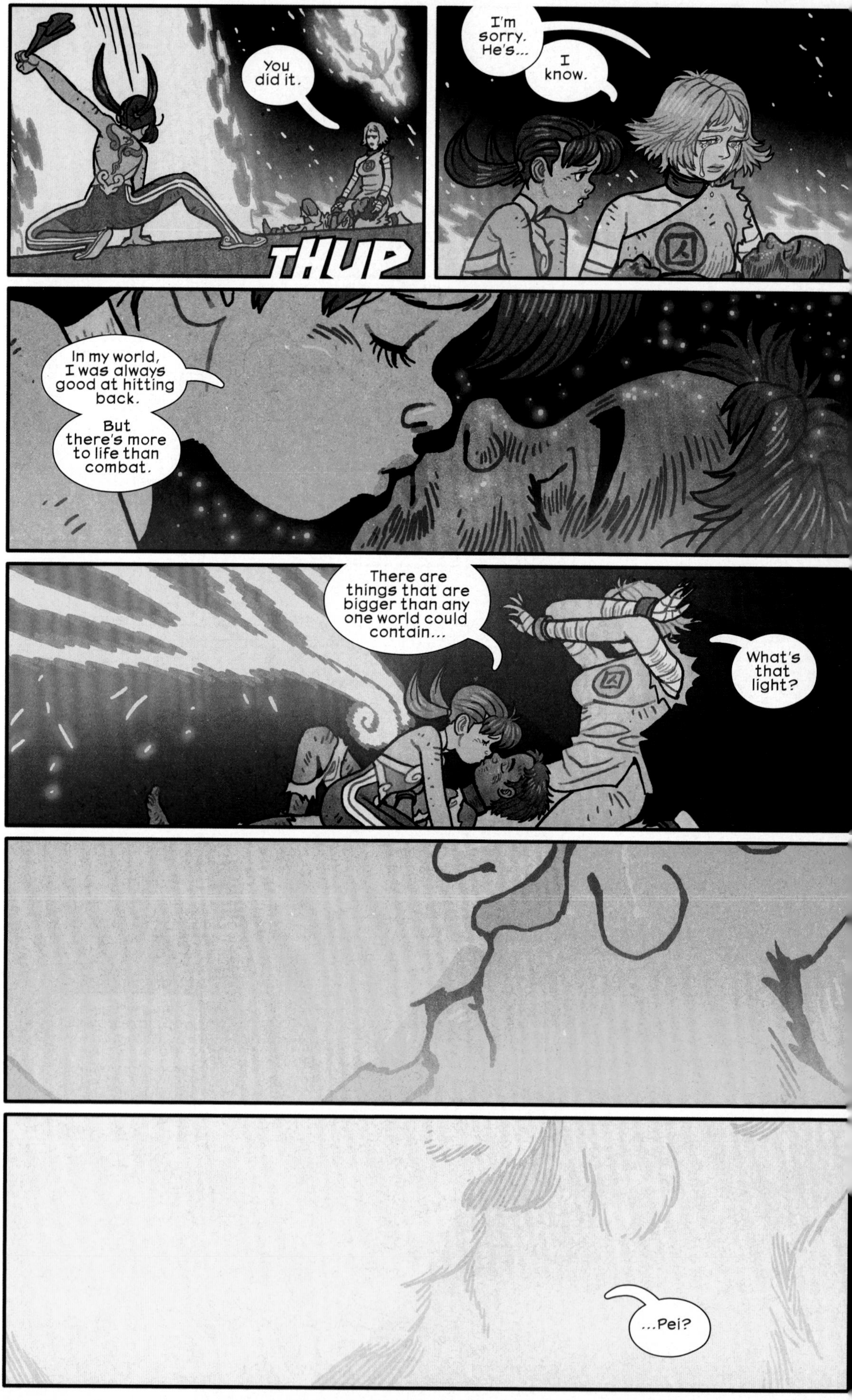
You did it.
THUP
I'm sorry. He's...
I know.
In my world, I was always good at hitting back.
But there's more to life than combat.
There are things that are bigger than any one world could contain...
What's that light?
...Pei?

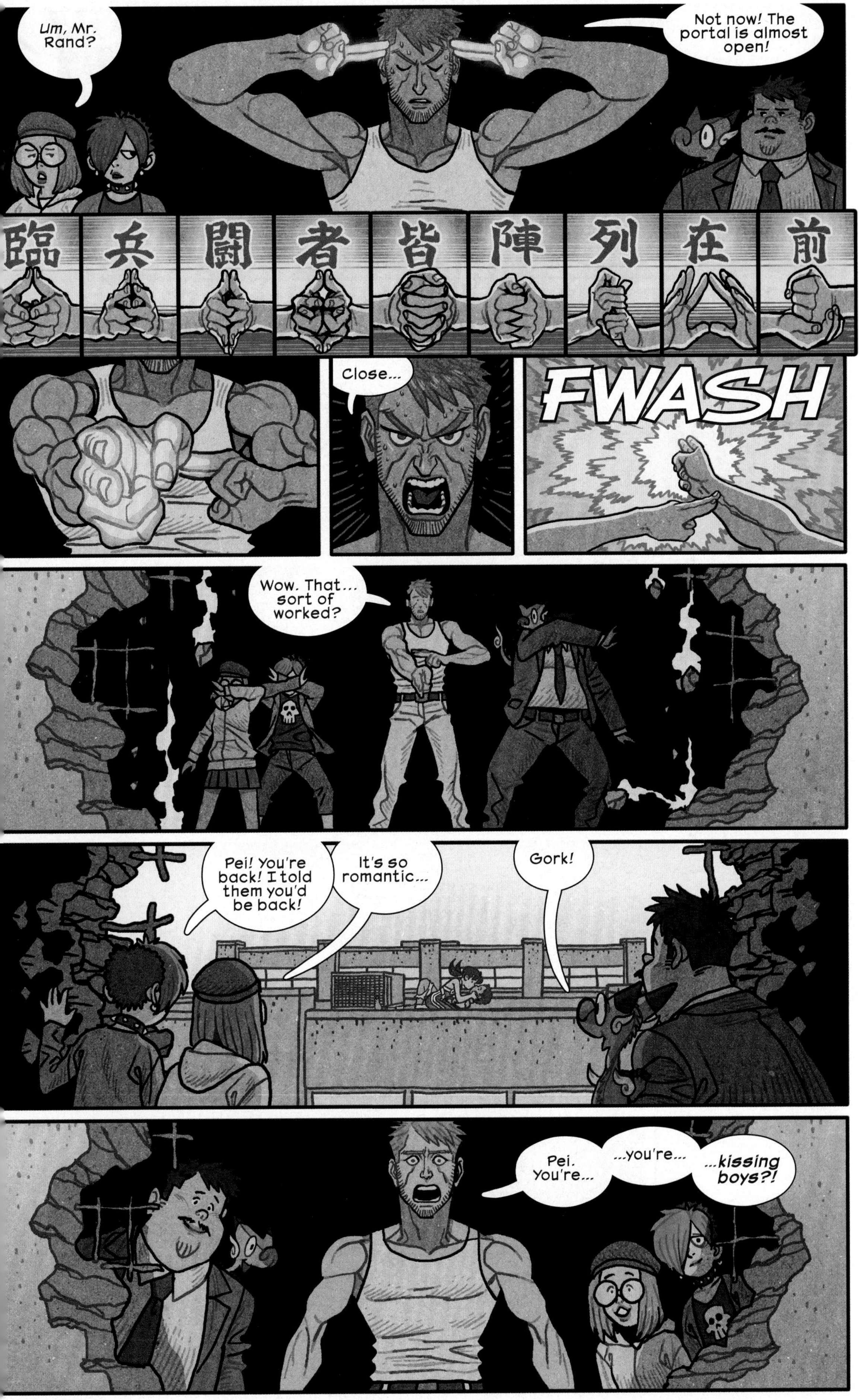
Um, Mr. Rand?
Not now! The portal is almost open!
臨
兵
闘
者
皆
陣
列
在
前
Close...
FWASH
Wow. That... sort of worked?
Pei! You're back! I told them you'd be back!
It's so romantic...
Gork!
Pei. You're...
...you're...
...kissing boys?!

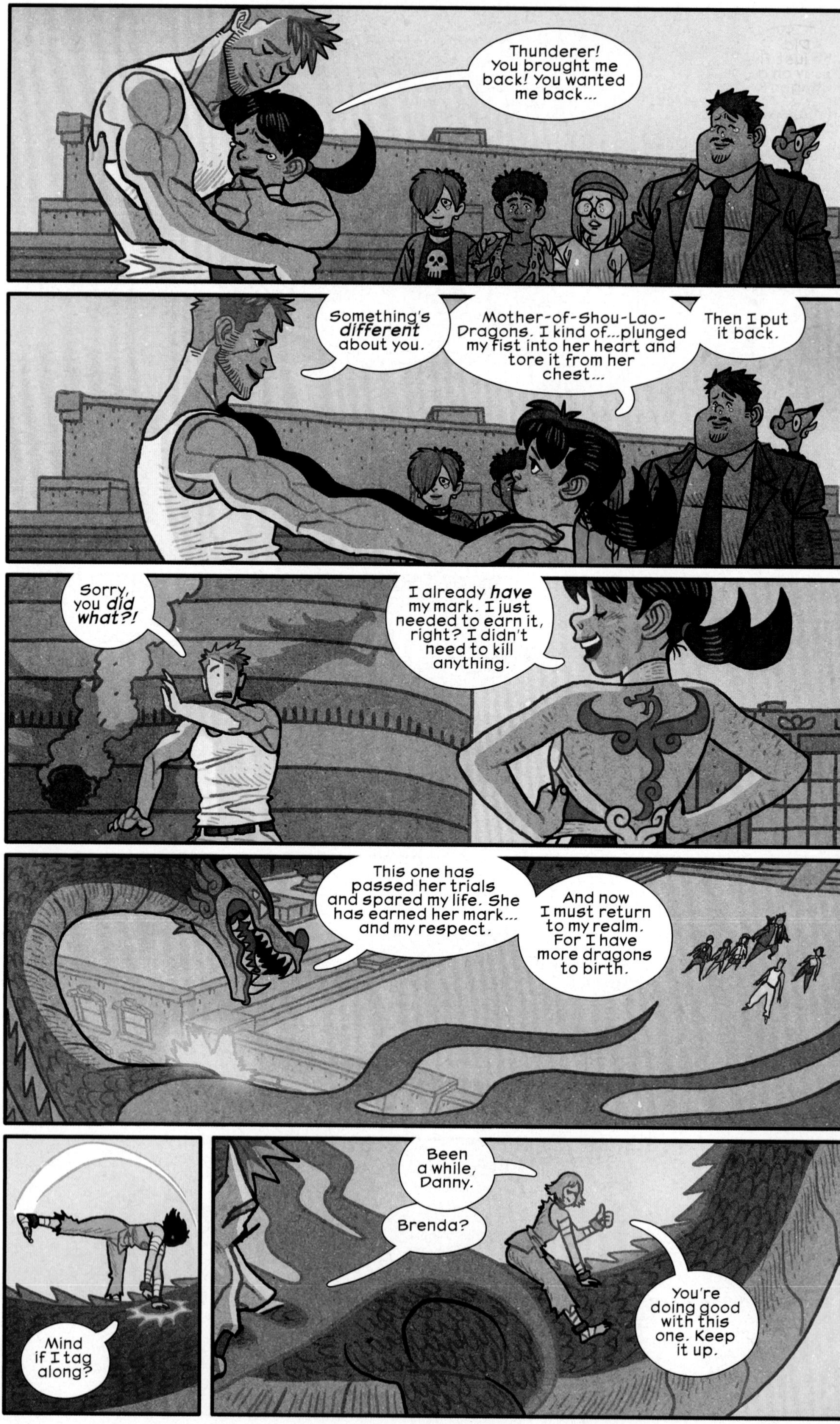
Thunderer! You brought me back! You wanted me back...
Something's *different* about you.
Mother-of-Shou-Lao-Dragons. I kind of...plunged my fist into her heart and tore it from her chest...
Then I put it back.
Sorry, you *did what?!*
I already *have* my mark. I just needed to earn it, right? I didn't need to kill anything.
This one has passed her trials and spared my life. She has earned her mark... and my respect.
And now I must return to my realm. For I have more dragons to birth.
Mind if I tag along?
Been a while, Danny.
Brenda?
You're doing good with this one. Keep it up.

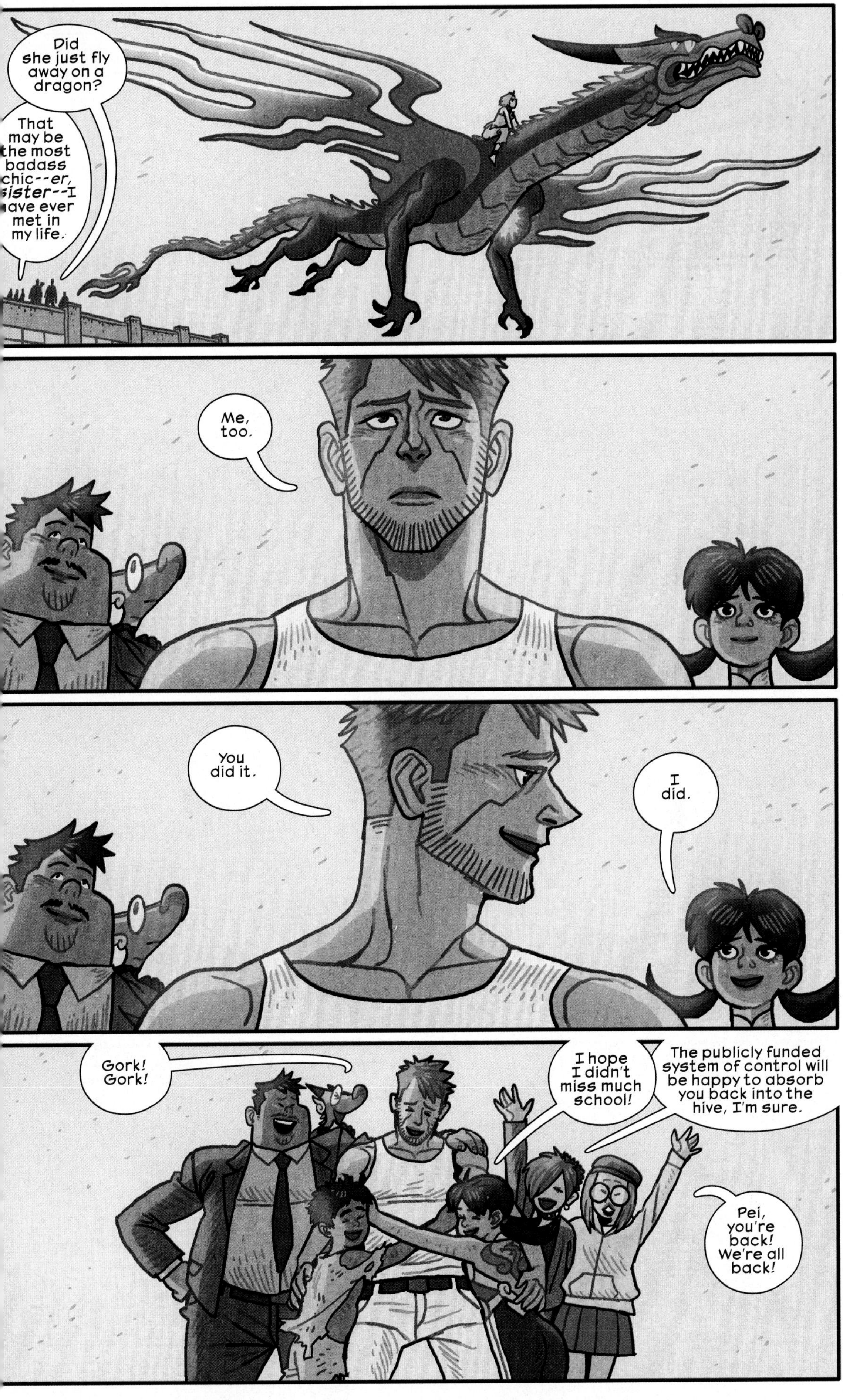
Did she just fly away on a dragon?
That may be the most badass chic--*er,* *sister*--I ave ever met in my life.
Me, too.
You did it.
I did.
Gork! Gork!
I hope I didn't miss much school!
The publicly funded system of control will be happy to absorb you back into the hive, I'm sure.
Pei, you're back! We're all back!

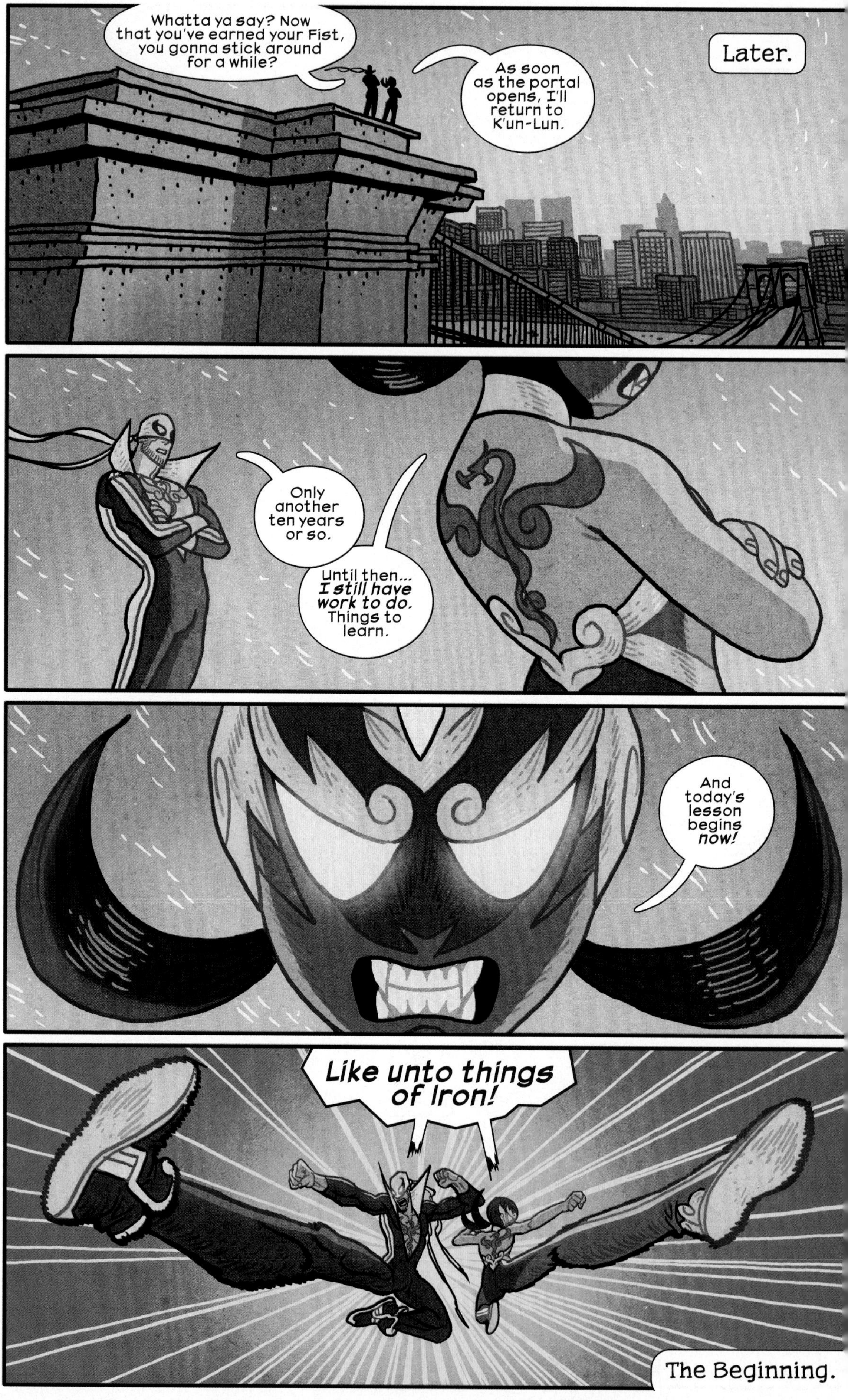

Later.
Whatta ya say? Now that you've earned your Fist, you gonna stick around for a while?
As soon as the portal opens, I'll return to K'un-Lun.
Only another ten years or so.
Until then... *I still have work to do.* Things to learn.
And today's lesson begins *now!*
Like unto things of Iron!
The Beginning.

CHARACTER DESIGNS BY
AFU CHAN

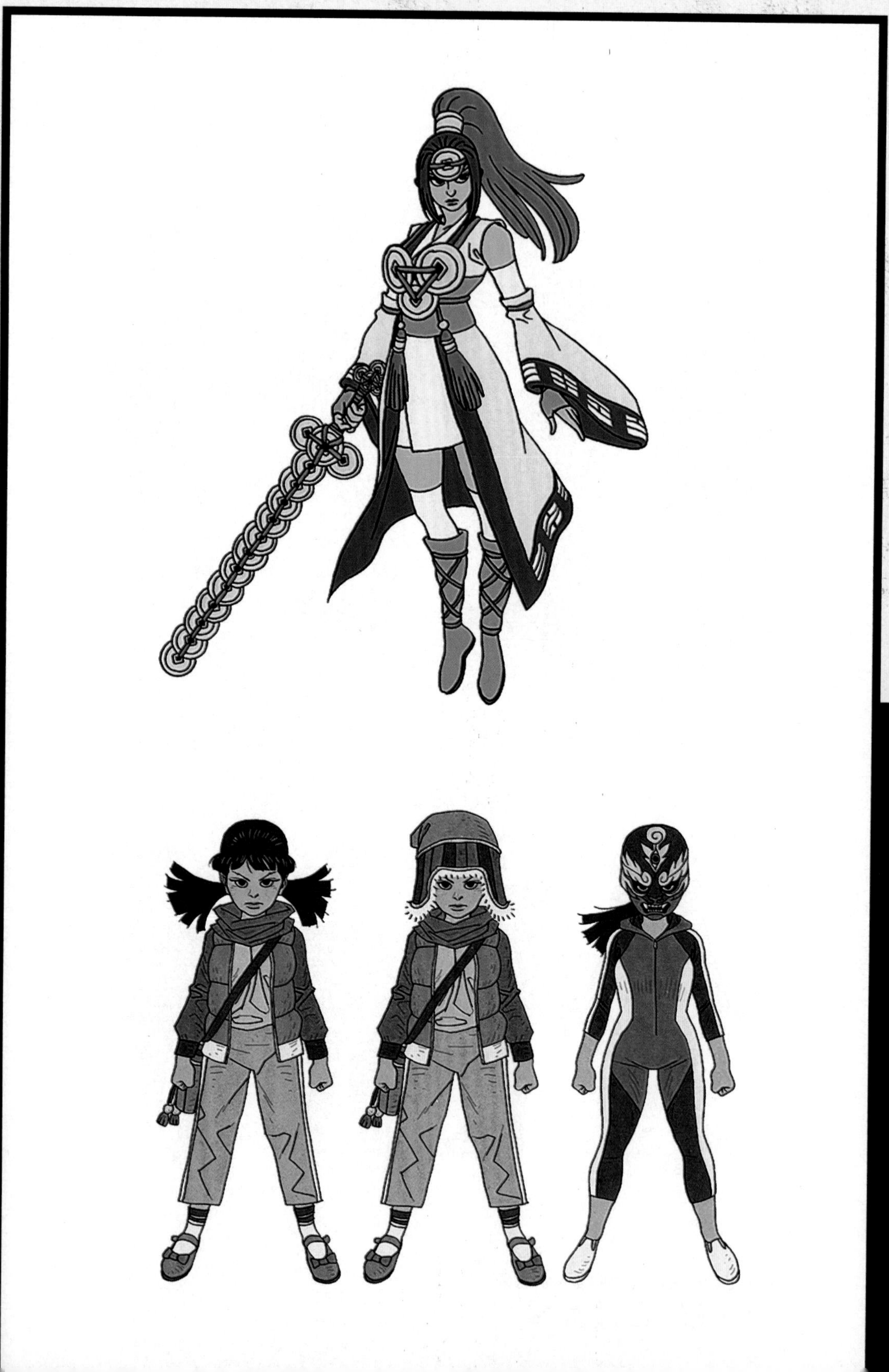

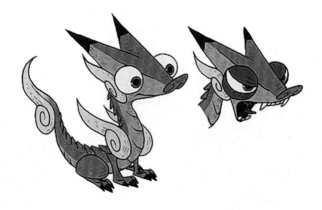

CHARACTER DESIGNS BY
AFU CHAN

CHRISTI-LYNNE   COOKIE   CANDACE

IZZY   RAY   JAYCE   JOCK#3   JOCK#2 (MIKE)   JOCK#1 (TODD)

CHARACTER DESIGNS BY
AFU CHAN

IN THE DOJO

AND SO IT ENDS HOW IT BEGINS — AND IT BEGINS HOW IT ENDS. SAYING GOODBYE TO CHARACTERS I LOVE. THANKFUL FOR THE TIME WE HAD TOGETHER AND HOPING THEY CONTINUE WITH RICH AND CREATIVE STORIES OF THEIR OWN.

THIS HAS BEEN A SPECIAL JOURNEY FOR MANY REASONS, NOT THE LEAST OF WHICH IS THE OPPORTUNITY TO COLLABORATE FOR THE FIRST TIME WITH AFU CHAN AND SHELLY CHEN AND CONTINUE ALONG WITH MY MAN JAKE THOMAS AND HIS PARTNER IN CRIME, KATHLEEN WISNESKI.

AND I APPRECIATE YOU, THE READER, MOST. I'M ONE OF YOU. WE LOVE THIS MEDIUM TOGETHER.

SEE YOU AROUND THE DOJO, DANNY. AND TAKE CARE OF THAT LITTLE MONK GIRL. SHE'S GOING PLACES...TRUST ME.

-KAARE ANDREWS

BEING A BIG FAN OF HONG KONG CINEMA AND *WUXIA* TV SHOWS BASED ON JIN YONG'S NOVELS, IT WAS MY HONOR TO WORK ON *IMMORTAL IRON FISTS*, A COMIC THAT WAS INSPIRED BY THOSE GENRES. IT WAS A BLAST WORKING ON THIS PROJECT, AND I'M SO THANKFUL FOR MY CREATIVE TEAM FOR GIVING ME ARTISTIC FREEDOM. THANKS TO EVERYONE WHO LOVED AND SUPPORTED THIS COMIC.

-AFU CHAN

IT WAS A VERY FUN EXPERIENCE WORKING ON *IMMORTAL IRON FISTS*. AS A CONCEPT ARTIST WORKING IN AN ANIMATION COMPANY, IT FELT LIKE I WAS COLORING FOR AN ANIMATED MOVIE. WORKING WITH THIS TALENTED TEAM WAS GREAT — THEY CAME UP WITH UNIQUE IDEAS AND GAVE ME A LOT OF ROOM TO EXPLORE. IT WAS NOTHING LIKE ANYTHING I'D EVER WORKED ON BEFORE. THANK YOU FOR READING THIS SERIES.